JUL 1 0 2001

Family Men

Family Men

Middle-Class

Fatherhood in Early

Industrializing

America

SHAWN JOHANSEN

ROUTLEDGE
New York and London

Published in 2001 by
Routledge
29 West 35th Street
New York, NY 10001

Published in Great Britain in 2001 by
Routledge
11 New Fetter Lane
London EC4P 4EE

Printed in the United States of America on acid-free paper
Design and typography: Jack Donner

Library of Congress Cataloging-in-Publication Data

Johansen, Shawn.
    Family men : middle-class fatherhood in early industrializing America /
    Shawn Johansen.
        p.   cm.
    Includes bibliographical references and index.
    ISBN 0–415–91786–7 (hardcover) — ISBN 0–415–91787–5 (pbk.)
    1. Fatherhood—United States—History—19th century. 2. Fathers—
United States. I. Title.

HQ756.J64 2001
306.874'2'0973—dc21
                                                                00–064036

For my parents,

Franz and Ruth Johansen

Contents

Preface

This work began over a decade ago when I started studying women's history in graduate school. Reading works that illustrated how gender had shaped women's lives in the past, I began to wonder how gender, as a category of analysis, could help us understand men's history as well. During these same years, I was struggling with the competing demands of graduate school at UCLA, part-time work, and being a husband and father. It was while working as a night security guard and trying to follow convoluted historical arguments at three in the morning that I discovered how different my school experience was going to be from that of most unmarried, childless grad students. While I found colleagues and professors generally encouraging and even sometimes admiring of my efforts to be both father and student, most did not understand the constraints on my time and finances. Few understood the logistical nightmare of something so simple as a spontaneous lunch meeting. Through it all I sought to balance these competing demands as best I could, and to my surprise I began to find sources of inspiration and help in my family. Childrearing not only fostered in me a balanced perspective that helped me endure the vicissitudes of graduate school but also gave me insights into families in the past. While learning in the abstract how parenting shaped women's lives through history, I came to understand from my own experience the degree to which having children could shape a man's life. It was not a great leap for me to begin to wonder how fatherhood shaped men's lives in the past.

A paper on childrearing and domesticity in the nineteenth century revealed to me that, contrary to what many historians at the time were writing, antebellum fathers were not deserting their families for the attractions of the industrializing workplace. After good advice from my advisors, I chose to further explore the story of fatherhood in my dissertation. As the lives of these nineteenth-century fathers unfolded before me, I realized that they no more thought of abandoning the benefits and responsibilities of fatherhood than I did. Yes they compromised, and yes their roles shifted, but fathering was too much of a part of their identity to abandon it.

As I studied beyond the stereotypes and simplistic myths that surround our view of fatherhood in the past, I found a surprisingly rich and complex story. The diaries and letters that I read revealed many different kinds of fathers and fathering behaviors. I was amazed at the poignancy of the emotions felt by fathers who grieved at the deaths of their children and wondered at the depth of the tension between some fathers and sons. I was surprised at the variety of ways in which fathers manipulated children and the subtleties of children's responses. I found fathers in surprising places (the birthing room) and tasks (teaching a daughter about morality)—roles that our current view of nineteenth-century fatherhood does not encompass. I have tried to be true to these fathers' story; the result is a complex picture of antebellum fathers that is engaging, perhaps undertheorized, and often exasperating in its variety.

At times I despaired of making sense of this complexity, but along with several organizing themes gleaned from scholarly sources, I found myself using my own experience. My interaction with my children is here in this book probably more than even I know—it makes my view of fatherhood both presentist and insightful. When I began formulating the chapter on men and birth, I planned for and worried over the birth of our third child. The experience helped me understand how men's romantic ties with their spouses made them care more about the health of their wife than the arrival of a new son or daughter. Similarly, while polishing the section on fathers with courting daughters, I stood helpless while my oldest, my beautiful daughter, blithely drove away with a young man on her first official date. In that moment I moved beyond intellectual understanding and *felt* the reluctance of antebellum fathers to let their daughters grow up.

Yet reading the journals and letters of nineteenth-century Americans frequently reminded me that these fathers lived in a culture quite different from my own. I might share with them certain experiences common to fathers of the last two centuries, but the meaning of fatherhood has changed in the intervening years. These men had more power to shape the lives of their children than I have. There seems to have been less of a cultural gap between the generations, as fathers had more to say about what their children believed and became. Religion was a more essential part of their fathering than it is for most of the fathers I know. I have tried to be sensitive to these differences and to the changes that shaped fatherhood over the period from 1800 to 1860.

Because of this variety, some of the fathers in these pages will be familiar to readers while others will not. It will be natural for some readers to find it difficult to accept this diversity, for we are all experts on the subject of fatherhood. Everyone has an opinion about fathers—even those who have been abandoned by them. Thus, our relationship with our own fathers, or lack of it, often colors our perceptions. Yet this expertise, based on experience with one or a few fathers, is myopic, and thus tends to be of the blind-men-and-the-elephant variety—correct in one context but not applicable to the whole and often opinionated in delivery. My own positive experience with my father requires me to guard against seeing all fathers as mostly wise and competent in their use of power. Understanding this tendency to extrapolate from one's own experience helps us approach the study of fatherhood with a more open mind. In the end, I hope that this study will aid readers in learning about their own father-child relationships as well as those in the past.

Much of what is valuable about this work is due to the excellent guidance of my dissertation advisor, Ellen DuBois. Without her keen analysis and encouragement it would have been a far inferior work. I am grateful to her for both her careful reading of this study and her encouragement to make this work my own. Gina Morantz-Sanchez read the entire manuscript and gave invaluable guidance in my study of family history. My dissertation group colleagues were, for several years, my most helpful critics and supporters. Thanks to Ernie Chavez, Mary Corey, Daniel Johnson, Margo McBane, and Pat Moore. Several historians have read and commented on all or part of this work in its various stages. My thanks to Sally Boniece, Holly Brewer, Paul Charney, Margaret Finnegan, Rochelle Gatlin, Donna Cooper Graves, James Hagen, Laura McCall, Connie McGovern,

Ruth Milkman, Nancy Osterud, Brenda Stevenson, and Albion Urdank. E. Anthony Rotundo responded to a letter from a lowly graduate student, and my work has benefited from his interest and trenchant advice. I have yet to meet anyone in academics who is more unselfish with his ideas and influence. My thinking about fatherhood and history has benefited from discussions with many friends and colleagues over the last fifteen years. I am particularly indebted to Randal Allred, Norm Barlow, Irene Bates, Herrik Eaton Chapman, Dana Comi, Greg Dundas, Barney Hadden, James Riding In, Phil Swirbul, Frank Towers, and Anne Ustach. I am grateful for the encouragement and assistance of colleagues at various universities over my short teaching career. Thanks to Nick Clulee, David Dean, Gordon Kershaw, Mathew Mancini, Betsy Perry, John Wiseman, and Nancy Beck Young. Finally, I would be remiss if I did not acknowledge the contributions to my understanding of history from Joyce Appleby, Daniel Howe, John Laslett, Melissa Meyer, Gary Nash, George Sanchez, and Bruce Schulman.

My thanks to Brendan O'Malley at Routledge for his patience and perceptive reading of my manuscript. I am also grateful to Cecelia Cancellaro, who saw the potential of this work.

Without the Huntington Library's wonderful collections, I would not have been able to pursue this topic. My thanks to the helpful curators and staff who facilitated my research in the two years that I was engaged there. I am also grateful for the Huntington Library's permission to quote from manuscript material from their collections. At the Newberry Library in Chicago, I was particularly fortunate to be given access to the uncatalogued Metcalf Family Papers, which proved to have a wealth of material on fatherhood. My thanks to the Newberry Library and its staff and also to Jeff Metcalf, who let me pry into the lives of his ancestors. I also acknowledge the Newberry Library's gracious permission to quote from their manuscript collections.

My thanks to Fred Strasburg and his Antelope Valley Institute of History for a job that allowed me to work in history during my last years in Los Angeles. I am grateful to Joan Gundersen, John Allswang, Lynn Dumenil, and Norm Cohen, who during my brief tenure as a Los Angeles "freeway professor" assisted with opportunities to grow as a teacher. Frostburg State University helped with a faculty development grant that freed valuable hours for working on the final stages of the manuscript.

Finally, I thank my family. My father, mother, sisters, and brothers taught me more about families than all the books I have read, and to them I owe a debt that I can never repay. My children Li Syin, Samuel, Thomas, and Jenna have been my teachers as well. The three oldest cheerfully endured the trials of poverty and graduate school with me, and now that they are growing old enough to know better, I ask their forgiveness. Last of all I thank Michelle, who through her contributions knows best the meaning of this work.

Introduction

The idea of fatherhood has occupied an ambiguous position in nineteenth- and twentieth-century American culture. In literature, an enduring image of nineteenth-century power is the Victorian patriarch. Austere, distant, and arbitrary, the Victorian father lorded over his children, whom he viewed as a distraction to his real business of earning a living and relaxing with the daily paper in the parlor. These men were so uninterested in children and family, one wonders how their offspring were conceived in the first place. Taking this view of fathers one step further, many nineteenth-century fiction writers frequently constructed stories around young protagonists with dead or missing fathers. Tom Sawyer's father would have taught him proper middle-class manners, thus squelching his boyish exuberance and genius; Jo Marchent could not have become so independent had her father not gone off to war; and Horatio Alger's Ragged Dick would not have been living on the street if he had been supported by a breadwinner. In the literary tradition of American individualism, heroes and heroines must find their own way in the world—the presence of fathers would have seriously disrupted the journey.

In contrast to these distant or missing patriarchs, our idea of twentieth-century fathers allows a nurturing element. The benevolent middle-class TV fathers of the 1950s took time after work to teach and discipline their children. These fictional fathers, like their nineteenth-century counterparts, were also symbols of power in the home (as in *Father Knows Best*), but their authority was tempered with kindness and understanding. Increasingly, however, many popular depictions of fatherhood point to a greater societal skepticism about paternal authority. The ineffectual Willy Loman in *Death of a Salesman*, *All in the Family's* bigoted Archie Bunker, and the buffoonish Homer Simpson are just some of the blatant portrayals of fathers' declining prospects. Unlike the wise and competent Ward Cleaver, these men stumble through their limited family roles.

In recent years, the idea of declining paternal authority has become central to the way we think about fathers. It is generally assumed that fathers no longer have the time or talent to rear children, nor do they have the authority to govern as they once did. A few highly publicized countertrends have surfaced, like fatherhood support groups and stay-at-home dads, and perhaps even the growing number of single fathers, but these are seen as eddies in the current of decline. More often we hear of absent breadwinners, dead-beat dads, and abusive fathers. In comparing cultural icons such as the Victorian father and Homer Simpson, one gets a sense of the radical shift that has occurred in American perceptions of fatherhood over the past two centuries. The popular mind has discarded fathering images of power and nurture for views of anachronism, powerlessness, violence, and absence. The concept of fatherhood's waning significance resonates widely across American culture.[1]

Behind the popular images spun by pundits, social commentators, and popular writers is usually a far more complex and contradictory reality, yet we continue to hold on to easily understood representations. Despite the complexity of our own families, we persist in seeing families in the past through nostalgic, simplistic lenses. We base our views not on sound history but on short-term cultural memory. Many Americans today feel that fathers in the past must have been much like the idealized 1950s middle-class father found in sitcoms, which means that the latest generation of fathers is inadequate.[2] It is seductively easy for us to seek to understand fatherhood by looking to a simplistic image such as the Victorian father or the 1950s TV father as a model for fatherhood. As a result, we constantly face disorientation and disappointment when reality fails to match mythical ideals. Indeed, in the face of numerous and conflicting images of past power and current decline, it is no wonder that some contemporary fathers despair of ever successfully fulfilling their role.

It is the purpose of this book to step beyond simplified and nostalgic representations to a more complex view of fatherhood based upon actual fathering behaviors. Through the use of letters and diaries, this work will illuminate the lives of over one hundred middle-class fathers during the years between 1800 and the Civil War.[3] This period saw many of the most important changes that have shaped American society: the growth of commerce and early industry, expanding urbanization, the rise of a middle class, and the dissemination of new ideas about the value of the individual. All of these factors contributed to the emergence of a new "domestic" family type that altered the cultural meaning of being a father. While these changes caused elements of men's domestic roles and power to shift and even decline, merely emphasizing decline without exploring the significant place men held in nineteenth-century middle-class families is to present a distorted view of the past. Throughout these upheavals, fatherhood retained a vital place in the lives of men and their families.

Historians' task is to delve below surface perceptions that make up historical clichés. Often, in light of their findings, we reevaluate our interpretation of history and discard long-held views. However, in the case of fatherhood, a primary reason for the persistence of the popular conception of declining fatherhood is the lack of a sound historical alternative. Despite the centrality of patriarchy in the lives of Americans in the past, and despite many years of male-centered history, there are few historical studies of fathers. Like masculinity, fatherhood has only recently become the subject of historical inquiry. Most of our current view of fathers in the past comes to us indirectly through studies of women, the family, industrialization, and modernization. Early women's history works by Anne L. Kuhn, Robert Sunley, and Barbara Welter sketched the outlines of a portrait that was later filled in by Carl Degler, Mary P. Ryan, and others in their studies on the American family.[4] With some limited variations, this view suggests that from a central, unchallenged position of familial power and moral authority during the colonial period, fathers fell to a peripheral status in the family as early as the mid-nineteenth century. The economic and social changes of industrialization and urbanization limited men to the distant roles of provider, disciplinarian, and occasional advisor, leaving them bereft of moral authority and daily influence over children. Mothers, schools, and the state took over the duties of the increasingly distant father, until by 1850, according to historian Mary P. Ryan, "the idea of fatherhood itself seemed almost to wither away."[5] The assumption has been that fathers never really recovered from this lost position.

Occasionally, at the urging of mothers and "experts," men have made half-hearted attempts to regain a domestic role, but the more important (and appealing) demands of the workplace soon thwart these efforts. This tidy portrayal of the decline of fatherhood has an attractive simplicity and logic that has made it the standard whenever historians have addressed families in the past.[6]

This interpretation rests on two primary historical arguments. First, that fathers were the primary parent in the colonial period—governor, teacher, provider, and moral guide all in one paternal role—and second, that the immense economic and social changes of the early to mid-nineteenth century almost totally undermined that dominant position. Since these two accepted notions are so influential in shaping our current historical view of fatherhood, we need to examine them and the evidence upon which they are built.

The image of a dominant, involved colonial father comes to us largely from studies based on New England Puritan religious writings and law. These sources emphasize that men in this society were to control their families' access to the community, the state, and God. Fathers had the responsibility to provide for the material welfare of their children, see that they married well, and supervise work, but authorities particularly focused on men's duty to catechize children and lead family devotions. Puritan leaders felt that men were best suited for this work because women were assumed to be morally inferior and more prone to indulge their children's tendency toward evil. At the same time, men controlled all family property and the labor of their children, placing them in a position of considerable economic power over wives and children.[7]

Colonial American society made it a capital crime for a child to disobey a parent, leaving little doubt that fathers held awesome power in their families. Is it any wonder, then, that historians have extrapolated that colonial children feared and obeyed their fathers? However, historical studies that use sermons and law will tend to emphasize order, authority, and convention over behavior. Ministers and lawmakers usually tried to sustain the status quo in power relations by preaching patriarchal responsibility and authority and emphasizing men's dominance over children and wives. What the people themselves did was often a different matter. Studies have found that New Englanders did not always obey the law or even enforce it. There is no recorded instance, for example, of a child being put to death for disobedience, and recorded births tell us that many young men and women violated the statutes against premarital sex.[8] Furthermore, as early as the third generation in some New England towns, land scarcity limited men's ability to control sons through inheritance.[9] These examples suggest that Puritan fathers' influence was probably not as dominant as the legal and religious records suggest.

Moreover, it is likely that men's childrearing role in the colonial period has been exaggerated by historians overly persuaded by the patriarchal nature of seventeenth-century Puritan rhetoric. Men may have had the official, God-ordained responsibility to inculcate morality in children, but women spent more time with young children. We must remember that this was a hierarchical society; wives were considered to be a legal appendage to their husbands and were represented by their husbands before God and the state. If a woman did much of the child-rearing, the father would still fulfill his duty, for his wife would be acting under his stewardship. Even the Puritan church acknowledged that parents shared teaching responsibilities; Cotton Mather wrote in 1699, "And let it be remembered, That the Fathers are not the only Parents obliged thus to pursue the Salvation of their Children."[10]

Without a clear view of colonial fathering behaviors—and thus an accurate and realistic beginning point of reference—historians have most likely exaggerated the differences between colonial and antebellum fathers. Indeed, scholars of the American family, following the lead of European family historians, have often worked under the assumption that the colonial American family represents the premodern, patriarchal family. They have assumed that in a few short decades in the late eighteenth and early nineteenth centuries, patriarchy as a form of family government gave way to a modern, usually middle-class domestic family system. But, as historians of the European family have shown, a developing market economy and other factors were shaping and changing the European patriarchal family system even before the first English settlers came to America. The American family did not experience a rapid progression from "premodern" to "modern"; rather, its history begins somewhere in the middle of that grand change. If modernizing forces precipitated the decline of men's domestic power, then the first European fathers built their homes in the New World well after the process had begun.[11]

This brief look at colonial fatherhood illustrates the need for more exploration of sources that reveal fathering behaviors before the Revolution. Historians of the nineteenth century, who have a wider range and variety of sources to use than colonial historians do, should be able to say more about fathering behavior, but until recently, they too have turned to commentary on manners and morals, primarily the advice literature that became popular after 1830. The growth of this genre stemmed partly from developments in the printing industry that made cheap books readily available for a burgeoning middle-class market, but it also drew upon popular American manifestations of the Enlightenment, such as ideas of human worth, self-improvement, and perfectibility. Americans began to realize that environment played an important part in successful childrearing. Self-styled experts on childrearing and family relations took advantage of this dawning realization by giving copious advice to parents, especially mothers, on a wide range of childrearing matters. However, a characteristic of this advice-to-parents source is its prescriptive nature—it does not necessarily reflect actual behavior. As Jay Mechling has noted, *"childrearing manuals are the consequents not of childrearing values but of childrearing manual-writing values."*[12] This literature can tell us much about the values of the writers, but little about parental behavior or beliefs. Nineteenth-century middle-class Americans consumed this literature, but it is still not established that they internalized its values and acted upon them. Even careful historians who have used this literature in their work have often forgotten this point, extrapolating typicality from the ideal family painted in these manuals.

Forming the foundation of this prescriptive literature were two intimately related notions that structured much of the advice, what historians have come to call the ideologies of "separate spheres" and "domesticity." As antebellum observers watched with mixed feelings the growth of commerce and industry with its waste, greed, wealth, and power, they began to see in the rising middle-class family an influence that could counter the worst effects of modernization. Home could be a place where values such as honesty, hard work, kindness, and respect for one's fellow man could be esteemed and taught. When changes in economics shifted the role of women and children from producers to consumers, authors of advice literature started promoting the notion that it was appropriate for men and women to live and work largely in separate arenas in society. Men were to dominate the public sphere, where breadwinning was done, and women reigned over children in the private sphere where consumption took place and values were taught. Thus, the notion of separate spheres described a perceived separation of the domestic from the rest of society while also advocating a structuring of gender roles.

This division of male and female into separate spheres served as an integral part of the concept of domesticity. The advice literature suggested that separating men's and women's primary roles was befitting and natural because men's masculine nature contained traits adapted for business and politics, while women embodied the gentle virtues relevant to hearth and home. Breadwinners needed to be aggressive, driven, and rational, while homemakers needed to be able to nurture and instill morality; thus, men and women were suited for the work that the new capitalist economy had given them.[13]

As scholars of the twentieth century began to study women and the family, they found both of these cultural constructions useful. Historians in the mid-1960s and early 1970s used the advice literature extensively, finding the metaphor of spheres helpful when mentally building their own view of nineteenth-century family relations. Consequently, as Linda Kerber notes, their reliance on this metaphor has dominated their history.

> Exploring the traditions of historical discourse, historians found that notions of women's sphere permeated the language; they in turn used the metaphor in their own descriptions. Thus the relationship between the name—sphere—and the perception of what it named was reciprocal; widespread usage in the nineteenth century directed the choices made by twentieth-century historians about what to study and how to tell the stories that they reconstructed.[14]

As historians adopted the concept of separate spheres, they became predisposed to see men only in public roles. If men were public beings, there was no need to study their limited private lives. Thus, the pervasiveness in historical writing of the idea of separate spheres meant that its unstated and unexamined corollary, the father's absence from the home, was just as widely accepted.[15]

The concept of domesticity also found its way into the sociology of the 1950s from which historians of the family drew. According to sociologist Talcott Parsons, as men's and women's work became increasingly separated, both of the sexes "specialized" in appropriate gender traits. Women, he argued, as the primary stewards of childrearing and emotional sustenance, refined the necessary "expressive" skills to fill this role. Men, on the other hand, being tied to the public realm through their work, specialized in "instrumental" character traits that enabled them to function effectively in the economic world.[16] While some historians were uncomfortable with the functionalism of Parsons' views, this "updated version" of the nineteenth-century ideology of domesticity became accepted by many.[17] According to historian Mary Ryan, "A father in a Victorian parlor was something of a bull in a china shop, somewhat ill at ease with the gentle virtues enshrined there."[18]

The acceptance of the ideas of separate spheres and domesticity has immense meaning for the history of nineteenth-century fatherhood. On one level, it has curtailed the study of fatherhood. Why examine the fathering role when it became a minor part of nineteenth-century families? Furthermore, by dichotomizing the roles of men and women into public and private spheres, historians have oversimplified the complex family and gender relations of nineteenth-century America. They have decided, for example, that if women's role in the family increased, men's role necessarily had to decrease. "As mother's importance waxed, father's inexorably waned," notes one historian.[19] With this either-or approach we are inclined to view men and women in opposition in their function as parents; there is no entertainment of the possibility that perhaps both roles increased and complimented each other. We assume that fathers lost domestic power during these years despite the limited study of actual power relations within the home. In other words, we have developed our history from extrapolation rather than research. Even two recent studies of fatherhood, Robert Griswold's *Fatherhood in America* and Stephen Frank's *Life with Father*, which present more complex views of fatherhood than previous studies do, are heavily influenced by these ideas. Griswold relies almost entirely on secondary sources for his view of nineteenth-century fathers; thus, not surprisingly, his work emphasizes the loss of fathering power and duties. Frank tries to combine into a unified history cultural ideals found in the advice literature with fathering behaviors evidenced in letters, diaries, and autobiographies. At times he succeeds in presenting a complex picture of fathers for whom fatherhood was an important part of their lives, yet often he undermines these findings by imposing on them the rigid ideals found in the advice manuals. These historians' use of the language and model of separate spheres structures their perceptions and limits their conclusions. In the end their works join the ranks of previous studies that emphasize a limited and undermined role for nineteenth-century middle-class fathers.[20]

To develop a clearer view of fatherhood in the nineteenth century, we must step beyond the constraints of the advice literature's view of fathers. We know enough about convention; now it is time to look at behavior. Doing so will provide us with a richer, more complex view of fathers in the past. To borrow a metaphor from John Demos, fatherhood in the past has many faces that can be studied.[21] Fatherhood itself refers not to a single role or position, but to a set of intertwined and sometimes competing duties and rights. Fathers both serve their children and have power over them. While the tasks that a father fulfilled in the nineteenth-century middle-class family were quite varied, they can be categorized into four essential roles: provider, teacher, caregiver, and governor. The provider role meant more than just supplying the necessities of life; it also included providing the opportunities, knowledge, morals, and means necessary for successful inclusion into the ranks of the middle class. Men, at times, exerted enormous effort to fulfill this duty. Their teacher role included the inculcation of values and religion, as well as secular knowledge and skills. Middle-class fathers in the antebellum period also cared for children. While their providing role took precedence, men occasionally acted as nurse, playmate, companion, and ultimately as confidant to mature children.

Men's role as governor, the way that they wielded power, is more difficult to both examine and interpret. Fathers traditionally shared with mothers the task of governing children—allocating resources, dictating workload, presenting and enforcing an ethical code, setting rules, and disciplining when those rules were broken. When men have been able to fill this role it is because they possessed two key attributes: the authority (or right) to govern and the power (or ability) to control. In other words, power and authority, although related, are different; parents' authority over children is legitimated by society (through religion, law, convention, and so on), while their power stems from such advantages as superior size, their role as breadwinner, and even the status that their authority gives to them.

If we compare the power and authority held by early American fathers to that exercised by fathers today, it is evident that men's ability and right to control their children has declined. Behind the colonial father, buttressing his position, were the church, the community, the courts, and the extended family. Fathers' power was evident in their ability to dictate marriage and occupation choices for their children; few fathers today presume these rights, and even fewer have the power to enforce them. Middle-class men today do not apprentice their children, nor do they usually require their children's labor for the success of the family economy. Many historians point to the late eighteenth and early nineteenth century for the origins of this decline. Some suggest that the Enlightenment and Romanticism challenged the arbitrary nature of fathers' moral right to govern children by emphasizing the worth of the individual. Reflected in the ideas of authors like Locke and Rousseau, the general estimation of children improved; no longer were infants in need of baptism at birth because of Adam's sin, nor of having their will broken by draconian methods to ensure their obedience. Newer advice on childrearing emphasized parents guiding children through the process of becoming rational, independent beings. Paternal tyranny was thought to be a major obstacle in achieving this goal, so commentators of the time advocated relinquishing overly strict constraints on children.[22] Other historians emphasize economic causes, suggesting that as family economies shifted from farming to commerce and manufacturing, fathers no longer had the time to rear children or the land to use in controlling them. These historians maintain that as the cult of domesticity flowered, men supposedly deferred to female authority on all domestic matters, as women became the governors of the private realm.[23]

These views, however, have tended to overemphasize the decline of men's ability to govern their children, partly because they have rested on one-dimensional definitions of paternal power. Further research into the lives of fathers reveals that they have had access to a variety of sources of power. While a father's influence over children in the nineteenth century no doubt had a strong financial component—control of land, tools, a business, funds for education or enterprise—it was by no means the only source of influence. Many fathers also appealed to their moral right and obligation to rear children, and some fell back on their legal rights to maintain control. Some were more likely than others to use their superior size and strength to intimidate children, while many, especially after 1800, seem to have employed the obligation that accompanied love as a check on their children's actions. Most historians tend to focus on only one or two of these sources and do not take into account the broad and varied foundation of paternal power.

As power is an essential component of fatherhood, much of this book focuses on its nature and persistence in middle-class fatherhood. The men in this study perceived maintenance of control over children as a component of their dominant place in the family and society and thus did not relinquish power easily. Does this mean that their families can be defined as patriarchal? We should remember that although fatherhood and patriarchy are related, they are not synonymous. The word "patriarchy" has a wide range of often charged meanings—a system of family government based on the dominant male member's control of either the means of production or the family's ties with the community, male domination of females in society, or merely a father's authority over his children.[24] To avoid the confusion that sometimes accompanies the use of the word, we should ask three questions: Did patriarchy as a system of family government persist into the nineteenth century? Did men's role as fathers contribute to their dominance over women? Did fathers control children by virtue of their paternal position?

These questions pose divergent paths of inquiry, and I have obviously chosen to pursue the last (paternal patriarchy) in this book. Still, the first two questions are also important and have relevance to this work. In regard to traditional patriarchal families, the antebellum middle-class fathers in these pages are not like their colonial counterparts. They did keep a firm hand on the purse strings, but by comparison they were not given to controlling children through inheritance, nor were they the gatekeepers of all of their children's paths to the larger society. By 1800 children for the most part were choosing their own spouses and could expect an equal portion of the family estate, and as the century progressed, sons were increasingly less dependent upon land inheritance for successful inclusion into middle-class adulthood. Nineteenth-century fathers' position as head of household and breadwinner did allow them a substantial measure of control over their children, but not to the extent of the patriarchs of the past.

The question of how fatherhood influenced gender patriarchy (male power over females) is more difficult to answer. Scholars have confused the issue by often failing to differentiate between power over women and power over children. While middle-class women and children were both dependent on men's earning power and each held a subordinate position before the law, their power relationships with men were different. With this distinction in mind, we can see that fatherhood contributed to the maintenance of women's subordinate position in nineteenth-century society in two different ways. By giving men power over the inculcation of values, fatherhood allowed them to teach children to respect and perpetuate gender divisions that benefited men. As we will see in Chapter 5, men used this power to their advantage. Second, because mothers and fathers both held authority over children, spouses could wield their respective positions to influence each other. Men could, for example, significantly shape women's workload by insisting on a certain kind of childrearing technique that women, who were the primary caregivers, would then be obligated to institute. On the other hand, women occasionally vetoed their husbands' decisions when they felt that their position of constant interaction gave them a better perspective on a problem. Thus, men and women shared and negotiated power over childrearing.

Which sex had the most influence in this sharing? Men with their tradition of control and varied sources of domestic power would seem to have the clear advantage in any negotiation over childrearing. However, because of responsibilities attached to earning a living and their secondary status in children's first years, men at times had no choice but to defer to their wives. Indeed, there were some men who gave up all childrearing authority to wives (and teachers and servants), although they were not the norm; middle-class fathers before the Civil War were often more involved than not. Determining the exact nature of the division of domestic authority between antebellum fathers and mothers, however, is problematic. The power relationship in marriage was complex; it was shaped by romantic expectations, changing views of gender, and the variety of childrearing behaviors. This book will throw some light on this key family dynamic, but much work still needs to be done. The relationship that the men in this study had with their wives, like much of our picture of the private life of men in this period, has yet to come into complete focus.

Those who read this work hoping for definitive answers to the question of men's and women's domestic power in the family will be disappointed. However, by clearly showing that it was shared, this work lays groundwork in the effort to answer a conundrum that has bothered historians for some time: If childrearing represents the transmission of culture, and women controlled childrearing, then why did they continue to teach values that actively contributed to their own subjugation? Why not take advantage of the opportunity to undermine male domination? Historians have usually answered this question by appealing to the concept of hegemony, which is supported by the fact that many women actively upheld and propagated the notion of domesticity during these years. However, by bringing fathers into the childrearing equation, both as inculcators and as an influence on their wives, the conservative nature of childrearing becomes more understandable.

To fill the need for a clearer view of nineteenth-century fatherhood, this book examines what it meant to be a middle-class father in the northern portion of the United States from roughly 1800 to 1860. I have included in my sample men who had a legal father-child tie with their children—biological fathers, stepfathers, and fathers-in-law. I included the latter because many antebellum Americans viewed this relationship as essentially the same as a father-child relationship, complete with similar obligations and privileges. I have indicated when the tie was through marriage rather than blood. Men who mentored children could act much like fathers but lacked paternal rights and powers and thus are excluded from the sample.[25] The dates 1800–1860 are approximates because lives and primary sources obviously are not as tidy as our periodization. To understand context or trends, some material is used from the decade before and the decade after this sixty-year period. I chose the antebellum era because many historians of the family feel that this was a pivotal time in the history of the family, when industrialization and commercialization altered family patterns and the father's role experienced its greatest erosion. Carl N. Degler, for example, asserts that in the period between the Revolutionary War and 1830, the modern American family emerged, complete with a separate spheres ideology.[26]

The period of sixty years was originally chosen in the hope that it would be short enough to provide a meaningful focus, yet long enough to show change over time. My research shows that some critical shifts occurred that will be outlined in the following pages. However, changes in parenting and family patterns come slowly. Philippe Ariés, noted historian of the European family, has found that "[t]he difficulty for the historian lies in being sensitive to changes, but yet not being obsessed by them to the point of forgetting the great forces of inertia which reduce the real impact of innovations."[27] Despite the dynamic development of society during this period, the continuities in fathering are more striking, suggesting that changes in men's roles were not as pronounced as historians have thought. Time spent with children may (or may not) have declined, but most middle-class fathers in this sixty-year period found time to fill the roles that colonial fathers did: They advised children, taught them how to work, and instructed them about gender roles, morality, and other values. Formal schooling increasingly became part of children's lives, but many fathers retained the role of tutor for their children. The parental role of mothers increased in significance, but fathers in 1860 seem just as likely as men in 1800 (perhaps even more so) to advise their wives on childrearing. Thus, it seems that fathers retained most of their duties and much of their authority during this sixty-year period. Fathers added a few new responsibilities associated with the birth of their children and expanded their role in the area of breadwinning, but they generally maintained the same duties that they filled in earlier times.

While we should beware of exaggerating changes to fatherhood, the variety of fathering behaviors needs to be emphasized. This study focuses on a fairly homogeneous group—white middle-class fathers from New England, New York, Pennsylvania, New Jersey, Ohio, Indiana, Michigan, and Illinois.[28] This geographical area had a population consisting largely of white Protestants, the majority of British ancestry. Yet within this group important distinctions exist. For example, occupations determined fathering patterns to some extent. Sea captains and traveling salesmen obviously had to have a different approach to fathering than did farmers and accountants, who usually saw their children every day. Likewise, urban fathers had constraints on their time unknown to rural fathers, and they occasionally abided by different value systems. Fathering also changed over the course of a man's life. Fathers had different needs, duties, and pressures on them at different stages in their lives. Thus, fathering meant something quite different for the father of an infant child than it did for the father of a marriageable daughter or son.

To protect this complexity from overgeneralization, this book does not attempt to represent "the" nineteenth-century father. Types are helpful, particularly in the early stages of study, but they can obscure and, indeed, have limited our view of nineteenth-century fatherhood for some time. By showing a wide range of behaviors, this book reveals that men were not restricted by a single set of conventions that kept them from participating in domestic matters. Rather, men responding to perceived duties drew on their authority to become involved with their families in a variety of ways. I have tried to let these fathers speak for themselves as much as possible and to show in their own words the complexity of their lives.

To further this objective, I have organized this work around the life course of the father, beginning with a chapter on the early provider role and continuing through to a chapter on the aging father's relationship with adult children. Fathers, if they lived long enough, experienced several key and often overlapping transitions in their relationships with their children—birth, sending a child away to school or work, the marriage of a child. At these junctures the life course becomes a valuable tool for understanding fatherhood, for it can reveal how men responded to these important changes. However, key issues, such as love, abuse, death, and authority, are not exclusive to any one stage. For the sake of organization, I have localized these issues in specific chapters, thus organizing chapters thematically as well as according to the different stages in men's lives, but these themes are occasionally discussed elsewhere and are relevant to all stages. Certain transitions such as the choice of a career, the birth of a daughter, or the marriage of a son were abrupt and often dominated the fathering experience at a particular moment. During other stages, such as the schooling and courting years, changes came slowly and less intrusively. Thus, in some chapters, particularly those that deal with the beginning and end of fathering years, the life course plays a prominent part, while in others it is hardly noticeable.

The first chapter concerns important early choices that young men made—occupation, home location, and family labor division—and also explores the power and responsibilities that came with the breadwinning role and how it shaped men's time with children. The second chapter looks at men's experience with birth control, pregnancy, and birth, distinguishing between first and subsequent births. The importance of the romantic ties men had with their wives is considered in this chapter. The third chapter studies fathers' sometimes ambivalent relationships with their infant children and also addresses responses to death in the context of the high infant mortality of the era. The fourth and fifth chapters each cover the long period between early fatherhood and the stage when children reached the threshold of adulthood; Chapter 4 addresses fathers' power and authority over children, and Chapter 5 examines the nature of men's instruction and leisure time with children. The final chapter shows the tensions and developments of the last years of fatherhood, from the maturation of children into the years when fathers occasionally turned to children for help in their old age. This life course framework allows exploration of how fathering was a process that extended over most of men's adult lives. It also shows how fatherhood exists only in relation to children. Thus, the stages of children's lives—birth, infancy, preadolescence, adolescence, young adult, and adult years—roughly identify the stages of fatherhood. Men usually had more than one child; therefore, these stages often overlapped. Yet the strength of this approach is its sensitivity to changes that shaped fatherhood over the course of fathers' lives.[29]

The life course structure is not without problems. Not all men's lives unfolded in the same way. Death, remarriage, career moves, and other life changes often altered the course of fatherhood. A man, for example, might marry a widow with children, becoming a father overnight and perhaps never even experience raising young children. Transitions like the departure of sons and daughters from home did not have the regularity of those stages rooted in biological change. However, even after taking into account exceptions like these, the life course provides considerable flexibility in illuminating the complexity of men's place in families.

This work, through the use of the life course model and a reliance on sources that reveal the lives of actual fathers, will add to the growing number of works that have as their goal a more complete, nuanced view of men and private life. The key task of the very young field of fatherhood history is evident: to push beyond the simplistic conceptions that dominate our understanding of fatherhood and replace them with a fuller picture of men's power and involvement in the family. The rich variety of behaviors and values that emerge from the letters and diaries of antebellum families will assist us in bringing this more complete view into focus. With time and increased understanding, we will be able to discard the blunt models of family history that have led us to ignore and distort fathers in the past.

More sophisticated views of antebellum fathers will allow us to see how families were structured throughout history. As we come to understand that fatherhood can contain significant degrees of domestic power and weakness at the same time, we will see more clearly how men, women, and children negotiated the division of domestic power. If we illuminate the range of paternal feelings felt by nineteenth-century fathers—everything from apathy to ambivalence to passion—we can begin to understand the complex motivations behind actions and attitudes. In the end, a study of fatherhood is also an exploration of gender relations, personal politics, and cultural change. If we are truly to understand the relations of the sexes, if we wish to have a clear view of how culture is passed from one generation to the next, and if we are to understand the interconnectedness of the public and the private—all questions that deeply interest more than just historians—then we need a clearer picture of men's role and power in families, both past and present.

chapter one

"Oh Ambition!"

CAREERS AND HOME

By his forty-fifth year, Lincoln Clark had come to regret career choices made earlier in life. Born in Massachusetts at the turn of the nineteenth century, he had ventured to Alabama in 1837 with hopes of establishing a law practice in a developing region of the country. By 1845, however, he was tired of the itinerant life of the circuit court. "I am becoming to believe that I am the greatest home man in the world," he wrote to his wife Julia, "and this I think speaks well for me and better for you. I sometimes think I can not endure this judgeship, it will keep me so long from the only place at which I am satisfied."[1] Also worried about his children growing up in a culture dominated by slavery, Clark decided to return to the North. But not just any region above the Mason-Dixon Line would do. Having made a stagnating choice a decade earlier, Clark agonized over his decision. He wanted to return to live near family in Massachusetts but worried about the prospects for a law practice in rural New England. "I should probably get nothing but small business and should almost certainly be looked upon as of small importance, and to endure this I have too much pride, and my habits and associations revolt at it; we had place, character and influence in our circle and I must have it still in order to be satisfied."[2] Clark finally chose to move his family to Iowa, where, ironically, his ambition eventually pushed him into politics, a career that often kept him away from home for months at a time.

Ambitious, geographically mobile, and working long hours away from home, men like Lincoln Clark seem to be forerunners of the modern absent fathers who abandon wives, children, and home to do battle in the male "sphere" of business and politics. Yet domestic concerns clearly influenced his decision to move; in Alabama, he felt that his job kept him too often away from family and that there were negative cultural influences on his children. Was he attempting to mold his career around the needs of his family, or were these mere excuses, justifications of a guilty conscience that had chosen opportunity and public power over domestic bliss? Was Lincoln Clark a status-seeking lawyer and politician, a concerned father, or perhaps both?

These are important questions to the historian of nineteenth-century fatherhood. Scholars of the family and of women argue that one by-product of the immense economic and social changes of nineteenth-century industrialization was the growing isolation of the middle-class family from the public world of work and politics. The fate of men in the face of this widening gulf has prompted little debate. Historians assume that as the domestic "sphere" became separated from public life, men of the new middle class were less and less to be found at home. No longer farmers in a slow-paced agrarian world, these men spent long days in the brutish, demanding, and sometimes venal world of business. Many historians believe that this retreat of the family away from the public arena contributed to a divergence of the masculine from the domestic. Indeed, for men, involvement in the masculine working world meant contact with the perceived evils of industrialization. According to historian John Demos, "maleness itself seemed to carry a certain odor of contamination."[3] Since men spent more time working away from the home and thus increasingly were alienated from domestic life and values, fathers were no longer childrearers. Even if they had wanted to fulfill this role, these men no longer had the time or ability to raise children.

Like most of our historical images of nineteenth-century fatherhood, however, the concept of the absent father is based on largely unchallenged and untested assumptions. Three come to the fore in the narrative of fatherhood's diminishing prospects. Among the most enduring is the idea that dramatic changes in work patterns greatly decreased fathers' time with children. Usually, the new patterns of work proposed by historians look suspiciously like those that structured the life of the stereotypical 1950s suburban father. These men, responding to economic forces, were unable or unwilling to manipulate their work environment to maintain a strong presence in the home. They spent their days commuting, working, and entertaining, and had little time for anything else. Powerful pressures such as love, attachment, and the desire to influence their children's lives played little if any part in this equation. These stereotypical men were merely economic beings spending long hours engaged in the culture of work because corporate America provided the only yardstick to measure their success. The second assumption stems from the perception held by nineteenth-century observers that the work-related values of the industrializing nation were less pure than the older, agrarian values. Historians assume that, as middle-class men imbibed new ideas of competition and cutthroat individualism, they became tainted and thus incapable of acting as the moral center of the family. Women, by virtue of their separation from "public" values, became repositories of traditional morality. The third assumption, that childrearing became solely a feminine duty, asserts a strict division of labor between the sexes along public/private lines, thus exempting public men from domestic chores. Finally, underlying each of these assumptions is the notion that men were willing to relinquish domestic influence in exchange for public prestige and power. With these arguments in place, it seems logical to conclude that as men abandoned families for the world of work, there was, as the historian Mary P. Ryan states, a "transfer of functions from male to female as mothers' concern for child care expanded into the vacuum left by the indifference of fathers."[4]

This book, and this chapter particularly, challenges these assumptions through a discussion of antebellum middle-class men's work. Diaries and correspondence reveal that, in many ways, work actually linked men to their families. For most middle-class men, acting in the role of provider usually created strong emotional bonds that tied them to their wives and children. Fathers were more than providers, but even this role had many facets aside from just an economic one. The same sources also show that many middle-class men regularly performed domestic chores, suggesting that the boundary between public and private was not strictly equivalent to the gender line. Careful examination of family relations among the middle class also shows that men did not relinquish all of their domestic power and moral authority to women. While antebellum women saw their influence over childrearing increase during these years, men strove to retain the rights and privileges that they held in relation to wives and children. Throughout the antebellum period, men exercised considerable influence over the running of homes, the raising of children, and the allocation of family resources.

One cannot deny, however, that work patterns played an important role in shaping middle-class fathering. Indeed, this study begins with the issue of work because it was so central to men's identity and authority.[5] When young men made a career choice, they often determined much of their future as a father; work shaped men's daily routine, including the number of hours they would spend away from home and how many opportunities they would have to interact with children. In addition, by putting men in the position to control most of the family income, work formed a significant source of men's power over family members. By locating the origins of changes to fatherhood in the shifting economy, family historians acknowledge these important ties between work and fatherhood. However, by assuming that work pushed men from domestic affairs, they have ignored a basic tension in the lives of antebellum men. A close look at the correspondence and diaries of middle-class families reveals that fathers strove to balance their often conflicting roles in the workplace and the home. For many, this task exacted the price of substantial psychic stress. Lincoln Clark wrestled with his career dilemma for at least two years before finally choosing opportunity over proximity to family by moving to Iowa instead of New England. The stress of maintaining public and private roles, instead of showing decline, actually illustrates the strength and conviction of men's commitment to both arenas. To deny middle-class fathers any significant role other than that of an economic provider rejects the complexity and authority of nineteenth-century fatherhood.

When young middle-class men ventured from home and school to find work in the antebellum North, they stepped into a world quite different from that known by their grandfathers. In the commercializing economy of the nineteenth century, the path to middle-class success lay not on the farm, but in the emerging industries and enterprises of consumer capitalism. Although some found middle-class status on farms where cash crops were grown, young men were more likely to find jobs with rhythms set by the time clock rather than the round of the seasons. Business historians have shown that commerce, which had been dominated by the all-purpose merchant before the early nineteenth century, saw the proliferation of specialized merchants in the Jacksonian period. Importers, exporters, brokers, jobbers, manufacturers' agents, freight forwarders, bankers, insurance company officers, credit reporting agents, retailers, bookkeepers, and the ubiquitous all-purpose clerks were just some of the white-collar occupations that flourished in the commercial growth of the antebellum period.[6] Often, young men had little choice but to seek these jobs outside of their community of origin. New Englanders were particularly prone to leaving the rocky farms of their homeland. Some sought more lucrative opportunities in the new businesses of the South and West. Others found positions that required constant travel on the burgeoning transportation systems of the industrializing nation, moving about far more than their forefathers would have thought possible.

Changes to work patterns were more fundamental, however, than just new kinds of occupations; the very culture and value of work took on new meaning. Diligent labor was venerated in America before 1800, but nineteenth-century men took this value a step further than their colonial counterparts by considering work an end in itself. At the death of his father, George Templeton Strong, a New York lawyer who produced an extensive diary over his lifetime, wrote, "It was from higher than money-making motives that he toiled early and late, and denied himself relaxation and holiday. It was from the feeling that what work he had to do ought to be done thoroughly, promptly, and well."[7] Behind Strong's statement was a panoply of values and incentives pushing men to revere work. The Protestant work ethic held that labor was ennobling and character-building by nature, not to mention that it also kept men from the sins of idleness and dissipation. Work also produced material rewards. John Pintard, founder of the New York Historical Society, wrote in a letter to his daughter in 1819, "To labour incessantly is the doom of man. 'In the sweat of thy face shalt thou eat thy bread,' was denounced on Adam, but a merciful God tempered the sentence of vindictive justice by giving bread as a never failing reward of industry."[8] To some observers, acquisitiveness certainly had a hold on the minds of middle-class men. "Most men are too much devoted to money-making," noted William A. Alcott, the author of a book for young wives. "Nor is this the worst. They are not merely desirous of becoming wealthy, in a reasonable time and in proportion to their own diligent efforts; for were it so, the evil would be more tolerable. But they are in haste to be rich."[9] George Templeton Strong wondered, "Is it the doom of all men in this nineteenth century to be weighed down with the incumbrance [sic] of a desire to make money and save money, all their days?"[10] This was certainly true of Rinaldo Parker, a schoolteacher incongruently driven by the desire for wealth. Writing to his mother in 1837, he verbosely observed, "There is but one solitary star that emits any directing or attractive raye [sic] through the long & dubious perspective of coming years. There is but one desire—one object that stimulates, enerves to action my paralyzed & sluggish energies—it is the acquiring of what is called competence & wealth."[11] Parker admitted that his "fevered thirst for power" was excessive, even destructive, yet still the thirst remained.

Men of the nineteenth century often viewed work as a path to the wealth and opportunities that formed the building blocks of social power. "Work was a means to independence and self-advancement," writes historian Daniel T. Rodgers.[12] A man's job determined to a large extent his status in the community: The amount of money he made usually correlated with the extent of his influence. At the same time, as Rodgers argues, "Work was an outlet for self-expression, a way to impress something of oneself on the material world."[13] Work, then, was very attractive to men in the nineteenth century because it was the arena in which they expressed dreams, pursued ambitions, and sought self-aggrandizement.

Men also valued work because it had its altruistic side. At the very least, it was understood that work fueled the economy, and thus contributed to the common good. Some occupations like the ministry and medicine were particularly valued for their chance to serve mankind. When a young man, like William Potter of Massachusetts, faced the choice of his life's work, he asked himself where in society he could "do the most good."[14] Potter's sense of duty to his fellow man led him first to teaching and then eventually to a position as a Unitarian minister. "I find that the only sure way to contentment with one's lot," he wrote trying to convince his Quaker father, "is patient & persevering effort to discharge faithfully one's daily duty."[15] Yet men felt conflicting pressures when it came to their sense of duty. After hearing that his baby was ill, Thomas Kilby Smith, an Ohio legislator, wrote, "My position as a public officer renders it imperative for me to remain at my post, happens what will. I must stifle my heart & my feelings towards all ties & live only to the performance of my duties."[16] While Smith's anguish dramatically illustrates the tension between public and private duties, the two were closely intertwined. Robert Griswold has shown that in the divorce court records of California, "nothing more detrimental could be said about a man than that he did not support his wife and family."[17] Although Griswold's evidence comes from the West and the last half of the nineteenth century, the same can be said of the antebellum East. Violation of the expected provider role brought the censure of the community, which in turn jeopardized the reputation and social standing so vital to the livelihood of middle-class men.

Since work occupied such a central place in the lives and identities of men, it is tempting to see it as the defining characteristic of nineteenth-century fatherhood. How could men take an interest in fatherhood when they were so mesmerized by the opportunities available in this new economy and bound by its rigorous demands upon their time? The chance to choose one's own career, travel, earn a hefty paycheck, negotiate the intricacies of commerce, or wield power in the influential industries of nineteenth-century America were all heady opportunities seemingly more attractive than anything that the domestic realm offered. Capitalist society seemed to measure men's success in terms of hard work and income, not the kind of children they raised. It is no wonder, then, that many historians suggest that men's attention wandered from home during these years. The new types of employment seemed to be at cross-purposes with involvement in the home.

One must, however, be careful about drawing simplistic conclusions about the relationship of work and fatherhood. Obligation, love, mutuality, and authority, although frequently tied to the economic functioning of the family, often worked independently of these pressures and needs.[18] Men's love for their children or sense of duty to wives or God pushed them to nurture and care for children at times when purely economic motivations would dictate that they do otherwise. The provider role linked men not only economically but also emotionally to their families. "The new businessman might in fact be caught up in the excitement of building his ventures," writes historian Peter Stearns. "Yet even to himself, and certainly to the outside world, he phrased his personal goals in terms of his family."[19]

There is no doubt that men keenly felt the responsibility to provide. In colonial society, where the home was a place of production, men shared with women and children the task of producing the necessities of life. In the antebellum period, however, men's wages formed the basis of the family economy, as middle-class families primarily became places of consumption. Women's and children's labor, although important for domestic chores, was no longer needed for production. Even farming families, through the shift to commercial crops, became more closely tied to the market and patterns of middle-class consumption during these years. As production moved out of the home, families became dependent upon men's income; without it the family economy collapsed. Given the limited occupational opportunities and wage-earning capacity for women and children in the antebellum period, middle-class families needed a man to fill the role of provider. Nothing made this more tragically obvious than the death of a husband and father. After her husband died in 1832, Sarah Ayer's family began to disintegrate: She lost her home to creditors and was forced to live with her brother-in-law. Unable to support her children, she put them out with other relatives.[20] Some widows more fortunate than Sarah Ayer managed to find ways to keep their families together, but they faced an uphill battle. The few jobs available to women paid such low wages that widowhood usually meant a decline in class status. The reasons women remarried were compelling; middle-class families needed a provider, and in the nineteenth century that role was a de facto adult male role.

This universal and abiding need of middle-class families to have a male provider underscores a side to men's work not often acknowledged. In addition to the advantages of power and self-expression available in a career, men faced the unceasing pressure to provide; men were, in effect, bound into a role of service to their family. This strong obligation to provide came to characterize men's personal and public identity in the nineteenth century.[21] Keith Spence, a purser in the Navy, wrote to his wife, Mary, in 1801, "A man may never starve: But a helpless woman and Six Children may. I consider myself as nothing, only as an Instrument necessary to your & their support."[22] Two years earlier, when troubled by debts and unable to earn enough for his family, Keith wrote to Mary, "Can I think of your and the children[']s situation, and my own inability to assist you, without being oppress'd with sorrow?" He vividly added that her criticism of his inability to provide was "like probing a bleeding wound with the barbed arrow that inflicted it."[23] Only incapacitation or death honorably released a married man from this obligation; abandonment was the disgraceful alternative.

Even before starting their families, men began to feel the weight of this responsibility in their choices. Only certain occupations guaranteed a proper middle-class standard of living; therefore, young men who had middle-class aspirations were limited to careers that could provide the income and status necessary to meet this goal. After spending several years in the South teaching school, William P. Eaton decided to return to his native New England, but only if he could find a different kind of work. "I am willing to do anything, consistent with social position & personal integrity," he wrote to his father.[24] Eaton's occupation of teacher did not fit both of these criteria in New England, for although a respected profession, teaching could rarely provide the income needed to maintain a home. Understanding this, Eaton studied to become a lawyer.

Young men were taught early on to forge their own way in the world, but they were also aware that their work determined the social position of their families. E. Anthony Rotundo writes that the "self-made man of the nineteenth century made not only himself, but his family as well."[25] A man's personal failure, for example, could severely influence a whole family's standing. John Pintard spent a year in debtors' prison in 1792, but he paid for his failed investments the rest of his life. Even as late as 1818, he blamed his daughter's poor marriage prospects on this early bankruptcy. "Never was a young female more secluded than yr Sister," wrote Pintard to his oldest daughter. "Not a single friend or acquaintance, as visitors, in this place. How many miseries does early misfortune entail on a man & his family."[26] The fortunes of the entire family depended on the man's ability to provide, and men like Pintard and Eaton keenly felt this responsibility.

While recognizing the coercive pressures of the provider role on men, it is clear that it also gave them a strong economic foundation from which to exert authority in the family. Men controlled the bulk of the funds that purchased homes, land, and material goods and provided education. As the middle class' reliance on these latter two increased, men's authority in this area grew. Men drew from this source of power at key times in their lives to ensure their position of dominance in the family.

This interplay of obligation and power found in the provider role was one of the shaping tensions of middle-class fatherhood and masculinity. Men keenly felt the obligation to provide for families, but they also enjoyed the power that came with that role. This dynamic is well illustrated in the task of buying a home. Middle-class status demanded home ownership, and it was the responsibility of the provider and family head to purchase and maintain that house. In the early years of marriage, some young couples lived with parents or in boarding houses, but most hoped for their own house. While courting Augusta Halleck, James Bell wrote to her, "I have always said that I would never get married unless I could give that one 'whoever it would be' as good a home as she has always had."[27] John Pintard's early bankruptcy made it difficult for him to purchase a home later in life, but he still felt the obligation. "The price of lots & buildings are so extravagantly dear," wrote Pintard to his daughter, that he wondered if he could afford to purchase a home. The burdensome payments made him fear that they would "take all my life till 70 to redeem should my years and health be spared so long, but there is nothing like trying & I am resolved for her [his wife] sake to make every reasonable effort."[28] Wives probably had input into the choice, but the purchase of the house was seen as a provider's duty.

Aside from evaluating their own economic opportunity and professional requirements, when looking for a home men also took into account other family members, considering such factors as opportunity for education, the salubrity of the climate, and proximity to friends and loved ones. When Charles Ray contemplated moving his family to Chicago after accepting a job as editor for the *Chicago Tribune*, he expressed his worries to his wife about the location of their new home. "A house I can get anywhere; but the thing is to get [one] in a quiet healthy location for the babies, where they can have opportunity for the open air and exercise, outside of the crowd and hurryskurry [sic] of a city like this. I will not put you in a close and dirty street where the children are liable to every epidemic that comes along."[29] Occasionally, the health of a family member took precedence over any and all other considerations. "Our present locality was chosen with a single eye to Jodie's [his son's] health," wrote William Eaton in 1851.[30]

Sometimes class expectations determined where men located their families, as the case of Lincoln Clark demonstrates. Clark's class concerns were in conflict with his desire to continue ties with his extended family. "It has always been a source of extreme regret to me, that our parents . . . should have remained on the comparatively barren soil on which they live," Clark wrote to his sister. "Had they removed to some location of the western country, I doubt not they would have been in better circumstances—and even if they had not, we should all have derived this advantage of remaining together while we live in the world. It never has been an idle spirit of adventure that has kept me from the land where I was born and educated, the land of my most interesting associations, but pure necessity."[31] For Clark, the West represented a place unlike New England, with plenty of future economic opportunity, and thus he could hope that his children would not feel the need to move away as he had done.

The responsibility to provide the right kind of house, however, was not only a heavy obligation but also an important opportunity. Home location and occupation choice were usually linked. Some made the career choice to stay on the family farm, but many others felt the city's lure of opportunity. Aaron Burr expressed a popular faith, "A young man who can greatly distinguish himself by his talents cannot fail of success in this city [New York] and for such as one the Largest or wealthiest City is always the best location."[32] Other men of the time disagreed with Burr, looking to the West for wealth and opportunity. When it came time to make the choice, it was the men who ultimately made the family decision to move. For example, John Faragher and Christine Stansell's study of families on the Overland Trail found that because the decision to migrate was primarily an economic one, men introduced the subject and made the final decision.[33]

Isaac Metcalf, an engineer and land speculator from Milo, Maine, was one of the many who left New England looking for greener pastures. His quandary over where to locate his family illustrates the competing demands of opportunity and obligation. Not long after his marriage, he wrote the following passage to his wife while away from her on business, illustrating the various considerations a man had when making the decision of where to put down roots.

> Sometimes when I stop & think I am much at a loss what to do with myself. If there were not two or three things—or persons—which make life so beautiful to me . . . probably, I should be plunging into business wherever I could find it, going south, or going any where my profession, and my advancement in it, might call me. But as it is, I hesitate; I think not only of my profession, not only of myself alone. The happiness, the comfort, the health, the best interests, of others are still dearer to me.[34]

Metcalf desired to make the best choice for his career, but at the same time he had to honor his responsibility to establish a healthy, well-positioned home where his wife and children could be happy. At times these goals were compatible for men, but often tension arose from the competing demands. For much of his early years of fatherhood, Metcalf supervised land investments in Illinois, housed his wife and children in a home in Ohio, and frequently visited family and friends in Milo, Maine. Although dissatisfied with these arrangements, his responsibilities and competing expectations gave him little choice but to continue in them.

Metcalf, like most middle-class men, understood that the purchase of a house had far more meaning for him and his family than the mere buying of a building. Providing a physical residence was an integral part of establishing an emotional center for the family. John Wesley North, on his way to take the office of Surveyor General of Nevada, indicated as much in a letter to his wife. After a day of contemplation he wrote,

> I spent much of the time revolving in my mind our future destiny, and how we could soonest and best, secure the reunion of our happy family. And then I fancied myself once more securing a spot that we could all call home; and a comfortable dwelling, with the conveniences, comforts and pleasant surroundings with which we still hope to be blest. And then I thought how we should vie with each other in diffusing joy around the loved centre of our hearts and hopes until 'every dimple in the face of home should smile.'[35]

North linked material comforts with family joy. At the very least, he felt meeting material needs constituted a prerequisite for family happiness. In this, North was fairly typical of most middle-class men of the time who pursued economic success with the idea that it would bring happiness to their families.[36] Men did not view their provider role in merely economic terms; a complex web of emotional bonds, pride, social expectations, and other less concrete influences all played into how they perceived this function. Economic activities like the purchasing of a house and the furnishing of material necessities and comforts were inseparably tied to the family's emotional welfare.

If the ties of the provider role—even the complex emotional ones discussed here—were the only links binding men to family, then middle-class antebellum fatherhood certainly would have been one-dimensional. But men participated in the domestic realm in many more ways. The division of labor and the nature of personal relationships in most homes actually encouraged men to engage in some domestic work and childcare. Most historians of the family have assumed that as the family became increasingly privatized in the nineteenth century, male work was done in the public arena, while female work comprised all that had to do with the private. A few historians have acknowledged that men did do some domestic work. Carl Degler, for example, reported, "It was not unknown for young husbands to be helpful to . . . their wives," while older husbands assisted in some domestic work and childcare.[37] Degler and others regard such incidents of participation in domestic work as either vestiges of an old order of economy or as historical anomalies.[38] A close examination of letters and diaries reveals that these incidents were more predominant than previously thought.

A simple dichotomization of the family's work along gender lines ignores the fluidity and complexity of the family. Men participated in some domestic tasks, including tending, teaching, and caring for children; washing dishes; caring for the sick; tending fires and furnaces; supplying firewood; cleaning house; drawing water; washing clothing; cooking; decorating rooms; and fixing broken household items.[39] The nature and extent of men's participation in childcare will necessarily be left to the remaining chapters, but a brief discussion of the other chores reveals something of men's participation in domestic labor.

Some housework, like cooking and dishwashing, was considered female work under most conditions. The few instances of men engaging in these activities were usually couched in terms of assistance to the wife. Pregnancy or illness, for example, could spark such help. During the second month of his wife's first pregnancy, Samuel Cormany recorded, "I helped Darling wash and polish all the dishes, and do the cleaning up of affairs."[40] When the need arose, men gave temporary service in the domain of female work. Some domestic tasks, however, were almost exclusively male work, such as supplying firewood and mending broken furniture or other household items (boys could also perform these tasks if they were old enough). While away from home Isaac Metcalf hired someone to do the work he normally did around the home. "I guess Rollin will take care of things pretty well if [you do] not reprove him. I have instructed him about the Furnace &c."[41] Such tasks were probably considered men's work since they required outdoor activity and extensive physical strength or tool use. Some jobs like drawing water for washing clothes were also often performed by men for the same reasons.

While some tasks had fairly rigid gender assignments, others, like tending the ill, proved to be more fluid. Although contemporary observers felt that women were better at caring for the sick,[42] necessity often made men perform this duty. Although their ability to do so was often limited during business hours, assisting sick children, wives, or other relatives was a common act for men. When Antoinette Metcalf and her son Wilder both became ill, Isaac Metcalf nursed them both and provided childcare. Antoinette wrote in her journal, "Wilder very troublesome. Isaac taking care of him all day."[43] Six days later she wrote again, "Isaac at last getting away from care of Baby," but the following day Isaac was again "in care of Baby."[44] Young Jane Elfreth of Philadelphia wrote to her father, "I am much obliged to thee for that borax thee gave me this evening it has [al]most made my mouth well."[45] When mothers were well and able to attend sick children, fathers would often take their turn after work; illness in most families meant an increased workload for both parents.[46]

During the antebellum period, the gender assignments of some chores were in a state of flux. Faye Dudden has argued that men dominated the task of shopping for groceries well into the 1850s, but thereafter it began to be controlled by women.[47] The example of George Templeton Strong supports Dudden's contention; Strong recorded in 1848, "I've taken to rising at seven and only want to acquire the faculty of going to market to become a model Head of a Family."[48] In some families male participation in chores like shopping was episodic but still common. When John Pintard's servant went on vacation he had to "rise with the dawn, make 3 fires, run to market, shave and get breakfast to be in my shop by half past nine."[49] Four years later Pintard purchased the family groceries often enough to engage in a detailed discussion of food prices with his daughter.[50] While women began to take over the purchasing of food items in the latter half of the nineteenth century, acquisitions that required a considerable outlay of cash, such as furniture or livestock, were usually still made by men.[51]

This list of tasks performed by men should not be construed to mean that men shared equally with women the work of the domestic realm. Women, after all, did the lion's share of domestic work, and with the ready excuse of their breadwinning duties, men had more choice about the work they did and did not do at home. Evidence does suggest, however, that their routines regularly included some domestic service. Even the popular prescriptive literature of the time, so often used by historians to delineate the boundaries of the separate spheres, offers examples to counter this simplistic dichotomy. Describing the disposal of refuse in less than neat families, the author William Alcott exclaimed,

Look at the cellars, the kitchens, the drains, and the yards! See the putrefied vegetables and fluids, the half spoiled meat, the offal matter, the heaps of manure, the vaults! . . . You may say that all this belongs to the husband, rather than the housewife. Granted it were so, it can do no harm to remind the housewife of it, that she might remind him. He is busy here and there and may overlook it; but organs of sight and smell, of those who are hourly annoyed, will not so readily permit this. It is not true that the matter belongs exclusively to the husband. It belongs to both.[52]

Alcott makes no distinction in this passage between manure from the barnyard and scraps from the kitchen, nor who should remove them. Health and olfactory well-being required both spouses to take out the garbage.

Historian Laurel Thatcher Ulrich has shown how the fluidity of role behavior in early America gave Puritan wives the responsibility to occasionally act as "deputy husbands." When family need arose, and when husbands directed, these women had the right and responsibility to oversee their husbands' legal and business matters. When called upon, women could act in the male sphere without challenging the reigning gender divisions in society.[53] Likewise, some of the chores that antebellum men performed in the domestic arena did not seem to undermine established gender divisions. When men washed dishes, did laundry, cooked, or cleaned the house, they were usually acting for their wives, who because of absence or illness could not perform the task. Antebellum couples functioned much like colonial husbands and wives in this regard. Yet much of men's domestic work cannot be seen as merely filling in for their wives—some domestic tasks were men's to do, and others were regularly shared because the family needed the father's labor. Without the supports enjoyed by families today—insurance, pensions, government assistance, modern public school systems, daycare centers, and charities—antebellum families performed a wider range of functions, and fathers played an integral part in the family system. It is likely, as Robert Griswold has recently argued, that breadwinning increased its significance in many fathers' lives at this time, but we must also see that obligations and chores kept men involved in domestic matters.[54]

A common argument of historians suggests that new work patterns in the nineteenth century prevented fathers from having time to spend with children, thus effectively limiting their ability to participate in childrearing.[55] This notion has received little critical attention. It rests on two assumptions: First, that old work patterns, primarily farm labor and artisanal work, gave men the time and opportunity to teach and rear children, and second, that in the early nineteenth century, industrialization and urbanization produced new work schedules and patterns that prevented men from participating in home life.

An in-depth examination of the first notion is beyond the scope and time period of this work, but several inconsistencies can be pointed out in the assumption itself. Most damning is the fact that daughters in the preindustrial economy were generally under the tutelage of their mothers, not their fathers. Daughters might assist in farm work or participate in cottage-industry work, but the teaching of domestic skills—a daughter's primary education—was left to the mother. Men primarily instructed sons in the skills needed for success in the preindustrial economy. But even in the case of sons, there are problems with this view. Only those families where all sons followed in the father's occupational footsteps could fathers be said to have had the opportunity to educate sons extensively. Many artisans in the colonial period felt diversification was desirable or at least inevitable since sons had different interests and labor needs fluctuated as the economy changed. Because many artisan fathers bound their sons out to apprenticeships, they had little control over the day-to-day training of the child. Benjamin Franklin's father seems to have exercised this option with many of his numerous sons.[56]

Farmers were perhaps more likely to have sons follow them in their occupation, but just how often children worked on a daily basis with farming fathers warrants further examination. The sources used in this study reveal that farmers and their children frequently worked apart from each other at different chores. Younger children performed menial tasks such as weeding, chopping kindling, running errands, and herding cows—jobs that could be done by one person. Fathers supervised but did not usually perform work alongside young children. Older sons engaged in the same work that fathers did—plowing, harvesting, felling trees, clearing land—but some of these chores were not the kind that threw sons and fathers together. Plowing, for example, often required only one individual to manage the team and plow. Most farmers understood the value of their sons' labor by dividing with them the farm's numerous chores.

A look at the daily account books of two farmers, one from the year 1796 and the other from 1859, show that men in agricultural life spent a significant amount of the time away from the farm. These two accounts also suggest the continuity of work patterns in farming over this period of six decades. During the course of a single year, each of these men spent portions of approximately one hundred days visiting neighbors, running errands, and fulfilling political and community duties.[57] Including time spent working for others, the farmer in 1859 spent a total of 136 work days away from his own farm. Whether this meant time away from children is not clear, but it suggests that the image of the farmer and his children working daily together close to home in a teacher-pupil relationship needs further examination.

The vision of the rural, preindustrial father as a constant, instructive presence may or may not have any relation to historical reality; however, the question still remains: Did new work patterns indeed take fathers away from children? A writer in *Parents Magazine* in 1842 condemned the "new" father, who "eager in the pursuit of business, toils early and late, and finds no time to fulfill . . . duties to his children."[58] Historians of fatherhood have embraced this image. Even if fathers in the North "tried to forge emotional, companionate bonds with their children," notes Robert Griswold, "breadwinning obligations sabotaged such efforts."[59]

A close look at some of the middle-class occupations of the nineteenth century, however, suggests that historians have exaggerated the impact of new forms of breadwinning on childrearing. Most work patterns, even the new commercial occupations, usually allowed occasional opportunities for fathers to interact with children during the day. Jacob Elfreth was a Philadelphia bookkeeper with five children, who, although only earning $800 annually in 1840, owned his own home. A special letter-book that Elfreth kept with his family suggests that his workday was neither so regimented nor so long that it kept him from interacting with his children. During the workweek his hours were flexible enough for him to take time off to visit his son at school and also take his daughter to the dentist. His children were also familiar with his workplace. When his employer leased a new building, Elfreth's son helped the company move, making himself "very useful" in the process. Before and after work, and on days off, Elfreth had time to purchase shoes and school books for his children and, with the older children, to take frequent walks, attend lectures and church, and visit friends and relatives.[60] In this letter-book Elfreth described the domestic activities of one evening's interaction with his daughter. "Thee spent this evening with me, and I helped thee wind a skein of knitting cotton, and thee sat by me knitting thy stocking while I cut up some cabbages to pickle, and [thee] held the light afterwards while I salted them in the cellar."[61] In a society still in the midst of modernizing, an accountant found nothing strange about spending an evening pickling cabbages with the help of his young daughter. While most of Elfreth's interaction probably took place outside of working hours, the evidence indicates that if needed, a bookkeeper could suspend work to take a daughter to the dentist or visit a son who was away at boarding school. Elfreth's case also suggests that it was not unusual for a young son to accompany his father to work occasionally.

Nineteenth-century work patterns sometimes allowed men to combine childrearing and work. Deliveries, errands, and business trips provided prime opportunities. Eleven-year-old Frances Hodge recorded a day accompanying her father on his errands.

> Father and myself went to Blackrock this morning to see about getting some ice. I saw them get the ice out of the water and I amused myself a while by sliding on the ice. Then Father and I took a walk on the ice on the west side of the harbor and saw a man fish with a net. Then we went to the slay [sic] and we got in and rode down the harbor about half a mile where they [sic] was some men filling a large ice house. Then we got out of the slay and walked around a while then we got in the slay and went to Mr. Allens. He was not at home so we got in the [sleigh] and started for home when we got to Delaware Street, father turned down the street and went to Mr. Wesplals [sic]. There we saw a owl, peacock and some guinea hends [sic], turkey hends, dogs and a cat and we went in to the greenhouse. They have not got any flowers in it now. Mrs. Wesphal gave me three little pots with Cactus in them then we went home.[62]

Frances' father Benjamin was the owner of a plant nursery with a seasonal workload allowing him to have days when going for ice and visiting a fellow horticulturist could be combined with a sleigh ride and a walk on a frozen Lake Erie with his daughter.

Often times a new baby facilitated interaction, pressing a father to spend more time with his two- or three-year-old child. After twins were born into his family, three-year-old Mayo Metcalf's father thought him old enough to take along on errands and short business trips. During one of the latter his father wrote home, "Mayo behaved like a regular old traveler both by Rail and Steamer, was as good as could be; few companions of any age or sex could be less trouble."[63]

While many of the new commercial occupations allowed men to spend time with children, some middle-class occupations did require long hours and constant attention to work responsibilities. Among the most demanding were traditional, task-oriented professions, such as medicine, law, and the ministry. In her diary, Sarah Connell Ayer illustrates this point when she juxtaposes her childrearing trials with her physician husband's work schedule.

> The children have been less noisy, and read more. I find it very difficult to keep them under suitable restraints. To day I have felt more the necessity of seeking Divine assistance to enable me to discharge my duty to them. Last Tuesday my husband return'd from Calais, left Doct. Whipple better. Wednesday he was sent for to Deer Island. Mr. Emery dangerously ill. Came home Thursday morning, return'd again in the afternoon, and staid [sic] with him till Saturday. Left him better. This evening he has gone to Dennisville. Was sent for to Mrs. Hobart, who is very sick.[64]

A lawyer's working day, although perhaps involving less travel than a doctor's, could be just as long. Some lawyers recorded that evening hours, in addition to morning and afternoon hours, were typically used for work. Likewise, ministers' obligations to their congregations often required constant travel when not studying and writing sermons. One early nineteenth-century minister's son remembered, "As our father had so little time to be with us, our mother, who had us almost constantly with her in our early days, understood our special needs better than he."[65]

Not all ministers, doctors, and lawyers, however, were quite so busy. Clergymen, for example, often felt strong obligations to find the time to shape their children's souls. New Yorker John Pintard critically noted that a young pastor of his acquaintance "does not study, as one determined to excel, ought. But this is somewhat a family failing. . . . He is too fond of playing with his children in the Nursery."[66] Professionals who lived in small towns or who possessed limited ambition usually had free time for children. John Wesley North practiced law in a small Minnesota town and felt that having his office nearby allowed him to be involved in family affairs.[67] This shows that work demands on a man's time varied according to more than just type of career.

This evidence of complex patterns found in old and new occupations suggests the need for a clearer view of the correlation between breadwinning and time with children. The professions of law, medicine, and the ministry, for example, were hardly characteristic of the new industrial work patterns, having been around long before the economy industrialized, yet men in these jobs were among the busiest of fathers. The country was still in the midst of the transition from an agriculturally based economy to a modern commercial economy, and many of the new jobs had not yet been influenced by the rage for efficiency and long hours that became popular in the post–Civil War period industries. Although familiar in name, we cannot assume that the occupations of clerk, salesman, accountant, and merchant functioned according to present-day patterns. A good example of this is men's travel time to and from work. Commuting and professional middle-class work became virtually synonymous in the twentieth century and substantially contributed to fathers' time away from children. But the physical and psychological distance between home and work that commuting enforced had not taken hold in the antebellum period since the suburb was primarily a development of post–Civil War America. Sam Bass Warner, Jr.'s, study of Boston shows that even though the "streetcar suburbs" had their origins in the 1850s, the technological, commercial, and municipal factors for suburbanization did not converge until after the Civil War, with the largest growth coming after 1870.[68] Another study has shown that even in post–Civil War Philadelphia, a large majority of the white-collar workers of several selected industries still lived within one mile of their workplace.[69] Commuting probably became a factor in the fatherhood equation after mid-century, but for most men in the antebellum period, the time spent traveling between work and home was negligible. As the century progressed, urbanization and industrialization affected the rhythms of work for most middle-class men, but the sources show that fathers working in a wide range of new and traditional occupations found time to spend with their children.

If, as historians have suggested, absence from the home and involvement in the harsh world of business were the two principle forces behind the decline of men's role in the family, then it stands to reason that men who spent the most time away from their families because of their careers would have had a negligible, if any, domestic role. The truly absent fathers were sea and riverboat captains, businessmen whose work required frequent travel, miners who left their families for the gold fields, and politicians and military officers who lived away from home. The railroads, steamships, and new ways and volumes of business increased the number of these kinds of jobs, although many of these occupations had a basis in an older tradition. Absent for months and even years, these men lived and worked in the rough, male world of politics, commerce, mining camps, and the military. But despite long separations from their families and no involvement in day-to-day affairs, even these distant fathers retained a great deal of authority over family members and felt strong obligations to teach, provide for, and direct their children. Fortunately, because of their absences, these fathers were the most likely to leave a record of their relationships with their wives and children.

Their writings reveal that their absence was a hardship for their families. Wives of these men often expressed regret for the lack of a father's participation in day-to-day childcare. Albina Rich stayed with her three children in Milo, Maine, running the family farm for several months, while her husband Charles worked for a railroad in Illinois. Although she had a servant girl to help her, she still missed Charles' help with the children. "They are good children but they need their Father to help govern them. I sometimes have my hands full to take care of them all especially when any one is here, but I get along very well."[70] A week later she wrote of their oldest son, age six, "Charlie is a real driving boy. He begins to need a Father to manage him. I shall be glad when you get home. It is a great care for me to take the whole care of them day and night."[71] Elizabeth Thacher wrote to a friend in 1836, "I am wearied of living alone. Instead of getting used to it, I find it becomes more & more of a trial & then it is so bad for the children. I am fully convinced that they need a father's care & instruction as much, if not more, than a Mother's."[72]

A few of these men came from families with a tradition of work that required their absence, as in the case of maritime and military families. For them, separation from home was a part of the established rhythm of work and providing, and although often regretted, men and their families accepted these separations as part of life. But more often, men who absented themselves from home in the antebellum period did so specifically for economic opportunity or personal prestige. Some sought the chance to free themselves from debt in order to retain a middle-class standard of living; more than one miner went to California hoping to strike it rich to release the family farm or business from debt. Others, like politicians, were more concerned about honor, often hoping to add to their own standing in society. Lured by the dynamic economy of the West, many men took advantage of the improvements in transportation to do business on a geographical scale larger than ever before possible. While some men could claim family need, family tradition, or civic duty to justify their absences, it was obvious that ambition was keeping most of them from their homes. Fortunately for the historian, family correspondence preserved many conscious discussions of the conflict between career and domestic roles.

Christopher Pearce, in his early years as a steamboat captain, came to an awareness of the tensions between family and career. On one occasion he wondered in a letter to his wife about the appropriateness of his career choice. "I feel almost consciencious [sic] that I am committing a rong [sic] by being separated from you. While on the other hand, I see the cause produced from the purest m[otives] of m[y he]art . . . the intrust [sic] and welfar[e of] those [w]ho I claim to be protector, and guardian for. Although I have taken [this] argument for granted as truth, without any defense."[73] With time it became obvious to Pearce that the two ideals of a good family man and a good provider were incompatible in a riverboat career. He later gave up the river trade to become an insurance agent.

Other men also came to understand the conflict between fame and family. "Oh ambition! Ambition!" lamented Thomas Lyon Hamer, "how much of the sweets of life have you taken from man!"[74] Hamer spent most of his adult life away from his home as a politician and army officer, yet he often wrote that he was happiest at home.

I have resolved so often, that I would abandon the vain pursuits of worldly honor, and sit down in the peaceful quiet of my domestic circle, there to 'live and move & have my being'—enjoying and enjoyed—that I am afraid to make promises on that subject. But I do think now, that I will at least spend two years at home voluntarily when my present service is done. I cannot reconcile it to my feelings, to wear out my few days in the turmoil and uproar of public life—to the entire distraction of my own happiness and the happiness of those who are dearer to me than life. It is too great a sacrifice. It is one which ought not to be asked of any man; and when asked ought not to be granted. It shall not be by me.[75]

It might be argued that these statements of Pearce and Hamer were merely rhetorical regrets, evidence of changing domestic roles for men—the last throes of guilt as they embraced the public world. However, the strength of these sentiments shows the enduring nature of the conflict between ambition and home in absent fathers' lives—the ties between men and their families did not usually deteriorate because of absence and involvement in the work world. Although Hamer could not stay away from public office, he also could not free himself from a sense of duty and emotional attachment to his family. It was not uncommon for middle-class men like Hamer to struggle with this dilemma for much of their adult lives. After spending years away from home in political office, Lincoln Clark could still write concerning his children, "My greatest solicitude is for them. I care less and less for office and place the longer I live. They bring distraction and leanness of soul, and impart a poor preparation for that end to which all must come—the power of ambition is blighting in every respect and can never be satisfied."[76]

The strength and durability of the obligations absent fathers felt toward their families can also be seen in the extensive advice, counsel, and commands they gave to their children in their correspondence. Most of these men relied on their wives to govern and care for home and family while they were gone, but they did not abdicate all responsibility; as we shall see in the following chapters, fathers who saw children only weeks or days out of the year gave advice to them on issues of work, manners, health, exercise, education, diet, dress, and a host of other practical matters in which they thought children needed direction. Many of these fathers dictated from a distance children's work schedules, education, and preparation for careers or marriage. Usually, a father's desire to act as father remained strong despite time or distance.

Nor did these fathers feel that their involvement in the world of work tainted them or disqualified them in any way from giving counsel on moral or religious matters. Men agreed that the public world of politics and business was indeed filled with corruption and immorality, but few admitted to succumbing to these influences. Men who behaved unethically in this realm were not going to let their families know; such an admission was tantamount to a rejection of their middle-class identity. While serving as a New York state legislator, Daniel S. Dickson pined for his family but wrote that the Albany environment was not "a suitable place for children and so much as I would like to see them, I am glad ours are at home."[77] Yet Dickson did not feel that he was in any way morally deficient because of the immorality he saw around him. Indeed, no matter where they found themselves, fathers who wrote home usually showed more concern about their children's moral character than anything else. Despite living in the rough-and-tumble surroundings of a California mining camp, William Swain felt quite capable, indeed duty bound, to advise his wife on how to inculcate proper moral values in their infant daughter.

> In relation to the manner of discipline, it may be well to say that it is my belief that government of children should be effected by impressing upon the mind ideas of right and wrong, propriety and impropriety, and good and bad, and these principles once impressed upon the mind will constitute the most reliable means of directing the acts of infancy. But these are not always adequate to counteract the will and subdue the temper. . . . Restraints are necessary, especially in early infancy, and unless they are timely and judiciously resorted to, the omission may be the cause of great evil to the child and trouble to the parent. No less the good of the child than the duty of the parent requires restraints and punishments.[78]

Swain saw no irony in writing of parental duty while he himself was hundreds of miles away—he did not perceive himself negligent in his fathering. In outlining for his wife the proper way to establish a child's good character, Swain felt he was delegating, not abdicating, his childrearing responsibilities. He wrote to his wife concerning their daughter, "[I have] the fullest confidence in your judgment and ability to train her aright," but he also felt compelled to give copious advice.[79] In this manner, he was able to exert authority in matters of childrearing even when his wife performed all of the childcare.

There were limits, however, to how long men could stay away if they wanted to maintain the integrity of their position in the family. Most likely because of debts incurred while a young man, Keith Spence lived away from his wife and six children for eighteen years, most of this time as a purser in the Navy. His correspondence with his wife and children shows that he rarely visited home. In one letter to his wife Mary, Spence asks her to tell him the ages of their children for he could no longer remember them, and on another occasion, he did not recognize the silhouettes of his daughters that his wife sent to him.[80]

The duration of these absences led to an obvious decline in Spence's paternal role. Without a father at home, his sons relied on other men for guidance and promotion in the world, much to Spence's chagrin. "I am jealous & fearful that their affections will be drawn from me, to others more fortunate and deserving. I trust, however, they will ever be attach'd to Virtue, and virtuous men; & that they will endeavour to become so themselves."[81] On issues in which other fathers far from their families retained a significant voice, Spence deferred to his wife. After suggesting that their oldest son should learn the skills to become a merchant, he wrote to her, "if you approve of it—for I have no right nor will, to dictate to you in this, but only to advise."[82] When he finally decided to move the family to New Orleans where he had obtained a Navy appointment, Mary refused, and Keith spent the last three years of his life in New Orleans without his family.

If we are to believe Keith Spence's stated reasons for his long absence, "fortune," "Providence," and his provider role kept him away from home. Throughout the separation Spence maintained that he had little control over the arrangement. His real purpose, he claimed, was to free himself from debt and restore his place in the family. "I never shall know peace or rest on this earth, until we all come together again, and to bring this about as soon as possible, I shall never cease my endeavours."[83] At the same time he also wrote, "necessity has sometimes . . . made me act contrary to my expressed intentions, and innumerable times, contrary to my inclinations."[84] Thus, according to Spence, "necessity," or paternal duty to provide, kept him away from home. His wife, however, suspected that there were other reasons for Keith's absence. At times Keith failed to send home enough money to take care of family needs. During one such lean period, Mary accused Keith of not supporting his family and not wanting to come home. He in turn claimed that even though fate kept him from properly filling his provider role, she was not supporting him, as a wife should. At one point, between Naval commissions, he accused her of writing "cruel" letters to him that blamed the decline in family fortunes on him, claiming that if she did not cease, it would kill him.[85]

But despite his frequent remonstrations and appeals to fate, Mary held him responsible for their position, not because of his failure in business, but because of his choices that kept him from his family. Her understanding of middle-class propriety did not allow her to forgive Keith for remaining away; rather, she saw it as a violation of established norms and husbandly obligations. In a sense, Keith Spence abdicated his paternal position by violating the belief that men should not live apart from their families indefinitely. Without regular visits home to ensure his position, Spence lost his right to direct his family's affairs, and, knowing this, Mary made her own choices. Mary often felt some obligation to follow his advice, but when his counsel on important issues conflicted with her own judgment, the distance between them allowed her to choose her own way. So, unlike the other distant fathers who managed to maintain their place in the family despite absences, Spence made choices that prevented him from achieving this balance.

Even with these limitations, however, Spence continued to exert some authority in the family. Through his wife, he cautioned his daughters about public decorum, gave them a curfew, and planned the education of a second son. He arranged to have his oldest son, who had joined the Navy, assigned to the ship on which he was serving. The situation allowed Spence to give the guidance he felt the son was missing, as he mentions in this note to his wife. "I have several times thought fit to give him very pointed and warm advice."[86] Despite nearly eighteen years of almost continuous absence from home, and despite acting contrary to his wife's and the community's expectations, Spence exercised some power over his children's lives.

Keith and Mary Spence's story, when combined with the accounts of other distant fathers mentioned in this chapter, reveals that men's authority over childrearing in middle-class families in the antebellum period was based on far more than daily interaction with children. In most cases, the task of daily childcare allowed women a primary role in discipline and immediate decision making. Yet even fathers far from their loved ones still maintained a significant role in childrearing decisions because the source of their authority over children was not based on daily contact. As we will see in the remaining chapters, men could and did get involved in the day-to-day process of childcare, but men's authority was more often based on control of production, perceived intellectual superiority, and the remnants of a patriarchal tradition than on constant proximity to children. While there were clear shifts in men's responsibility when they left their families for extended periods of time, they continued to function in an advisory role and women in a caretaking role.

Still in its infancy, the study of fatherhood remains prisoner to generalizations. Few are as enduring as that of the preindustrial father working alongside his children, instructing them in moral and intellectual matters, who is then pushed by industrializing forces to leave his family for work in a more demanding world where he can no longer fulfill his paternal duties. The idea of domesticity offers a seemingly convincing corollary, arguing that into this "vacuum" stepped mothers willing to fill the defunct father's childrearing role.[87] The tendency of historians to assume that antebellum middle-class fathers immediately took upon themselves the characteristics of the stereotypically alienated twentieth-century counterpart ignores not only the vastly different texture of antebellum life, but also the complexity of men's lives.

Part of the problem stems from a limited definition of men's work. Expanding the idea of male work to include both public chores, such as the purchasing of goods, and private ones, such as periodic caring for children and the sick, would help to restore a more realistic picture of men's role in the family. In comparison to women's extended domestic duties, men's were obviously limited, but these duties still played a key role in involving men in their families. Even breadwinning work served to bind men to their families by giving them both power over family income and the obligation to serve the family. With the right to leave the home each day for the world of work came the responsibility to return with a middle-class income. This relationship of power and duty, illustrated here in the provider role, permeated many other aspects of men's private lives. We acknowledge the constraints that family structure placed on nineteenth-century women—and rightly so, for a woman's domestic responsibilities shaped much of her life—but we also need to see the domestic obligations that controlled much of men's lives as well. Men's ability to act and govern in the family was continually being mitigated and shaped by the obligations that stemmed from class expectations, religious attitudes, and emotional attachment. When we understand the strength of these responsibilities, then we can see that men's provider role during this era was more complex than it is often portrayed. When we raise the issue of changes in fatherhood and masculinity, we need to look not only at how the growth of a commercial economy influenced men's roles, but also at the changes in the social and emotional factors that governed the use of men's power.

chapter two

Husbands as Fathers

PREGNANCY AND BIRTH

N ot long after the birth of his son in 1846, Illinoian Isaac Chauncy Haight expressed his joy at the event. "[I am] mindful to thank God that he has given me a son to bear up my name . . . may he live to be an instrument in the hands of God in doing much good and a polished shaft in his quiver to assist in establishing the Kingdom of God on Earth."[1]

George Templeton Strong, a young New York lawyer, had a very different experience with the birth of his first child. Soon after waking one April morning in 1849, George found his wife, Ellen Strong, in the midst of a convulsion far more violent than labor pains.

> I sent off the servants as fast as I could for help, and then held her, we two alone together, for near twenty minutes. Some of the ladies came up from No. 24. She was quiet then, only half-conscious, clinging to me and now and then looking at me with a bewildered, appealing kind of gaze. I was telling her that I really would not go downtown at all that day when came more of the same dreadful convulsions that began the illness.[2]

The convulsions continued sporadically, even long after the stillbirth had brought an end to Ellen's labor, until finally,

> At two Tuesday morning came the announcement from Johnston and Robeson that it was hopeless—pulse failing, inability to swallow.

I can't write about it. At seven I made one last effort with ice and some brandy and water from a rag, and she swallowed—and the tide had turned. I believe that rubbing her rigid lips and the inside of her mouth with ice saved her life—if God will yet spare it—for they [the doctors] had ceased to do anything and said she could not live two hours, that her speedy death was inevitable. Since then there has been steady improvement.[3]

Strong would remember that fateful event as the "noche triste, the dark and perilous night" that cast a shadow of worry over his wife's subsequent pregnancies and births.[4]

These two accounts show the range of emotions felt by Northern middle-class men about the birth process; Strong focuses on his feelings about the near death of his wife, while Haight emphasizes maintaining his family line and potential service to God. Haight's account, indicating no action on his part, is full of joy and pride, while Strong's, showing extensive involvement, is heavy with fear and relief. The birth of a child could evoke in new fathers joy, sorrow, happiness, anxiety, pride, and even apathy. Not surprisingly men frequently expressed ambivalence concerning birth. This ambivalence was occasionally based in the perilousness of childbirth itself; the possibility of the death or sickness of a wife or child was not far from the nineteenth-century father's mind. But men's conflicting emotions and attitudes toward pregnancy and birth were also rooted in the changing and sometimes conflicting expectations and values of nineteenth-century middle-class society. Men viewed the coming of children through the lenses of romantic love, masculinity, religious belief, and class expectations. Most historians of American family life agree that what it meant to be a man, a husband, and a father was in flux in the antebellum period. Therefore, some of men's anxiety and fear associated with childbirth in this period came from new expectations surrounding romantic love, family limitation, and the breadwinner role. Older economic and religious imperatives still enabled some men to welcome the arrival of children with pride and relative tranquility, but these newer expectations increased men's emotional investment in the birth. Thus, a conflicting set of older and new ideas pushed middle-class men in the North in several directions at once.

Because discussion of reproduction was not common, determining what antebellum couples thought about the issue is difficult. For example, only four of the collections used in this study contain records of men discussing birth control with their wives, which is certainly far below the proportion of middle-class couples that historians suggest were practicing it at this time. This chapter does not attempt to generalize about a single nineteenth-century male role in the reproductive process. Instead, the sources allow us to explore something of the range of male behaviors and attitudes present in middle-class society before the Civil War. These letters and diaries clearly reveal that these men did not adhere to a set of conventions preventing them from participating in the most private of events, the birth of children. If indeed women did live in a sphere separate from men, then pregnancy and birth would have been far removed from men's concerns. Gender conventions circumscribed men's and women's lives in the nineteenth century, keeping them apart in many ways, but such an important event as the birth of a child brought men and women together in ways that historians of the family have overlooked.

Views of reproduction in colonial New England and the mid-Atlantic region were grounded in an agrarian economy and Protestant religious culture that dominated colonists' lives. Ministers preached that pregnancy and childbearing were part of the "curse of Eve," which all women inherited because of Eve's transgression. While women's perspective may have differed from that of the clergy, they agreed that childbirth was their concern. As a woman's time drew near she asked advice of other women and called on women to assist in the necessary preparations beforehand and attend the birth. Women offered support and encouragement, delivered the child, and provided postnatal care to mother and child. In all this men were rarely present; as one historian notes, in the colonial period childbirth was "a thoroughly feminine event."[5]

What little we know about becoming a father in colonial America suggests that for men, childbirth was more a matter of fulfilling male duties and meeting family needs than of playing a direct role in the process. The birth of a child gave evidence of obedience to the biblical injunction to "multiply and replenish the earth"; pregnancy was not only the curse of Eve but, as Cotton Mather preached, also "to be esteemed a Mercy of God."[6] Perhaps most importantly, children constituted the necessary labor supply for the family farm, and under the patriarchal system of familial obligation, parents could depend on children for support in old age. For these reasons, men in the colonial period generally viewed the birth of a child as a favorable event and the abundance of children as a symbol of status. Men were not wholly insensitive to the pain and danger of their wives' childbearing—especially since death or disabling injuries were not uncommon occurrences in childbirth—but the needs of men, women, and children were subordinate to family, community, and God.[7]

The tradition of thinking of birth as the 'presentation' of children by the wife to the husband typified colonial attitudes. Far into the nineteenth century some men still used this phrase to describe birth. When George Phillips' child was born in 1844, he wrote in his journal: "This day my dear wife presented me with a young daughter. It is a fine looking healthy child. O, what a matter of thankfulness."[8] This view implied that mothers produced (carried and gave birth to) the infant, which they then presented to the father, who had a stronger legal and moral right to the child. For men with these attitudes, birth could mean the preservation of the family line, the proof of male virility, and the fulfillment of God's commandments. None of these, however, required male participation in the birth process beyond conception.

By the nineteenth century, however, religion and communal obligation were becoming considerably less influential in shaping the way men viewed children and birth. Middle-class families were increasingly the locus of strong emotional attachments, especially intense romantic love between husband and wife. As a young man began his family, his feelings about the birth of his first child usually were influenced more by his relationship with his wife than by his position in the community and before God. During courtship, as Karen Lystra suggests in her study of nineteenth-century romantic love, the partner was all important; "the experience of love created a mutual identification between women and men that was so intense that lovers repeatedly claimed to have incorporated a part of their partner's inner self into their own inner life."[9] Such a tie seems to have left little room for others, including future children. Early nineteenth-century lovers' focus on each other can be seen in their love letters, which were consumed with the revelation of the self and exploration of inner feelings. The letters rarely mention other people and never discuss the prospect of children. On the day of his wedding, Samuel Francis Smith, a minister, enumerated seven necessary virtues that he and his bride needed for a successful life together. These qualities ranged from maintaining the proper place of affection in their marriage to recognizing the importance of God's work in their lives, but not one of the seven concerns was about parenting. There is not even the faintest hint or anticipation of the almost inevitable birth of a child in the first years of marriage.[10]

The primary reason for men's (and probably women's) reticence about future children during courtship seems to have been a desire to have the partner all to oneself. Isaac Metcalf evoked images of the solitude of the Garden of Eden when he wrote to his fiancée while on a business trip, "I had on the way some delightful visions of a snug little cottage in one of those quiet villages, made happy by a sweet & loving wife, as my home & Earthly paradise for a year or two at least."[11] Metcalf viewed the period of marriage before the arrival of the first child as a blissful, although ultimately temporary, state. Likewise, the exclusive conjugal intimacy of paradise attracted Nathaniel Hawthorne even after his marriage to Sophia, "How happy were Adam and Eve! There was no third person to come between them, and all the infinity around them only served to press their hearts closer together."[12] If we carry Metcalf's and Hawthorne's Edenic metaphors to their logical conclusions, marriage was paradise until children came, representing part of the fallen state requiring toil and pain in the mundane world. The natural result of the partaking of the forbidden fruit is that which "comes between," an Abel or a Cain—both bringing pain, the one through death and the other by murder. Men expressed this desire for an exclusive relationship with their wives before and during the pregnancy by focusing on their wives and often openly stating a reluctance to cross the threshold into fatherhood.

Despite the "paradise" of the childless phase of early marriage, antebellum couples generally did not try to extend this period for more than a year or two. Children generally came early in nineteenth-century marriages, and couples that practiced birth control did so later in their marriages. Unfortunately, because nineteenth-century Americans rarely discussed such matters, historians have found that the "sharp decline in birthrates is a phenomenon easier to describe than to explain."[13] Historians can state with some accuracy that the average number of children born to a typical white woman in America decreased from 7.04 in 1800 to 5.21 in 1860, but they are still not exactly sure what caused this change to take place. Indeed, even determining which sex was most responsible for the decline has proven elusive. Women had the most to gain from the reduction in family size, since the desire to control their sexuality and reproduction, as well as their work situation in the home, provided strong motivations.[14] But men also had significant reasons for wanting fewer children. Historians like Richard Easterlin and Morton Shapiro have argued that men began supporting limitation because a smaller family reduced the pressure on them to provide for their children.[15] Men took their new responsibility as sole provider for the family seriously, often going through intense anxiety and doubt about the fulfillment of this role, and occasionally they did acknowledge the link between family size and career. After the birth of his sixth child, William Lloyd Garrison wrote, "I would not have the number of our children less, but it is difficult to look after so many, and at the same [time] to discharge the duties of my position as a 'leading' abolitionist."[16]

Middle-class men's motivations for keeping their families small, however, were not solely economic. Of the four men of the 110 in the sample who wrote about limiting the size of their families, each seems to have acted out of a mixture of love for his wife, concern for her health, and dependence on her contributions to the family.[17] Tradition still dictated that men find joy in the arrival of a child, but because men had considerable emotional investment in their wives and because childbearing was a painful and dangerous undertaking, the wife's well-being during childbearing years was foremost in their minds. These men were acting in accord with the self-appointed experts of the antebellum advice literature who supported the practice of birth control if the health of the wife required a cessation of childbearing.[18] A politician from Ohio, Thomas Lyon Hamer, stated such a concern, although in a rather bucolic manner, when writing to his wife Lydia:

> Your constitution never firm—has been shattered by rapid childbearing & suckling your children—& therefore requires careful nursing for some time. . . . You are like a field that has produced a crop of corn every year for ten or fifteen years. It must be uncommonly strong land if it does not require to be laid down in clover for two or three years to renew its strength.[19]

Despite his unfortunate choice of metaphor, Hamer's concern for his wife's health seems rooted in a strong romantic relationship. Only one month later he wrote to her, telling her to take care of herself at all costs. "Do not talk to me of property lost or wasted—or educating children. I tell you again and again—that you are dearer to me than all else. . . . If you throw away your health & life—I am a miserable wretched man."[20]

Over and over again in nineteenth-century family letters husbands and wives admonished each other to protect their health. As Henry F. Hitch wrote to a friend, "When a good loving wife sees that the happiness of the man she loves depends upon her life, she then sees the necessity of the greatest possible care of herself not merely as herself but as her husband[']s happiness in this life."[21] The complex intertwining of love and economic interdependence meant that husbands joined in their wives' fears concerning the danger of childbirth. Men like Hamer seem to have taken the logical step in dealing with this apprehension by participating in the practice of birth control to contribute to their wives' well-being.

Whether men's involvement in controlling births was prompted by a concern for economic status, by affection for wives, or even by some other reason is still very much open to interpretation. However, it is clear that this shift increased men's involvement in the private realm. Of far-reaching significance was the increase in men's sense of responsibility for conception. In colonial New England, multiplying and replenishing was a commandment, and thus when conception occurred the responsibility lay not with the soon-to-be-mother or father, but with God. Remnants of this attitude did persist into the nineteenth century. Richard Henry Dana, Jr., for example, believed that "having children or not ... seem[s] to be placed quite beyond the sphere of our determining."[22] As the century progressed, however, people increasingly believed that children came not according to God's will but as the result of conscious choices of the parents. Samuel Cormany, while contemplating the pain his wife would experience in the birthing room, acknowledged men's part in conception. "O that I could take upon myself every pang she has to feel and could suffer for her ... because in a sense I am the cause or occasion of much of her pain and miseries."[23]

A new cultural construction of sexuality perhaps intensified men's sense of responsibility for conception. "Middle-class men ... were confronted by two ethics of sexual conduct," writes E. Anthony Rotundo, "one urging the 'natural' expression of aggressive impulses and the other demanding stringent self-control."[24] Men had so-called conjugal rights to their wives' bodies, yet were taught to respect their wives' "purer" sensibilities. Thus, when they acted according to one impulse and impregnated their wives earlier than the desired interval, they felt guilty for their lack of control. Moreover, if, as some historians suggest, the contraceptive method of choice in most marriages was *coitus interruptus*, then when an unwanted conception occurred, the blame most likely fell upon the husband for failing to prevent conception. Likewise, men in the nineteenth century seem to have had less control than their wives when couples tried to use abstinence to curtail fertility.[25] The diaries and letters used for this study do not reveal how or if these factors contributed to tensions at birth, but clearly men keenly felt some responsibility when the pains and dangers of birth came.

While historians can only surmise about how this new sense of responsibility shaped the majority of men's lives, it is clear that it placed considerable strain on some men. Only nine months after his wife almost died in childbirth, George Templeton Strong learned that she was again pregnant. "There's no longer any doubt about the subject of my last ten day's anxiety and wretchedness. God preserve my poor little wife or *take me*, that is all I can write about it." A week later, although his wife was ill with a cold, he was so immensely relieved "by finding that we've been mistaken about Ellie's state of health in one particular that I feel as if all the rest were nothing."[26] Strong's phrase "*take me*," indicates he felt himself at least partly, if not wholly, to blame for the feared pregnancy.

This developing awareness of their role in conception perhaps contributed to changing perceptions of family size. After the birth of his eighth child, Calvin Fletcher noted that although he himself wanted a large family, "it is not fashionable to be the parents of many childrin [sic]."[27] A large family, which to a colonial father would have been seen as a blessing, might to a nineteenth-century father be a trial. In 1845, Tench Fairchild writing to Charles Ray ridiculed a mutual friend of theirs for having eight children and a "dried up" wife; their friend, Fairchild noted, had seemed ashamed of his family.[28] Not all men had this kind of antipathy for large families, but the notion that too many children could be linked to men's irresponsibility made such contempt possible.

Perhaps to deal with these tensions, men sought greater understanding of and control over the factors influencing reproduction. Men turned to the growing number of medical advice books for "scientific" methods of managing health. Armed with the latest theories, these men were able to discuss intimate physical issues confidently with their wives and be present when birth occurred. Some, like Charles Ray, studied medicine, and thus had the authority of education to cross the line that kept men at a distance from traditional female concerns. After his wife wrote that she was not menstruating (she was nursing their second child), Ray confidently allayed her fears and advised her against the use of an abortifacient.

I hardly think Dear Jennie that you need take anything to bring on your monthly periods. The fact that you have sufficient nourishment for Master Penn, and that you do not increase in flesh accounts for the non-appearance of what you were visited with after Minnie's birth. It is not possible that you are in that way.[29]

While some men read contemporary scientific literature to gain knowledge about women's gynecological and obstetrical matters, others simply became more conversant in these issues through the course of marriage. Lincoln Clark, a Northern lawyer who lived in Alabama for several years, grew more capable of discussing such matters over time. After the birth of his first child he wrote to his mother-in-law, "I suppose from hints droped [sic] in my hearing that the tiny little emigrant was a month before its time."[30] At this first birth, Clark was not privy to such simple information as the approximate date of conception. Thirteen years and several children later the situation had changed. By this time the Clarks were practicing an unstated form of birth control, and Lincoln was beyond the stage of catching dropped hints when he wrote to his wife, Julia, in 1851:

I feared you had some such trouble as you mention. I think it must be the result of exposure and cold at Springfield—that it can be the existence of a 'condition' I do not believe—there has been in my opinion no adequate cause. Neither do I believe it to be the result of age. You had best lose no time in consulting Dr. Collins—you might pay severely for delay or false modesty.[31]

A shared language needed to develop before couples could cooperate to limit the size of their families. In the Clarks' case, the passage of time and the need to protect Julia's health enabled the couple to discuss such matters later in their marriage, and thus practice birth control more effectively. This pattern seems to be borne out in demographic studies of the nineteenth century that show the interval between births increasing near the end of some women's reproductive years.[32] Because of the immense meaning and impact of birth on families, couples like the Rays and the Clarks seem to have cooperated in preventing conception to some extent.[33] Just how women and men made decisions concerning family size, how they controlled the timing of births, and what methods of contraception they used during this period still need more study. However, birth control changed the meaning of becoming a father for many men in the nineteenth century, adding a new sense of responsibility by involving men in intimate family decisions and processes.

After conception, men's biological participation in the reproduction process obviously ends. Women conceive, carry, and bear children and face the fear, pain, and danger of childbirth. Men experience everything from the first indications of pregnancy to the actual birth as an observer, or at best a supporter. In the nineteenth century, tradition combined with nature to limit men's participation. Childbearing remained a central event and rite in the lives of most women. After 1800 women began to choose to have male doctors, and in some cases husbands, participate during their deliveries, yet women still dominated the scene as long as birth remained a home-based event. Men were outsiders, to a large degree, in pregnancy and childbirth.[34]

Pregnancy demonstrated for many men the strength of ties between women. Pregnant women turned to their female relatives and friends for advice, and many women traveled great distances to be together at the hour of delivery.[35] Along with relatives, female friends and neighbors often helped during and after the birth. Some middle-class men in the antebellum North held that birth and everything with it was a God-given responsibility of women and not the affair of men. These men accepted the limits on their participation in pregnancy and birth as part of a natural and appropriate division in society. And just as they believed that women had their own place during this process, these men busied themselves in the male world of work, politics, and male leisure when the time drew near.[36]

An engineer and land speculator from Maine, Isaac Metcalf, provides a good illustration of men who chose to maintain the traditional gender division that surrounded pregnancy and birth by emphasizing things masculine at this time in their lives. Metcalf had twelve children by his first wife, Antoinette, and after she died, he fathered five more children by his second wife. He seems to have viewed this fecundity with pride. In 1855, three to four months into Antoinette's second pregnancy, Metcalf left her with his mother and went with male friends and relatives on two extended fishing trips that would today be called "male bonding" experiences.[37] On the second trip, Antoinette recorded making "gingerbread & cake" and "doughnuts & fried meat" for the men, who "started on a loaded sled with buffaloes [sic] quilts, boxes of edibles, gun, & fishing tackle, about ten o'clock in high glee."[38] The trips included fishing, shooting, and tales around the campfire. "Evening in camp and . . . plenty of Moose hunting stories. Old Chase is a mighty hunter. Inherits it from his father Old Capt. Chase the original first settler of Sebec. Stories of . . . hunting away up the mountains; hardships and exposure."[39] While Metcalf's fishing trips might have been spurred by other factors aside from his wife's pregnancy, the events just prior to the birth also reveal a pattern of turning to masculine roles at this time. Just four days before the birth Metcalf spent the whole day fishing again, and on the day of the delivery, even knowing all day that his wife was "not very well" (a euphemism for labor pains), he pruned trees and went to vote at the town meeting. At nine that night Antoinette gave birth to twins.[40]

The motivations for Metcalf's seemingly nonchalant behavior are difficult to determine. Men turned to work, leisure activities, and politics at such junctures for a variety of reasons. Still, the equanimity expressed in Metcalf's actions during the pregnancy and his terse journal entry recording the birth contrasts sharply with the intense emotional involvement and actual participation in the birth process that others of his generation recorded. Men like Metcalf were influenced by the traditional view that bearing children was the fate of the "Daughters of Eve," and, except in case of an emergency, outside the consideration of men. These men, whether from callousness or from gender or cultural barriers chose to forgo personal involvement in childbirth.

More often than not, however, the men in this study chose to become more directly engaged in the birth process. Spurred by strong emotional relationships with their wives, they sought greater participation, usually to continue the sharing, support, and control that had characterized their marriages before the pregnancy. Some of these men saw the unborn child as an expression of love. Historians have noted that both in literature and among actual couples, men and women occasionally identified their future children as "love tokens" and "pledges of their mutual love."[41] For example, Samuel Cormany confided to his diary in 1861, "In a whisper! It is now settled that we are to have a little pledge of our love and affection."[42] Among the fathers in this study, this is a rare acknowledgment of the child before birth, but the focus of the comment is on the marriage relationship and, in fact, shows considerable ambivalence about the child as an individual.

Many of these fathers expressed concern for the health of their wives and, perhaps implicitly, for the health of the fetus. The popular literature of the day suggested that a mother's physical and emotional state during pregnancy could be transferred to the fetus.[43] Men encouraged their wives to eat properly and practice good hygiene for the sake of their own health and that of the unborn child. Mary Smith, for example, while pregnant and spending time at her parents' home, reported her eating and sleeping habits in letters home to her husband so that he could rest assured that she was taking care of herself.[44] Anxiety and overwork were thought to cause premature labor, so some men took steps to ease their wives' domestic workload. Usually this meant arranging for a servant or nurse, but occasionally when money or circumstances made such arrangements impractical, men stretched traditional boundaries of labor division by assisting with women's work. Men were more likely to help with heavy chores, such as drawing water for washing clothes, but they also occasionally cooked, cleaned, and washed dishes. While pregnant, Ann North wrote that without the domestic help of her husband she would not have been able to manage the affairs of her home.[45] While in the same condition, Jane Pearce expressed her desire for her absent husband's company and assistance: "I am still anxious to be with you and in my present situation I feel that it is very necessary to have your society and attention occasionally."[46]

Men who responded to pregnancy and birth in new ways did not entirely discard more traditional responses. Many also turned to work, the established male avenue of expression. Work could be a catharsis for the anxiety that stemmed from their increased emotional involvement in the birth process. George Templeton Strong provides an eloquent statement of this sentiment. Although he was often concerned about his financial status, the imminent birth of his first child seems to have made him particularly anxious about his ability to provide:

Ellen better, thank Heaven; that's one bright spot at least. Wretchedly nervous, anxious, and uneasy for the past few days, gloomy and oppressed, with a perpetual fifty-pound weight of foreboding on my breast, looking forward to all sorts of nameless calamities, and first and worst that standing bane of man's existence on earth—the fear of the want of money—tenfold worse than the reality, bad as that would be. Perfectly without any tangible reason, too; that makes it still more unworthy of a man who ought to have faith and hope in something beyond dollars. But it's a periodical disease with me, a causeless attack of insane, gnawing, corroding, burning, suffocating anxiety and despair about my own resources and prospects, my ability to fight my way through the world and carry my little wife through it in comfort and honor. When the disease is upon me I'm a pitiable case, sick at heart, disgusted with myself, and able to exist only by working hard and drinking coffee.[47]

The differences between the older and newer male views of childbirth should not be overemphasized. Some men expressed elements of both perspectives. Lincoln Clark, who cooperated with his wife in practicing birth control to preserve her health, nevertheless also demonstrated a belief in more traditional values when writing to Julia, his wife. At the time he held a seat in Congress while she was caring for their four children in Iowa and was probably pregnant.

> I fear the effect of the care and noise of so many children upon your constitution. . . . I do not know what can be done. Had they all a permanent good home it would be better for them. But I will not say a single word that shall lead to their neglect—If it breaks you down, and undermines your constitution, perhaps it is a duty and a providence which must be borne. It is a weary life, but there should be no complaint.[48]

This was the same Lincoln Clark who wrote to his wife, "I wish you to be more cautious than you have been and not break your back while it is weak—if you can't get others to do the work let it go undone at least for a while."[49] Later, he took over childcare and home duties to allow his wife to spend time to visit relatives and rest away from her family.

Most middle-class fathers remained close at hand by arranging their schedules to be near during the birth. George S. Phillips, a Methodist minister, responded typically when he wrote in his journal just three days before the birth of his daughter, "Remained at home. Wife in delicate health."[50] Men with occupations that required extensive travel, such as boat captains, circuit judges, salesmen, and land speculators, often scheduled trips around the birth. One whaling captain left off whaling for shorter lumber trips to be with his wife when the birth took place.[51] Most of the births that occurred while the husband was absent were premature or the result of poor planning. Gregory Yale's wife gave birth to a child while he was in California, but from evidence in his letters, it is clear that he did not know of the pregnancy until reaching the gold fields.[52] When the time drew near, fathers usually went for the midwife or doctor and escorted attendants to the lying-in room. All middle-class men, regardless of their particular attitudes toward childbirth, found their public lives affected by developments in the private sphere in the months and hours before birth.

If women's and men's activities were becoming increasingly differentiated in the nineteenth century, as some historians suggest, then middle-class men should have had even less to do at the culminating event of birth. After all, the birthing room, like the kitchen, had always been women's domain. Some men did keep their distance during the labor and birth, but as the nineteenth century progressed, more middle-class men sought greater participation and emotional involvement. Nothing illustrates this new approach more than the presence of husbands in the privacy of the birthing room. Samuel Cormany, a farmer and erstwhile teacher, illustrated some of the complex emotions that these men experienced. After the birth of his first child he recorded in his diary his exhilaration at witnessing the event,

> She said several time[s] 'Oh! I cannot stand it'—'It will kill me.' I responded Oh no Darling, soon you will have relief—Do your utmost at expulsion—and our rejoicing will start in—9 O['clo]ck! The Little Pet came.... A sudden thrill flew through us all when Darling spoke out 'There it is'—the Moment—I knew it was here. I felt like pressing my Dear precious Rachel to my bosom and covering her with kisses—I did give her quite a number—and so now we have our desire—a Baby!—a dear—Innocent—Angel Angelic—precious Baby. The pain it cost was great but, ah! how dear, how precious it is—Worlds could not purchase it, the little household pet—and it a little girl, a dear pretty little girl— and all our own—with such a sweet, round face, and such sparkling eyes, and hair like its Pa ... Pa ... Pa ... how funny that sounds. Me a Pa![53]

Cormany's sense of belonging in the picture is evidenced in his declaration that the "precious Baby" was worth the great pain that not he but his wife felt.

Nor was Cormany alone. The diaries and letters reveal that other middle-class men attended births in the 1840s and 1850s, and one study has found that physicians began reporting husbands in attendance at births in the medical literature published after 1830.[54] A few writers urged obstetricians to prohibit husbands from attending, but most allowed the practice for the benefit of the mother. One wrote concerning the support a husband could give to a wife in the grip of labor:

Here too is an ample field for the exercise of the endearing blandishments of a husband's love; and whose presence, we ask, can be more acceptable, or conversation more agreeable, or kind offices more consoling, than his, to the dispensing wife. To whom can she with so much freedom, and with so much confidence disclose her thoughts, and unbosom her very soul, as she can to an affectionate companion who gives ample evidence of his anxiety to alleviate all her cares?[55]

This supporting role, according to these writers, was the primary justification for men's attendance at birth.[56]

This conclusion is corroborated by the sources used for this study. Men who attended births amused their wives during the tedium of the early stages of labor. George Templeton Strong recorded, "Elie was very bright through the morning; played a game of chequers with me, read aloud, and so forth, her pains occurring every ten minutes or thereabouts. She dined here in the library, and by six o'clock the pains were much more frequent and began to be severe."[57] In the final stages of labor, these men stayed beside their wives, holding their hands and whispering encouragement.

Occasionally men gave more than just moral support to their wives during labor. Historians have found that some men physically supported their wives during labor, holding the wife as she reclined in his arms. This seems to have been more popular in the rural and frontier regions, however, and none of the sources studied for this work yielded any evidence of this kind of assistance.[58] Some husbands also may have been present in the birthing room to see that the doctor acted with propriety. Nineteenth-century codes of modesty made simple procedures like a vaginal examination a delicate matter. Some medical manuals instructed doctors to ask the husband or another third person permission to proceed, and then to perform the examination by touch and not by sight. At times, no one in the room saw the actual birth since it took place under the cover of a sheet, with the physician performing the delivery by touch alone.[59] On rare occasions some fathers were present because a sudden birth or other circumstances demanded that they act as midwife. Most couples, however, took great pains to assure that this did not happen.[60] Regardless of the reason, however, men's attendance at births marked a significant involvement in the private realm.

This newfound role in the lying-in room shaped men's perceptions of the birth process. Men who attended gained an increased understanding and appreciation for what women experienced during birth.

Richard Henry Dana, after witnessing the birth of his first child, recorded his awe at his wife's suffering. "There is surely no pain like it in the world. Poor S., who has great self command, screamed again & again as the last & heaviest came on. All self control is gone & the woman lies a mere passive instrument in the hands of an irresistible power. It is the rending asunder of all but soul & body."[61] The respect that came with witnessing this pain led some to ridicule the practice of describing birth as a presentation to men; Lincoln Clark, for example, called it a "vulgar old phrase."[62]

Fathers-to-be in this study also began to share some of the fear that, according to one historian, "remained central to women's perceptions of their birth experiences" throughout the nineteenth century.[63] Instead of viewing suffering during birth as the natural lot of all daughters of Eve, some men supported women in their efforts to ease the discomfort and pain of pregnancy and childbirth. After a difficult first birth, Ann North and her husband "had both come to the conclusion to have her take chloroform" on her second birth. When the time arrived "the Doctor gave it to her," wrote her husband to Ann's parents, "and she is perfectly delighted with the effect of it. She is very comfortable and happy that she has got along so finely, and that the child is so well. And you can easily imagine how much I am delighted and *relieved*—from anxiety."[64] In addition, the growing preference among middle-class women for male obstetricians was supported and possibly encouraged by husbands as a perceived means of lessening the danger of birth.

Some men were not content to play a passive role in the birth. Samuel Cormany's enthusiastic participation illustrates the extent to which a husband and new father could try to exert control over decision making in the lying-in room. He recorded this disagreement with the midwife during the course of his wife's labor.

> Too vigorous an effort was made by the Lady to have Pet— 'Press'— 'Pull on the towels fast to the bed-posts' 'Beardown'—&c. I remonstrated that there was too much hurrying of nature—take time— I urged—give nature a chance—so I prevailed—6 O['clo]ck in the morning—all went to breakfast. I comforted Darling—she was so glad I stayed with her.[65]

The labor went so smoothly that, during its course, Cormany was able to tell his wife that "all was going on perfectly—according to 'The Books,'" which he called the "authority." Samuel also took over much of the postpartum care of his wife, bathing and feeding her, while his wife's mother and sister cared for the baby. His hydropathic penchant for washing led him into an argument with the midwife and his in-laws over the proper time to bathe both his wife and child, but in this disagreement Samuel lost to the combined opposition and authority of the women.[66] Cormany's challenge to the female control of birth represents the extreme in the spectrum of male participation. The men who recorded attending births seem to have been prompted more by the desire to give comfort and encouragement to their wives rather than to oversee the process. Birth still remained largely controlled by women during the nineteenth century.[67]

Most of men's attempts to influence the birth process seem to have focused on guaranteeing the health and safety of the mother even over that of the child. That men could maintain a certain detachment from the child can be seen in their attitudes toward stillbirths. Unlike the mother's nine-month carrying of the fetus, men obviously had less invested in the child to be born and usually responded with limited emotion. While living for a time in Alabama, Lincoln Clark's second child died in birth, and a relative recorded that the corpse was "buried in one corner of the garden by moonlight the same day."[68] "I have had some affliction in my own family," writes Clark to a relative. "Julia had a child the other day which died in the birth. The Mother was very low, but is now recovering."[69] More information would help to better understand Lincoln's emotionally distant response to this event, but it seems from this instance, and from similar deaths in other families, that without the bonding period, some fathers did not need to mourn the death of children who died in birth or soon after. Men occasionally responded in the sentimental terms of the antebellum period, as one man did in describing his stillborn nephew to his brother, "He is finely formed, dark hair, a bright dark eye, perfect arms & hands folded across its little breast, and is every way truly a sweet little object to see."[70] But the wife's well-being appears to have been the primary concern of men. Samuel Furber voiced such worries soon after the birth of a son: "The little one does not seem so well to day as usual. I have many fears in regard to it, the effect of its death upon Lucy would be very much to be regretted."[71]

The relief felt by fathers at successful births was partly founded on a concern for the integrity of their own masculinity. Men began to feel a certain responsibility for initiating a pregnancy, and thus felt guilt for contributing to the pain and potential death of their wives. Men's masculine image of themselves came under conflict during pregnancy; they saw themselves as their wives' protectors, and also as somehow responsible for the potential endangerment of their loved ones. Combined with romantic love, this anxiety explains men's ambivalence about pregnancy and their periodic desire to question and challenge conventional wisdom regarding birthing. Men turned to a variety of sources—science, religion, their breadwinner role, their position as father, and, most importantly, their exclusive, romantic relationship with their wives to direct or influence aspects of the reproductive process.

Contrary to what the separate spheres model would lend us to believe, men could and did get involved in the most intimately domestic of matters: pregnancy and birth. Although some middle-class fathers adhered to their traditionally distant and limited roles, many others, spurred by love for their wives, became closely involved. The often intense reactions of these fathers to the births of their children, coupled with the influence that men had on the birth process, demonstrate the inadequacy of the separate spheres notion as a tool to think about men in nineteenth-century families.

Most middle-class men in the antebellum North faced the birth of a child several times throughout their lives, but the first was usually the hardest. After the initial birth, men no longer viewed themselves only as husbands, but also saw themselves as fathers; thus second and third children did not involve as traumatic a shift in how they thought of themselves. Over all, however, reproduction was increasingly becoming an anxious process for men because their emotional investment—primarily in their wives, but also in their children—began to outweigh their more traditionally detached role. Men still found joy in the arrival of a new son or daughter, but fear usually preceded the joy. This ambivalence toward birth occasionally carried over onto the newborn child, affecting the developing relationship. But as new fathers began to see their infant children as individuals and attribute an identity to them, the emotional ambivalence from the birth experience seems to have waned in the face of new pressures.

chapter three

Oedipus Forgiven

INFANCY AND EARLY CHILDHOOD

In the antebellum era, the stage of childhood that provided the fewest opportunities for a father's involvement was infancy. Women performed the necessary chores of feeding, diapering, bathing, clothing, and tending, and later guided a toddler's efforts to eat solid foods, walk, and speak. Nursing obviously fostered a close bond between mothers and children. Convenience and conventional wisdom encouraged middle-class mothers to breast-feed their children—wet nurses and bottles were largely used when a mother could not lactate.[1] The flourishing prescriptive literature of the day, such as advice manuals by Lydia N. Sigourney, William Alcott, and Almira Phelps, strengthened notions of the preeminence of the mother-infant bond, arguing that nature had given women the ideal mind and disposition to teach and nurture, along with the body to bear and feed children. According to these writers, allowing others to care for children, particularly nurses or servants, but also fathers, would result in children getting less than the best care.[2] It is tempting to accept this antebellum rhetoric as proof enough to deny men any role in their infant children's lives. Indeed, for over half a century historians have asserted that nineteenth-century fathers had little, if any, interaction with their infant children.[3]

A careful look at infant-father relationships—not the idealized relations of the advice literature, but actual behavior of men and infants in families—reveals complex connections that were more substantial than previously thought. While apparently not giving much thought to a child during pregnancy, after birth men were constantly reminded (even in the middle of the night) of the child's presence, having little choice but to make accommodations to their new situation. Not surprisingly, most seemed psychologically unprepared for fatherhood. Their exclusive relationship with their wives and the intense feelings brought on by the birth process left middle-class men ill-equipped to deal with a third member joining the family. Most had little, if any, experience dealing with infant children, which exacerbated their unease. Initially, new fathers struggled with their unfamiliar role, but as letters and diaries show, within a matter of weeks, the distance closed as fathers began to see their children as individuals. Naming and gender assignment were the initial threads that bound men to their young children, with play and some childcare soon following. Even though women had the responsibility for performing most day-to-day care, young fathers did participate in this duty, although to a limited extent. These activities helped men perceive their infant daughters and sons as individuals and foster emotional attachments to them.

The role children themselves played in creating a relationship with their fathers should not be underestimated. In thinking about family dynamics, we often erroneously assume that all influence flows from parent to child. But as sociologists have noted, children "initiate and affect parental responses" as well, even in the first years of their lives.[4] The fathers examined here recorded many instances of this type of behavior: Infants often expressed joy at the sight of their fathers and sadness in their absence. Men, on the other hand, demonstrated their emotional ties by playing with their babies, caring for them, and grieving when they died. The first two years of a child's life were unquestionably an important stage in the development of a relationship with the antebellum father.

The first weeks of fatherhood were a time of turmoil and transition for most middle-class men. Men who had become accustomed to being half of a married couple suddenly found themselves forced to redefine and readjust many aspects of their lives. Couples rarely envisioned themselves in the role of parent during courtship, and men's concern for their wives during the pregnancy and birth process seems to have restricted contemplation of the coming child. As a result, some fathers' references to a newborn show that they were having difficulty initially accepting the child as both an individual and a member of the family. For example, Wellington Burnett, a transplanted Connecticut lawyer in California, still identified his infant child with his wife when he wrote to her in 1857: "I see you together; and I see you separated but near each other. You are my life darling, and I cannot look upon our baby, except through you. My love for him does not arise from consanguinity alone, but roots deepest in the soil of love I bear my wife."[5] Some men referred to the infant at this stage as their wife's child and only later called him or her their own. George Templeton Strong, the New York lawyer whose wife almost died during her first delivery, even referred to his child as "that baby."[6] This is different from the colonial practice of calling the child a "stranger," which historians suggest indicated distrust of the character of the child (influenced by the idea of children born in sin). In the nineteenth century, the appellation "young stranger" was used more in jest than as a serious reference to an infant.[7] Nonetheless, referring to the child as "her baby" or "it" shows that these fathers had not yet recognized the child as having an identity of its own, nor had they established a personal relationship with the infant.

In these early weeks men participated in the rituals that society demanded of them. They basked in the good wishes of relatives and friends, and they felt pride in their ability to father children. But after the congratulations came the realities of an infant in the usually modest-sized middle-class house. Newborns usually slept near their mothers to facilitate feeding at night, and, in the natural course of events, fathers, even if they slept in a separate room, often heard more of their young sons and daughters than they liked. George Templeton Strong remonstrated when his first child became colicky, "Went to bed with both my ears stuffed full of cotton, a precaution against the turmoil of that baby, which has got into one of the habits of the Noctivagous Mammalia, that, namely, of howling at night like the felinae, the great apes, jackals, hyenas, and wild dogs picturesquely described by travelers in tropical parts."[8] There were other sources of tension as well. Young fathers may have projected some of their sexual frustration onto children during these first weeks. Many couples refrained from intercourse during pregnancy and certainly most did in the first weeks after birth. And if these same men also adhered to the popular belief that "carnal relations" spoiled mothers' milk, then these young fathers may have felt considerable resentment toward the cause of these restrictions. At the very least, limits on sexual expression probably heightened the tensions men felt during these months.[9]

Not all fathers responded with resentment to the changes and intrusions accompanying a newborn child. Samuel Cormany, who had been fascinated by every facet of the pregnancy and birth, involved himself with equal enthusiasm in the care of his newborn daughter. Having obviously read many of the nineteenth-century advice manuals, Cormany approached this role in a "scientific" manner. Believing, as did some writers and birth experts of the time, that his wife's colostrum (the milk secreted in the first day or two after childbirth) would be harmful to the child, he tried to feed his daughter watered-down cows' milk the day after birth.[10] In addition, he recorded bathing and feeding patterns as the days progressed. Three months later he wrote in his journal, "all the world and the rest of mankind would be as nothing to me in exchange for my dear little daughter."[11]

By seemingly avoiding the tensions of the transition period, Samuel Cormany represents a minority among new middle-class fathers. During these first few weeks, most exhibited ambivalence toward their role and toward the new child. Gradually, however, most fathers warmed to their infant son or daughter, many eventually matching Samuel Cormany's intense interest and love. Fathers who initially referred to a child as "it" soon were writing about "my" child to friends and relatives. This budding relationship often took time to develop since it did not have the immediacy or significance of the bond between the nursing mother and child. As men responded to social conventions, like those that gave significance to naming, baptism, and gender assignment, their perceptions of their children as individuals became increasingly stronger.

The earliest stone laid in the foundation of this relationship was gender identification. We can see this best in the language that fathers used to describe their newborn children. While men occasionally referred to infants in the gender-neutral "it," fathers usually began using the terms "girl" or "boy" soon after the birth. Indeed, it is possible that men's use of "it" may have partly been a carryover from the period before birth when they lacked a better gender-neutral term to refer to the future child. This seemingly simple use of words had vast meaning for the father-child relationship, for it began the long process of sexual distinction that shaped men's developing perception of their young children. Not long after birth, fathers wrote of sons as "strong" or "robust" (or "sickly") and described their daughters as "small," "sweet," or "precious." While not as important as the gender-specific inculcation that later shaped a child's identity, this early distinction laid the foundation of gender difference in the minds of the people around the child.

Some historians suggest that expectant fathers hoped for sons over daughters, raising the question of whether or not preference might have shaped their view of the infant child.[12] Through the course of their lives, fathers of the antebellum era expended greater time and effort on sons and often interacted more with male children. This closeness did not always mean a more satisfying relationship, but it did mean that men's relationships with their sons were usually more important to them than those with daughters. In traditional agrarian-based societies, fathers preferred sons partly because of the future labor they represented. Sons also continued the family name and assured men of an heir to the family property. Yet economic changes in the nineteenth century undermined the foundations of this preference for sons. As society shifted away from agriculture in the nineteenth century, the need for sons as workers and heirs declined.

Without the economic basis for the tradition, preference for sons seems to have diminished somewhat by 1800. After his wife had six daughters, Erastus Smith adopted a son to carry on his name, but when he wrote his last will and testament in 1829, he still gave only one-seventh of the family estate to him, the other six-sevenths going to the daughters.[13] Lincoln Clark illustrated the changing sentiments a decade later when he wrote to his mother-in-law after the birth of his first child, a daughter: "I suppose most young fathers would consider their pride and dignity, or it might be their arrogance, as somewhat more flattered by having for the first a son instead of a daughter: but I am more than satisfied, nay more delighted."[14] Gregory Yale, who postponed his career in law for a try at California gold, was the only man in this study to openly express a desire to have a son. And in his case (possibly because his first child was a son) he deferred to his wife's hope for a daughter, writing, "I desire that the child be a boy, for reasons often stated to you, but for your own gratification, I am in hopes it may be a girl. At all events it will be gratifying to me."[15] Unfortunately, Yale's existing correspondence does not tell us why he desired a son. It is likely that Yale's preference was not unique in the antebellum period, for patriarchal societies tend to place a higher value on male children, but if a large number of men felt greater joy at the birth of a son, or disappointment at the birth of a daughter, they hid these emotions in the sources used here.[16]

As with early gender identification, naming the child was another initial step by which fathers began to think of their child as a separate and distinct person. A named child need no longer be referred to as "it." Historians have noted the decline of necronymic naming practices—the practice of naming children after deceased relatives and siblings—suggesting that name choice in the nineteenth century reflected the growing acceptance of children as individuals. In earlier centuries, as prominent historian of the English family Alan MacFarlane has noted, "It almost seems as if the names were present before the children, who were afterwards fitted into them."[17] By the nineteenth century, rather than the child growing into a name, one was chosen to suit the child. Samuel Francis Smith, a Baptist minister from Maine, wrote in 1835 about the naming of his first child, "It is true a name is not a matter of much consequence. The thing is far more to be valued. A good mind in a decent body, with a name which will make nobody stare, is more desirable than all the cognomens of antiquity, and all the praise or the wonder which the taste of parents in naming their children could elicit."[18]

This shift should not be overemphasized, however, since naming children after relatives or friends continued, and the naming of children remained a "matter of much consequence" for most parents. Parents generally chose the name of their own children, only occasionally giving that privilege to another. Whether mothers or fathers predominantly held this right is not clear. Some instances clearly demonstrate that the father exercised this privilege. In 1821, William Brown's son was born while he was away at sea, and his wife waited until she received a return letter to learn the name of the child.[19] But mothers also occasionally decided their children's names. Sarah Ayer named her daughter "for the dear friend of my early childhood, the companion of my school days."[20] For most children the sources are silent about which parent chose or whether it was a collaborative process. Usually, however, the parents appeared to be in accord. William Sewall wrote of a case sure to please both he and his wife: "[W]e have concluded to call this son of ours Henry Middleton after his two grandfathers."[21]

One instance of disagreement over naming suggests that the mother's daily interaction with the infant could allow her to override a father's preference. Soon after the birth of his first son, Charles Ray, one of the early *Chicago Tribune* editors, wrote to a friend, "I am going to call him Sidney Penn, after Algernon of immortal memory and my other idol—the Quaker William."[22] His wife Jane, however, preferred the name Frank, and two months later Charles was still lobbying for the name he had chosen. "How is the boy to-day? Little Penn—by the way, I do not know him as 'Franky'; the name does not sound will [sic] for my boy; it is not manly; it is only the name of a lad or of some squirt like Frank Peirce or Frank Granger. Let us have . . . him called Penn and done with it."[23] Six months after the birth, however, Charles finally admitted defeat and the child was called Frank. His surrender, however, was not graceful in the least, for he complained to her, "With such a name as you persist on giving him, he ought to be sickly—perhaps to die of the diarrhoea."[24] Charles was frequently absent from his family, which might suggest that Jane's daily interaction with the child legitimated her claim to name the boy. Neither parent had the outright authority to name the child, however, and it took months of wrangling for the issue to be settled.

Names given infants were often too large and formal, and parents used pet names for everyday use. Men, even in the first months, began calling their young daughters "little girl," "little love," "little sweet," "little puss," "little blessed," "little one," " little chick," "little duck," "angel," "little cub," and "little pet;" they referred to their infant sons as "little boy," "little darling," and "little Treasure," among others.[25] The use of these terms of endearment indicate that most fathers developed a fairly affectionate attitude toward their infant children. In a few cases, however, tension lies beneath the humor and warmth of these pet names. Some men referred to their sons as the "young aristocrat," "the Dauphin," "the Czarevitch," or "the Prince of Wales."[26] These mock titles of nobility suggest a mild resentment of the place infant sons held in the family. Some psychologists and sociologists suggest that modern fathers often reexperience a kind of Oedipal drama at the birth of their sons that contributes to jealousy of the child. Some scholars claim that the tension is best described as a "Laius complex" (named after Laius, the father of Oedipus), where the father fears the potential power of the son.[27] Given the ambivalent attitudes toward the coming of a new child held by middle-class men in the nineteenth century, these theories provide a possible context for these gently mocking pet names.

Referring to their sons as royalty was not the only jesting way in which some fathers revealed their unease over their new sons. At least one father facetiously imbued his infant son with the capability for committing adult or adolescent mischief. Thomas Kilby Smith, an

Ohio lawyer who often used humor in his letters to his wife, wrote in 1854 about their less-than-a-year-old son.

> Speaking of guns does the young aristocrat grow? There seemed to be room for it when I left. I hope you do not permit him to stay out late at night & above all that you permit no improper familiarity between him & Mrs. Donald [probably a nurse or servant]. You should reflect that your son is still young & that those habits he now forms will cling to him through life becoming second nature.

Smith continued the theme later in the letter, warning of "improper familiarity" with a cousin. "I will not permit him to trifle with his cousin's affections & that if without serious intentions he persists in the course of conduct I have reason to believe he is pursuing I shall visit him with my most serious displeasure." In a play on words, he asked his wife, "By the way does he still drink? If so & you cannot break it up, beg him earnestly to conceal the fact & if he must indulge, urge him to do so privately & in your room or . . . he will certainly sacrifice his reputation."[28] Smith's humor may have masked his concerns for both his child's future and his own ability to raise the child. Philandering and drunkenness, while amusing in this context, nonetheless challenged middle-class norms and patriarchal authority.

Daughters were never joked about in this manner. Fathers playfully referred to infant daughters as small animals and angels—things pure, gentle, and usually diminutive, never using the domineering and mischievous names applied to sons. Men were already thinking of their children within the framework of gender traits, and as early as infancy the tension and attraction between father and son existed in some relationships. Thus, during infancy fathers' perceptions of their children as individuals contained the roots of complexities that would come to shape the future father-child relationship.

While the humorous names given to sons had some obviously Freudian underpinnings, looking at the relationship between father and infant only in these terms does not provide the entire picture. George Templeton Strong showed a resentment and distance in his early relationship with his son, but several circumstances beyond mere Oedipal conflicts contributed to this tension. Strong's terrifying experience with his wife's first birth may have tainted his early attitude toward his son, the result of his wife's second pregnancy. His resentment also increased when, as noted earlier, the child developed colic, which considerably irritated Strong. "The Psalmist speaks of the young lions roaring in the night; he was a bachelor when he wrote that psalm, or he would have cited young babies as the better instance of habitual nocturnal ululation."[29]

Strong's upper middle-class status also contributed to the distance between his infant son and himself. His ability to hire servants kept him separate enough from his son to slow the process of attachment to the child, and yet he was close enough to be disturbed by the bouts with colic. His emotional distance can be seen in the following passage that disparages the comments of those closer to the child: "The young boy . . . grows like a fungus and is said to have laughed, and to have begun to 'take notice,' and is a fat, moon-faced, 'flabby dobby hobby.'"[30] However, within three months the child was sleeping easier during the night and much of the tension dissipated. At six months Strong seemed a bit more sympathetic to the child's circumstances.

> The baby don't [sic] seem to suffer much from the hot weather so far, but I suppose he'll soon feel it if it lasts much longer—nobody but must. Think of the agony of having one's lower end muffled and swathed in the barbarous trappings for which the nineteenth century has invented no humane substitute! I should go mad in two hours under the infliction. An extra thick neckcloth on one of these hot mornings would be fearful, but words can't express the misery a perpetual state of diaper must produce. No wonder the unhappy infant remonstrates with Fate sometimes, as he's remonstrating now.[31]

Naming and gender assignment had more to do with a father's idea of a new child rather than entailing any actual interaction with an infant. A middle-class man could participate in these processes and still remain at a distance from a child. But they nonetheless helped fathers begin to accept the child as a person in its own right. Even men like Strong, who in the beginning were quite ambivalent, usually warmed to their children after a relatively short time. In order to flourish, however, this developing relationship needed actual interaction between father and child. One important type was the contribution men made to childcare, since unlike George Templeton Strong, most middle-class fathers either could not afford to hire a servant to care for children or did not feel it wise to allow anyone to supplant the parental role in childcare.

Contrary to the notion of separate spheres, men participated at different stages in a wide variety of childcare activities; however, a good deal of these fell within the context of their traditional male roles. Some of the more businesslike aspects of childcare were considered to be men's duties, such as the arranging and paying for medical treatments like an older child's visit to the dentist or a smallpox vaccination.[32] Any domestic task perceived as requiring business acumen or scientific knowledge was quickly becoming the domain of men. Fathers were often the ones who hired servants or nurses, since these duties involved money and communal connections. "My good husband offers to hire a girl anytime," wrote one woman to her parents, "but I see many objections to that"—all of them having to do with the high cost of help and the scarcity of servants, but none about the appropriateness of her husband doing the hiring.[33] Some men had a surprisingly cavalier attitude about the choice of a nurse; as one suggested, "Any kind body can get acquainted with the children in half a day. If not well acquainted, it makes little difference who puts off and on their nappys."[34] Others were more cautious: "I would always hate to leave a child much with any girl I was not fully acquainted with. The little Child cannot tell if it is abused, or if anything is wrong."[35]

In some cases when the nurse was to participate in the birth or fill the role of wet nurse, the hiring could be considered a "delicate" matter for a husband "to attend to."[36] Yet despite the intimately feminine nature of this task, some men performed this duty. One month after giving birth to a son, Dorcas Brown wrote to her husband, a sea captain,

> I am obliged to give up nursing the Babe, which is a great grief to me. I tried to nurse him 'till the Doc.r told me I must either give it up, or give up your [sic] own life, for I could not live but a little while. We have got along so far with a nursing bottle, but the poor little creature does not grow and it makes my heart ache to look upon him & if you were at home perhaps you would get a nurse for him—but it is expensive & I don't know what to do.[37]

The Browns' finances and family authority structure prevented Dorcas from feeling free to hire a wet nurse without William's permission and instruction. William, however, knowing his wife's state of health, wrote about the time the child was born telling Dorcas not to nurse the child.[38] Clearly, William Brown had an important say in the choice of hiring a nurse and even in the decision whether or not to breast-feed the child.

Making provisions for their children's financial well-being and material comfort often helped to foster a connection. One father increased his life insurance coverage $1000 for each successive child. Other fathers purchased or made items for the baby. In his spare time, railroad builder Isaac Metcalf constructed a crib for his first son. John Wesley North, a Minnesota lawyer and businessman, bought a crib and clothing for his daughter, including a coat much too large for her and a garish hat that her mother detested. Because the family was not truly a private institution, but linked to the public sphere at various levels, the range of fathers' participation in their children's lives could be quite broad.[39] But as we shall see, most men's involvement went beyond this level.

Most of the functions already mentioned, such as naming, purchasing items, or arranging care, could be done at a distance. However, men also participated in childcare that was highly interactive and well within the bounds of the traditional domestic sphere. When they were not working outside the home, middle-class fathers aided in the daily care and tending of infant children. This care was given by fathers at select times and was often directed at easing some of the wife's burden. John Wesley North wrote to his father-in-law, "I would write more but I have to take care of the babies a part of the time so as to relieve Ann."[40] Christopher Pearce, a steamboat captain, acknowledged the daily strain of childcare in a letter to his wife: "I expect you all have your hands full, to take care of her, if I only had her here occasionally, I would be pleased to give you a spell."[41] Likewise, Lincoln Clark was worried about his wife's health during the infancy of their first child when he wrote to her, "I regret that I can not be present to relieve you at least in the nightly care of the little chick that sleeps in the cribb [sic]. For I think you ought to be as much at your ease as possible."[42] Illness was common for women in the nineteenth century, particularly postpartum sickness, and the wives of at least two of the men mentioned here at one time or another had extended ailments. During sickness men gave considerable time and care to their children as the immediate needs of the family superceded proscribed gender roles.

Any extensive childcare that interfered with a man's career, however, was viewed as temporary. If a wife was unable to work for an extended period of time, then a husband hired a nurse or convinced relatives or friends to assist. Middle-class men seem to have been willing to play with children, rock them to sleep, or feed weaned or non-breast-fed children during the evening hours or on Sunday, but their breadwinning role still took precedence in the long term. Between his business trips, Isaac Metcalf's wife wrote in her journal, "Isaac home all day caring for the babies and reading."[43] One Chicago merchant wrote, "I do not feel very well to day, and therefore am obliged to stay in the house and tend the baby," who was seven months old.[44] When fathers were idle, childcare was an appropriate task. One wife, writing to a friend, commented on her husband's weekend help with an infant son: "He [her husband] is very good about taking care of him, he took care of him while I went to meeting this forenoon, also 2 weeks ago to day [sic]."[45]

John Wesley North, who occasionally cared for sick children, provides a good illustration of a father's participation in the care of his young children. North was a frontier lawyer, politician, and businessman who divided his time between his law practice, politics, investments, and family. More ambitious than most, his correspondence leaves little record of family matters, but instead is devoted to business ventures, land speculation, and politics. However, from his wife's letters we can see that even with these various masculine pursuits, North was a devoted father and often played with his five children and assisted his wife and his sister (who lived with them) in caring for the children. Still, during elections, community programs, business deals, or critical times in his investments, North had little time for helping with the children. After complaining to her mother of the difficulties of her work, Ann North wrote, "Of course Mr. North can be here but little, and generally when he is, there is some one [sic] here to see him."[46] After a particularly busy and ultimately unsuccessful business venture, North wrote to his father-in-law, "Ann is felicitating herself on the fact that I am to stay at home this winter. And I am by no means sad at the prospect. I hope to make myself somewhat useful in the care and government of the children."[47]

North's role as provider, with its complex trappings of masculinity, materialism, and ambition, took precedence over his family cares for much of his early fatherhood, but not without a price. Like other middle-class men at this time, North struggled with the conflict between his ambition to succeed in a business career and his view of a proper domestic life. At times in the first ten years of his marriage, he was able to balance the competing interests to the satisfaction of himself, his wife, and his children, but at other times his work controlled his time and physical energy to the point that he contributed little to childcare. Still, North and his wife saw his place as helping in the "care and government" of his children.

Exactly what this care of young children entailed and its extent is not completely clear. The particulars of the daily care of infants was not a common topic in the letters of either men or women in the nineteenth century; thus, the silence of men's letters could mean either lack of involvement or a level of familiarity that did not require mention of commonplace events. Yet some clues do emerge in the correspondence. For example, earlier statements in this chapter suggest that it was common for men to tend children to give the wife time for rest or other work. Lincoln Clark's letters indicate that he rocked his child to sleep and sat up with infants at night when they could not sleep.[48] Men's absence during the day meant that fathers usually tended in the evening and nighttime hours.

Another indication that fathers were involved in many of the more domestic aspects of childcare comes from the interest they exhibited in all the stages of infant development. William Swain, a New York farmer turned forty-niner, wrote to his wife, "In your letter, Sabrina, you have made frequent allusions to our little girl—her growth, her progress in walking, talking; her tricks of childhood; disposition; temper; attachments; etc., all of which are of great interest to me."[49] Thus, reports of teething, weaning, "pranks" and "prattle," health, thumb-sucking, sleep habits, diet, dress, and other news of children were enjoyed and encouraged by fathers.[50] William Swain, while in the gold fields of California, learned from his brother that his young daughter "still tends the wants of Nature on the floor, or rather lets them tend themselves. There a few minutes ago she scattered her water and her mother told her to go and get the mop and mop it up. Away she went and got and tugged at it till she had dragged it several times over the place as sober as a judge."[51] Such details are not proof of participation, but they do suggest men's emotional involvement on this level. Men were aware of their children's development, but how they participated in these changes in their children's lives still requires further study.

Play was an exception to the silence on childcare, and probably formed the most important part of men's participation in childcare. From the sources it is obvious that young children often viewed their fathers as playmates. Ann North wrote of her eight-month-old daughter, "She is full of frolic. As soon as her father comes in the house, she begins to spring, reach towards him; laugh, squeal, and halloo 'bra!

bra!'"[52] That North's children valued play with their father is evident in another letter written by Ann, this time about a son who was teething and cranky. "The only place he seems to feel quite happy in, is riding on his father's foot—I think he would do that and laugh, half a day."[53]

Not all facets of the relationship were playful, however. The ties that bind parents to children do just that at times—limit freedom. Further evidence that men were involved with their children comes from the inconveniences that children brought into their lives. Samuel Cormany's enthusiasm for his new daughter waned somewhat during a trip where he saw "many . . . interesting sights—but not half so many as we would had we not Baby to care for and keep comfortable." But he was able to say, "Still, Thank God for our Blessed Baby."[54] Thomas Carter, mentioned earlier as a merchant who tended his son while recovering from an illness, wrote to a friend,

> I shall be well enough to go to the store tomorrow and have taken the time to write, but a crying child does not help a person's ideas much. However, these are necessary evils and therefore [we] must make the best of them, but the evils in this Case are but Small Compared with the Satisfaction Such little plums Sometimes give. Sometimes they are a good deal of trouble but not always So.[55]

All these activities—from naming to play and care—were the matrix within which the father-child relationship grew. Within the context of these activities, it is important to note that infants actively contributed to the bond. Children's joy in playing with their fathers is one proof of the reciprocity of these relationships, but fathers recorded many other instances as well. Infants usually begin to start to form attachments, or enduring emotional ties, at around six months old. Attachment at this age is primarily based on need gratification, and thus the nursing mother is usually the child's first object of attachment. However, other factors that play an important role in the development of a child's emotional life include familiarity through physical contact, mutual interaction, and play. While the process of attachment may have been different in the lives of nineteenth-century infants, it is still safe to assume that the first relationships infants developed were with those who participated in gratifying their immediate needs.[56]

If fathers were quite separate from the childrearing process, then it is not likely that infant children would have formed significant bonds with them, yet a substantial amount of evidence indicates that infants did recognize their fathers and create and maintain bonds with them. Furthermore, children, fathers, and mothers encouraged and cultivated these ties. Through smiles, animated movements, and even crying at separation, infants began to demonstrate an emotional attachment to their fathers several months after birth. After the death of an infant son, George Borrowe wrote to his grandfather, "he had just begun to know his Parents, and we the joys of having such a treasure, when he was taken from us."[57] One mother wrote of her infant daughter's attachment to her husband, Charles, "She loves her father ... 'very dearly.' Every time that her father comes into the house she will look up into his face and laugh. That is the way she asks him to speak to her. That he can do very easy. Charles takes a great deal of pleasure in his children. That of itself pays me for my trouble."[58]

Fathers who left very young children and wives to undertake journeys often heard from home how the child missed them. One woman wrote that her four-month-old son continually expressed disappointment at mistaking other men for his absent father.[59] More typical, however, was the eleven-month-old daughter of William Swain, who missed her father after he left for the gold fields of California. His wife wrote,

> Sis slept very well, awoke in the morning, and looked over at me seemingly to welcome a spree with her father, but to her disappointment the looked-for one was absent. She appears very lonesome, and seems to miss you very much. She is very troublesome and will not go to anyone, but cries after me and clings to me more than ever. I received your daguerrian. . . . I think I never saw anything but life look so natural. I showed it to little Cub, and to my astonishment and pleasure she appeared to recognize it. She put her finger on it, looked up at me and laughed, put her face down to yours, and kissed it several times in succession. Every time it comes in her sight she will cry after it.[60]

While some of the wife's longing for her husband was probably projected onto the child, or even suggested to the child, it nonetheless appears that some of these feelings were genuine.

After Swain had been gone for several weeks, his unmarried brother George became the child's father figure. Swain's wife wrote to him, "Eliza is getting so she thinks a great deal of George. She calculates to have a play with him whenever he comes in."[61] Playing with the child seems to have increased the strength of the tie between the uncle and niece. Two months later, George wrote of Swain's daughter, "She and I have great times dancing round the house when I am at leisure."[62] In a father's absence a young child occasionally formed a bond with a man other than the father, suggesting that the ties described here developed naturally in the ebb and flow of family life. Fathers and substitute fathers were familiar faces to young children, and play, care, and other interaction strengthened the mutual connections between them.

While we have already seen men demonstrate their emotional involvement with their children through affection, care, and concern, perhaps the most powerful evidences of attachment came in the expressive responses to the sickness or death of a child. Depending on its severity, a child's illness could range from a minor vexation to a significant alteration in a father's life. Men helped nurse sick children, worried over them, and, when they died, mourned them. Fathers had an obvious obligation to become involved in nursing ill children—the cost of servants, the frequency of illnesses, and notions of privacy all encouraged men's participation. But the strong emotions of anxiety and sorrow felt by fathers during these times also reveal the real emotional bonds between fathers and their infant children.[63]

Some illnesses merely inconvenienced the father. While staying with his half-brother Isaac Metcalf, Charles Rich wrote to his wife of Isaac's young son, "The little boy is pretty well but is rather troublesome just now on account of being weaned so that Isaac is kept awake some nights in consequence."[64] Two years later, Isaac's wife, Antoinette, wrote in her journal of another bout of illness in their family, "Wilder very troublesome. Isaac taking care of him all day."[65] Since almost any ailment could become life-threatening in this age of limited and often inaccurate medical knowledge, even a common illness was cause for concern. George Templeton Strong recorded a particularly worrisome night prompted by the illness of his son:

A very anxious and painful time since my last entry. I was called up at half-past four Friday morning with the report that the baby was out of order; some sort of cold, so that he couldn't take nourishment. Found him in a half-stifled state, breathing badly and in great distress and discomfort. Didn't suppose anything serious the matter, but the mamma being in such trouble, I started for the doctor. It was a savage southeaster, pouring rain and wind that soon blasted my umbrella into the form of a wine glass. Knowing that Johnston wouldn't come out on any such demand on such a night, I invoked Peters, who said he didn't suppose it was anything of moment, but volunteered to go up with me. He at once said it was a grave affair, and that he wanted help. Off again, called for [Dr. J. Augustus] McVickar, who couldn't come; then routed up Johnston, who refused point-blank to do anything in the premises. Back again, and again off to find McVickar, who came up this time, and agreed with Dr. Peters that the case was nearly desperate. They called it 'thymus asthma' or 'Millar's asthma.' It was marked by spasm of the throat, inability to swallow, blueness of the face, etc.

At about 8:30 I went for Hawks, and the poor little insensible thing was baptized by the name of John Ruggles. Then as things grew still worse, I went for Dr. Gray, and after waiting for a long while, succeeded in obtaining an interview with that great man—and home again, not expecting to find the child alive. But I was met by Ellie at the nursery door with the news that he was better—the spasm had terminated.[66]

Strong often wrote with a future public audience in mind, and his focus on the storm and the hesitant doctors pretentiously aggrandizes his own image. But behind the wry humor is also resentment toward the eminent doctors' inability to help his son and a real anxiousness that eventually turned into relief over the outcome.

Inevitably some illnesses did not have such a fortuitous end. From the experiences of mourning for deceased infant children we get a glimpse of the strength and extent of fathers' emotional bonds. "Mourning reactions to the loss of a loved one," writes Peter G. Slater, "include shock, grief and pain, which develop as the survivor's ego struggles to cope with the experience. If an individual does not mourn the death of a family member, either he is suffering from an abnormal emotional condition or he has not been involved in an affective relationship with the deceased."[67] The grief that many fathers experienced after an infant's death is sad testimony to the existence of such an affective relationship. One father wrote, upon the death of an infant son, "we endeavour to bear the affliction with resignation to [God's] will; but it has been the most trying period of our lives."[68] To remember his baby daughter who had died, William Lloyd Garrison had daguerreotypes taken of the corpse before the burial.[69] In a similar vein, Samuel Cormany, fearing that the sickness of his daughter would be fatal, had a daguerreotype taken of her.[70]

Cormany's forethought was not uncommon, since the preparation for a child's death could begin during the illness with anticipatory mourning.[71] The frequency of infant death in the antebellum period meant that any illness could signal the beginning of the end, and many fathers dealt with this by unconsciously preparing for death. The sickness of George S. Phillips' six-month-old daughter brought on thoughts of mortality in his journal: "The little love has suffered much. What a trial it would be for us to part with her."[72] Because Lincoln Clark's son suffered from an unnamed illness for much of his short year-and-a-half life, Clark's letters through this period are particularly informative about the complex emotions evoked by an impending death. "The sickness of the dear little boy grieves me sorely. When I left him my hopes were mingled with great fears. I was unwilling to persuade myself that rest and cherishing would not revive him, and yet I could not evade the thought that I might never more see his pleasant, winning blessed little face."[73] From the beginning of the illness, Clark hoped that rest and care would cure his son, but his grief at the suffering of the child began to prepare him for the worst.

Clearly, the depth of sentiment expressed by fathers like Phillips and Clark reveals strong attachments to infants. Yet some historians writing in the 1960s and 1970s argued differently. Influenced by Philippe Ariés, whose work introduced the idea that parents' views of children in past time were culturally determined (and sometimes not very affectionate), they argued that many parents in the colonial period and into the nineteenth century refrained from growing overly attached to their infant children. Partly as a defense mechanism against sorrow if the child died, and partly the result of mistrust of the child's nature, fathers supposedly kept their distance during the first few years.[74] A few historians have since challenged this idea of parental detachment, showing that the connection between love and death is more complicated than a defense mechanism or a minister's advice. Peter G. Slater has shown how even Puritan parents' images of children "varied among positive and negative shadings"; at times Calvinist parents feared their children's natural tendency to evil, and at times they enjoyed their innocence.[75] Linda Pollock's study of 144 American diaries and autobiographies found that fathers and mothers showed as much emotion for sick or deceased infants as they did for older children. Age did not seem to matter—and this was true for the seventeenth and eighteenth centuries as well as the nineteenth. Many of the nineteenth-century men she studied, like the men mentioned here, exhibited deep grief and loss at the death of their young children.[76]

Antebellum religious culture cautioned parents against loving children too much. During his son's illness, Lincoln Clark wrote to his wife, "I have sometimes thought I loved the child too well, and that the gracious God would take him for that reason. I have loved him deeply, but have attempted to guard against idolatry."[77] Here then seems to be a mitigating influence on men's relationships with infant children; God stepped between father and child. "We should find it very difficult to part with our little Boy who is just Seven months old," admitted Thomas Carter to his cousin. "But we know not how Soon we may be obliged to part with him. And it is our duty to be ready for any event, and not complain at any of the dealings of a Kind & merciful Providence. It is well for us to feel that 'all things work together for good to them that love God.'"[78]

If we accept these statements at face value, then we might argue that fathers avoided loving children too much out of piety. Perhaps some fathers were able to distance themselves from their children, but most in the sources could not. Lincoln Clark indicates that although he did try to keep his love within the bounds God set for him, his fear that he "loved the child too well" shows that he was not successful. In an 1810 letter to a friend, Erastus Smith, Lincoln Clark's future father-in-law, noted, "My brother Cotton & Wife are much afflicted. Their only child, about eight weeks old, is near its end. . . . It was a promising little Girl—and perhaps the Parents loved it too well. They now appear to be in distress."[79] But after this criticism of excessive love, Smith in describing his attachment to his own daughter expressed fear that he too held his daughter as his own, instead of God's, gift. Parents were warned to be careful of loving too much, but most did not seem to be able to pay heed to the warnings. Indeed, these fears of loving too much indicate strong attachments to children rather than a lack of love. In the end, although this cultural idea of a jealous God shaped how fathers expressed their love, and even how they interpreted it, it did not prevent the existence of that love and the resulting emotional bonds with their infant children.

If we follow the lead of Philippe Ariés, we can say that the expression of emotions at the time of death and sickness increased and intensified as the nineteenth century progressed. The rise in strong and impassioned laments, the dread of death anniversaries, the remembrance through cemetery monuments, the idealization of the dead, and other manifestations of this trend indicate that middle-class nineteenth-century Americans were changing their view of death. If they indeed were imbuing their families with greater emotional importance, then, as Ariés argues, this "exaggeration of mourning" means that "survivors accepted the death of another person with greater difficulty than in the past."[80] We should not, however, view this new kind of mourning as mere ritual or a cheap stylization of "real" pain. The anguish and sorrow men expressed at the illness and death of infant children indicate a strong paternal attachment that in turn shows the importance of infant children in fathers' views of their family. While men felt some resentment at times toward their children, they also felt considerable love. Naming, gender assignment, play, and care all contributed to the development of a strong, reciprocating bond.

The first two years of the infant's life was a time of mutual learning, play, and growing love between child and father. This period of relatively friction-free interaction, however, was short-lived as children grew out of infancy into the early years of childhood. In this transition, fathers and children both developed new responsibilities—fathers to teach and govern, children to learn and obey. These responsibilities dominated the long years of relationships between fathers and their children, but they were built upon the foundations of love and interaction that were laid during the earliest years of the child's life.

chapter four

The Tyranny of Love

PATERNAL POWER AND AUTHORITY

In 1849, William Swain said good-bye to his wife and infant daughter, left his New York farm in the hands of his brother, and ventured to try his luck in the gold fields of California. As his daughter Eliza grew from infant to toddler, Swain's family kept him apprised of the child's growing precociousness. His brother informed him that Eliza was "Master of the House, does what she pleases, asks nobody's leave, hunts up mischief as fast as she had a hundred eyes. You'd laugh to see her go upstairs to pay her respects to the preserves."[1] His wife, Sabrina, less amused by the growing willfulness of the child, wrote, "as she grows older, the more I feel the need of a father's care and assistance in lightening the responsibility of governing and training her right."[2] William obviously felt something of this responsibility as well. Although he never before had been the father of a two-year-old child, Swain began to advise his wife from afar. "It is my belief that government of children should be effected by impressing upon the mind ideas of right and wrong, propriety and impropriety, and good and bad." "But," Swain continued, "these are not always adequate to counteract the will and subdue the temper. . . . Restraints are necessary, especially in early infancy, and unless they are timely and judiciously resorted to, their omission may be the cause of great evil to the child and trouble to the parent. No less the good of the child than the duty of the parent requires restraints and punishments."

Nor did William Swain's advice end with matters of discipline; he also expounded on physical regimen and diet:

Her physical development too, I hope you will not neglect. It calls for far more care than parents usually bestow on their child's development. Be careful not to cripple the power of Nature by hampering it with close clothes; let them be such as will assist Nature in the creation of [a] good physical system. Let her food be rather coarse and such that is easily digested, not too highly seasoned nor very salty. Milk is the best of all foods for young ones; and as little pork or grease as possible—it is the worst of all things for children except candies and sweets. Be sure not to allow her to sleep with a high pillow, for they cause round and stooped shoulders. Avoid anything that can have a tendency to induce curved spine. These will require your careful attention.[3]

Swain's instruction to his wife, although more detailed than most correspondence of this type, reveals a great deal about the power structure of antebellum middle-class families. It shows a tiered family system that placed fathers in a position of authority over wives and children in matters as fundamental as the inculcation of values and as mundane as the proper dress and diet for an infant. William Swain's admonitions exude authority demonstrating his right to advise. While the modern reader is struck by the irony of a man miles from home on a questionable venture giving detailed childrearing advice to his wife, obviously Swain felt too secure in his right to notice any incongruity. He expressed his views on a wide range of childrearing topics with the confidence of someone who believes he is correct and who expects his advice to be followed. At the same time, the situation suggests a family structure complex enough to allow for men and women to share authority. William directed and advised, but Sabrina, possessing her own stewardship, interpreted his advice and at times vetoed his long-distance instructions in order to implement her own views. And finally, we must also remember that power rested not just with Sabrina and William; Eliza's pilfering of the family jams and jellies suggests that she had a great deal to say about the success of her parents' childrearing efforts.

According to current historiography of the antebellum middle-class family, Swain's authority over childrearing matters seems anomalous. Historians like Carl Degler, Linda Kerber, Anne L. Kuhn, and others have argued that although nineteenth-century fathers did some disciplining and advising, they usually deferred to their wives in matters of moral and physical nurture.[4] If Swain had lived two hundred years earlier, he would make more sense to us. In the patriarchal culture of seventeenth-century America, society endowed fathers with considerable power. Puritan ministers taught that men's moral and intellectual superiority made them the parent best suited to discipline and inculcate values. Women were thought to be of a too indulgent and affectionate nature to effectively teach and govern children in a godly manner. Children needed the firmer, more rational hand of a man. Cultural beliefs like these formed the basis of New England law, which not only legislated children's obedience to fathers but also guaranteed men's control over property and marriage choice. As head of the household and property owner, the father represented the keystone in the foundation of the authority of the state, and Puritan leaders sought to ensure that fathers had not only the right to keep peace and order in their families (authority) but also the ability to do so in the form of law, property rights, and community pressure (power).[5]

Swain's authority seems anachronistic, however, because historians suggest that by the eighteenth century, several complex changes began to undermine traditional sources of authority. The rise of emotional religion, the challenge to political authority, the dissemination of Enlightenment ideas, and the growth of a commercial economy all conjoined (in a manner historians still do not fully understand) to produce a societal system based less on hierarchy and more on personal freedom. During this volatile era, the authority of the church and community waned, and fathers, the representatives of these institutions within the family, lost a key source of influence. Law remained protective of some patriarchal prerogatives, but in the new republic that emphasized the rights of the individual, older statutes, such as those requiring the death penalty for disobedient children, were repealed or ignored. Perhaps more importantly, according to historians, a key pillar of men's traditional authority—control over inheritance—weakened as farmland became less significant in the new more commercially oriented economy.[6]

According to historians, others stepped into the vacuum left by this shift in power. Mothers became the primary nurturers, taking over the all-important tasks of the inculcation of religious and civic values. School teachers, increasingly women in the nineteenth century, had authority over the teaching of secular knowledge. Doctors and self-appointed health experts, in the name of scientific progress, expanded their influence over children's physical care and well-being. Children themselves saw their power expand in deciding such matters as schooling, work, and marriage. This transfer of power was a gradual process, but the end result, according to historians, was that fathers no longer had the authority to rear children.[7]

What then to make of William Swain's authoritative advice? Despite historians' claims of declining paternal influence at this time, the tone of Swain's letter clearly shows him to be in a position of power, but wherein did that power lie? We often perceive power as elemental and thus simple (money = influence, size = strength, votes = a mandate, consent = subordination). Such generalizations help us make sense of an infinitely complex world. Yet to understand who held power within the Swain family, we must see that in the nineteenth century, familial power dynamics were more complex than can be expressed with the limited vocabulary these generalizations impose. Men, along with women, children, and other relatives, were intimately enmeshed in a familial web of rights, obligations, prerogatives, and duties. Thus, it is more accurate to see familial power as varied, shared, and negotiated, and even as something for which family members vied.

Although the nineteenth century saw increased limits on their ability to influence their children's marriage and occupational choices, fathers in the antebellum United States still controlled more of their children's lives than men do today, primarily because of the broader and more diverse basis of their power in the home. Historians rightly focus on economics when discussing patriarchy—usually the control of land and the inheritance process. Middle-class men, however, also appealed to other sources of power, including physical strength, intellect, love, religious belief, and even their authority as given them by society. To focus on changes to only one source of men's power neglects other aspects and gives us only a partial picture of fatherhood. One must look beyond just the economic to gain a clearer picture of how changes in law, new perceptions of emotional attachment, shifting societal expectations, and men's evolving breadwinner role affected fatherhood in the nineteenth century. Furthermore, men appealed to different sources of power at different points in their tenure as fathers. The physical manipulation that worked with young children gave way to financial incentives and appeals to duty with older children. To determine the extent of men's power in nineteenth-century families, we must examine the various sources men drew upon throughout their lives.

As we learn more about nineteenth-century families, the need for more complex views of fathers' power becomes increasingly apparent.

Such a view, for example, would help us better understand a key distinction that is often overlooked: How did men's power over children differ from that over wives? Scholars typically have lumped the two together under the rubric of patriarchy. A subtler view of fatherhood in the nineteenth century will differentiate between these related but distinct types of power. In this chapter we briefly examine how men vied with wives over who held domestic power, but most of the chapter addresses fathers' authority over children. We will see how antebellum men's broad and varied power base allowed them to exercise authority over the shaping of their children's lives.

Most middle-class men during their tenure as fathers felt a keen, long-term responsibility to fulfill their stewardship as governors over their children. Unlike our post-1960s society, which is disillusioned with those who exercise power, nineteenth-century Americans still saw obedience to authority as essential to the fabric of society. Although they had challenged the paternalism of King George and established religion, antebellum Americans were still not far removed from John Calvin and feudalism; deference and order were traits still valued by society. Where today we respect the father who allows children freedom and expression, nineteenth-century middle-class Americans valued the father who controlled and shaped. It is easy for us to see men like William Swain as merely domineering, and in doing so we forget that in the nineteenth-century they were being responsible, caring husbands and fathers.

William Swain's concern for young Eliza's well-being reflects an important improvement in the status of children during the nineteenth century. Influenced by Enlightenment ideas of equality and individualism, Northerners increasingly rejected the harsher Calvinist doctrines that consigned infants who died before baptism to Hell and living children to a lifetime of struggle against their own evil tendencies. Children were blank slates, according to John Locke, susceptible to environmental forces and in need of proper instruction. Economic changes also improved children's status; in middle-class families, where men earned a family wage, children were increasingly seen less as sources of labor and more as objects of affection and nurture. Popular literature that gave childrearing advice of the day abounded with gardening metaphors of cultivating and pruning; "just as the twig is bent," wrote one author "the tree is inclined."[8] As children's status improved, the responsibility to rear them properly also increased.

If children were indeed plants in need of pruning, weeding, and watering, then responsibility for the outcome of childhood no longer lay with Providence but with the cultivators of the family. Some writers of the time felt that not only the fate of children's souls but also the future of the republic were in the hands of parents. Utilizing the republican rhetoric of virtue, these writers argued that a virtuous citizenry, so important for the survival of the republic, was the product of proper childrearing and, in particular, the role of mothers.[9] Historians have explored in great depth what these societal shifts meant for women in the antebellum period, such as increased expectations and duties placed upon mothers; relegation of women to a formalized, constricting "sphere" within the private realm; and idealization and sentimentalization of women in the role of mothers. Accompanying these changes was an increase in women's domestic authority. The popular writers of the day, delineating the construct of domesticity, argued that women, who were thought to be more nurturing and religiously minded than men, were best suited for guiding the lives of their children. As society placed more emphasis on the moral nature of women, their childrearing authority increased.[10]

Some historians have suggested that this meant a corresponding decline in men's childrearing role. However, families were not zero-sum arrangements where authority neatly flowed from one party to another—as the mother's authority waxed, the father's did not necessarily wane. In some cases men did abdicate authority to their wives, leaving women in charge of all things domestic, but these men were decidedly in the minority. Most fathers shared in the same heightened sense of responsibility concerning childrearing. Sabrina Swain's comment that she felt "the need of a father's care and assistance in lightening the responsibility of governing and training" their child indicates not only her adherence to new views of childrearing with their high expectations concerning parental guidance but also her belief that William shared with her the weighty responsibility to properly govern their child. William likewise noted, "I sympathize with you in the great responsibility devolving upon you alone in my absence, for with you I feel the task of disciplining and guiding her mind is one of great care and anxiety and diligence, on which depends to great [sic] extent her disposition and happiness in future life."[11] Fathers as well as mothers felt the weight of a child's developing morality and "disposition." Perhaps writers of the day, in order to clarify women's political role in the new republic, stylized the ideal family as a place where the "republican" mother inculcated virtue in children, but in actual middle-class families of the time, fathers unquestionably felt this responsibility as well. Consequently, both parents exercised their right to control the upbringing of children.

Nor did most middle-class Americans feel that men were less fit than women for inculcating morality. Although work and involvement with the world outside the home brought many tensions into the lives of men, fathers usually did not perceive these influences as keeping them from being an effective guide in matters of virtue. Men away from home in the halls of government, on business trips, in the mining camps of California, in the military, and at sea did not hesitate to preach morality to wives and children. While sitting in the male domain of Congress in 1799, William Edmond wrote his daughter, "I expect when you read this you will consider it a little like an old story or a dull sermon, that Papa is always preaching how he would have me behave. But remember my Dear your future happiness and worth can alone be his object."[12] Steamboat captain Christopher Pearce, transporting and trading on the Ohio River, still could write to his wife, "relative to the government of our children I shall be pleased to assist you, and hope soon to be so situated as to do so."[13] Nor did men's wives feel that their husbands were morally unfit for this duty. Antoinette Metcalf, whose husband Isaac spent his days building railroads and speculating on railroad land, felt the responsibility of moral nurture to be a mutual one. She and her husband would "together train the little one for a useful life ... and for a heavenly home."[14] Some women felt sons especially needed a father's care. Ann Brown of Salem, Massachusetts, wrote her absent seagoing husband in 1825, "I feel it to be extremely desireable [sic], & important, that you should be more with your Children, particularly the Boys; they need your attention and often, your discipline."[15] The evidence in the correspondence suggests that women as well as men felt that moral authority in a middle-class family was shared.

Surprisingly, men also shared with their wives authority over more mundane childcare. One of the earliest issues that fathers and mothers had to settle was day-to-day care. William Swain's concern for his daughter's health was not an anomaly; many middle-class men expressed their interest in the physical welfare of their children by giving directions to wives and servants on daily care. Thomas Kilby Smith, a lawyer in Cincinnati before the Civil War, admonished his wife, "Now is the time as winter sets in to take great care of the little one, not to confine her too closely to the house. Let her have an abundance of open fresh air keeping her well wrapped up."[16] Feeding habits too could elicit instruction from an absent father. Christopher Gardner Pearce, the steamboat captain mentioned earlier, cautioned his wife about their child's diet, even though he admitted that he himself indulged her penchant for sweets.[17] Mothers and fathers both felt that they had a solemn responsibility to keep their children safe and healthy. In some marriages men exercised a great deal of power, and in others they left this responsibility to their wives. While in Illinois building a railroad line with his half-brother Isaac Metcalf, Charles Rich rarely advised his wife, Albina, on how to care for their children, mostly inquiring in letters home to Milo, Maine, about the state of the family farm. Nevertheless, although Albina obviously had the greater say in childcare, Charles still felt compelled to warn her, "the warm sunny days when the snow melts a little . . . is just the time for little ones to take cold by playing till they get a little warm & sweaty and then remaining out till they get cold."[18]

On the other end of the spectrum, some men gave copious advice and direction to their wives, even to the point of being patronizing. Again we turn to William Swain, whose letters home to his wife were replete with instructions on the rearing of their year-old daughter.

> As I am absent, the duty of taking care of our child will devolve upon you more than before, which was, I am aware, even then a great task to one in poor health. But I have not the least concern but what that duty will be properly discharged. This cannot, however, be properly discharged without the knowledge of the human system necessary to form an enlightened judgment. I would recommend therefore that you supply yourself with books on the subjects of teething, food and its effects on the system; and on dress and its effects. If you wish, get George to assist you on choosing these books. Form your own opinions from what you know; do what you think is your duty to the child; and leave the rest to the Almighty.[19]

Despite Swain's expressed confidence in his wife, it is clear that he felt the need to instruct her in detail on childcare and refer her to books on the subject (which his brother could recommend).

Most men tended to be more like Charles Rich than William Swain, trusting in the mother's ability to care for the physical needs of her own children. The division of labor in families meant that mothers had more day-to-day contact with children, while fathers' contributions tended to be more periodic. Naturally, women had greater opportunity to make decisions about childcare, but men clearly had the right, even the responsibility, to give directions to the wife when they felt it necessary. Unfortunately, we have few letters from women absent from their husbands and children; thus we do not know if women would have advised husbands in a like manner. In most families, men and women seemed to have nurtured in concert, with women more likely to perform daily tasks and men often playing an advisory role. Absent men, for example, often guided children through their wives, delegating the task of passing on fatherly admonitions. Since the most common advice given by fathers was to be good and obey mother, the effect was to present to the children a united parental front.

While the research on the topic is far from definitive, the evidence suggests that middle-class men in the nineteenth century had a more advantageous position in the childrearing hierarchy than their wives did. The record left by Bronson and Abigail Alcott gives us a rare window into the tensions and negotiation of power between a wife and husband, and ultimately shows the balance tipped to the father's advantage. Bronson Alcott was an educator and transcendentalist who kept an extensive journal of his efforts to use methods of his own devising in the upbringing of his young daughters, Anna and future writer Louisa May. Perhaps because of his desire to leave a perfect record of his experiment, Alcott's journal records the tensions in his relationship with his wife Abigail over childrearing. Bronson's approach often taxed Abigail's patience, as he required her to put his theories into practice even when he was unable to assist in childcare. At times he felt Abigail fell short in her application of his program, and even blamed her once for spanking Anna. "Had the children been under my supervision continually, had the principles of prevention been carried out in the nursery, I do not believe that it would have been necessary to have resorted to such methods."[20] Abigail, on her side, chafed under Bronson's unrealistic expectations, "Mr. A. aids me in general principles, but no one can aid me in detail."[21] Both parents had high expectations for themselves and their children—probably higher than most middle-class parents—which increased the strain between them.

Tension between spouses occurred within a context of romantic love, divided labor, and a hierarchical family system, all of which mitigated outward manifestations of tension and probably exacerbated inward strains. By mid-century, middle-class marriage was perceived as a union whose purpose was the emotional fulfillment of both parties. When tension arose that challenged the notions of blissful marriage, men could withdraw into their breadwinner or political roles to some degree or could exert more authority in an attempt to control the situation. Bronson Alcott used both methods; at times he was intensely involved in raising Anna and Louisa May, at other times he was absent from the family while working. Women, on the other hand, had fewer options for dealing with this tension; they could not step away from their childrearing duties with impunity, and their power over the actions of their husbands was limited. Abigail, for example, was discouraged and insecure in her role as nurturer, and suffered from fits of melancholy, suggesting, as historian Charles Strickland has noted, that this was her way of dealing with Bronson's demanding perfectionism.[22] Men like Alcott could direct and participate in the governing of children, even control it, and then retreat into a supervisory role while women continued the daily care of the child. This was a position of power; men could be distant yet exert authority at the same time.

The extent of men's childrearing influence vis-à-vis women can be seen in Keith Spence's long-distance relationship with his family at the turn of the nineteenth century. Spence's correspondence with his wife Mary, written while absent from his family for most of his married life, is permeated by a tension stemming mostly from financial problems and an unstated barrier to returning home that was probably the threat of debtors' prison.[23] Part of this tension, however, derived from disagreements over childrearing. Although he usually deferred to his wife's judgment, his long absences working as a purser for the U.S. Navy did not prevent him from periodically advising his wife, even criticizing her domestic decision making. As Keith's daughters approached womanhood, he cautioned, "[E]verything that can tend to their improvement, or accomplishment, will be agreeable to me, especially their going to the assemblies; but it seems to me there would be an impropriety in sending them, unless yourself, your Aunt Brackett or some other particular friend was with them." Yet, illustrating his unique position as a perpetually absent father, he added, "however, of these matters I cannot be a proper judge at this distance; and therefore leave it entirely to you; hoping, & nothing doubting, that you will embrace every opportunity, & use every means in your power, for their improvement, and accomplishment."[24] This passage reveals both his weakness and his power; his absence and the limits on his economic role in the family prevented him from firmly controlling Mary's decision making, but it did not prevent him from assuming he could still advise his daughters on propriety despite not having seen them in years. Other instances of Spence's instructions to his children via letters to his wife also illustrate the same kind of authority. Speaking of a son, he declared, "I am surpris'd, mortify'd and vex'd, at the trouble you have with that Boy to get him to school. What does he mean? Does he want to be an illiterate Blockhead and Blackguard, a burden to himself, and disgrace to his parents?" Spence then admonished the son to repent and become a good student in order to succeed in business someday.[25] While this sermon is directed at his son, an undercurrent of criticism toward his wife's childrearing runs through it and is continued in their discussion of an older son, Robert, who began to challenge his mother's authority while home on leave from the Navy. "He was too much his own Master," wrote Keith to Mary, "and what was worse, seem'd desirous of being yours also; besides his life was too inactive to be virtuous."[26] Taking matters into his own hands, Keith used his influence in the office of the Secretary of the Navy to get Robert assigned to the same ship upon which he was serving as purser, where he could impress upon the young man "with many various conversations and some severe lectures" the importance of improving his mind and soul.[27] Despite the tenuous position in which his lengthy absences put him, he still exerted authority over his wife in how his children were to be raised.

One of the truisms frequently stated in childrearing literature of any time is that childrearing plays a key role in transmitting culture. Control over the process is a form of power and should be an essential part of any discussion of patriarchy. Unfortunately, the notions of separate spheres and distant fathers have predisposed us to ignore the issue of childrearing authority in antebellum America. We have assumed for too long that men had a limited impact upon the domestic realm. Further hindering historians is the paucity of records. The voluminous writings left by the Alcotts, Swains, and Spences are the exception rather than the rule. Few nineteenth-century parents discussed their childrearing, and even fewer admitted having tensions over the issue. Does the silence mean that the contours of parental power generally were well delineated and thus not a source of tension? Or does it mean that parents were merely reluctant to leave for posterity a record of their conflict over the issue? The evidence that can be drawn upon suggests that men were fairly successful in having a say over the process. Although Keith Spence, writing at the turn of the nineteenth century, may have relied on vestiges of an older, patriarchal authority, it is nonetheless telling that a man who literally spent no time at home during his children's formative years, and often failed in his duty to provide, could still advise his wife on childrearing and shape his sons' training.

While mothers and fathers shared and negotiated control over childrearing, a child's actual behavior was the product of a triangular power dynamic between the father, the mother, and the child. During the first year or so of a child's life, men's role as playmate and part-time caretaker allowed them to avoid most of the tedious aspects of daily childcare. Most parents believed that children were not accountable for any misdeeds at this age, which helped to offset some of the discordant notes that stemmed from men's possible resentment left-over from the birth process. Once the bond between father and infant began to develop, most men enjoyed a year or so with their children free of any tension emanating from disciplinary concerns. Usually during the second year of a child's life, however, the self-assertion or will of the child became manifest. As children began to perceive of their identity as separate from their primary caregiver, they experimented with this newfound freedom in ways that were often disturbing to parents—strong demands, temper tantrums, disobedience, and so on. What many parents today call the "terrible twos" marked a change in the relationship, as both fathers and children became accountable—children for their actions and fathers for their duty to train their children and command their obedience.[28]

Colonial Americans held differing views on how to deal with this early assertion of the will, but most sought to quell it in some way to ensure that the child would develop a proper respect toward authority. From their perspective, letting a son or daughter persist in behaving in such a manner would be committing a great disservice to the child and the community. Middle-class men in nineteenth-century America, although probably not as religiously inclined as their fore-fathers, still lived in a culture dominated by religious forms and values. Not surprisingly, most fathers met this early assertiveness with a firm hand. New England evangelicals, heirs to the Calvinist doctrines of original sin and basic human depravity, seemed most wary of a child's early self-assertion. They believed in breaking the will so that the roots of rebellion would not find a permanent hold in the child's character. The submission to God so necessary for evangelical conversion required learned acceptance of authority, so yielding to a mortal father as early as the age of two was preparation for future submission to the grace of the immortal Father.[29] Other religious persuasions in nineteenth-century America, however, viewed the will of their children with less suspicion. Influenced by changing religious doctrines and also Enlightenment ideas, nonevangelical nurturing experts were less inclined to see sin and depravity in the assertiveness of young children. Some liberal religious writers, among them Unitarians, held that the child developed from an innocent state, thus stressing the importance of environment in the development of character.[30] Others, like the transcendentalists and Mormons, believed that children's spirits not only came to earth directly from heaven but also imbued their newborn infants with the goodness of nascent godhood.[31]

Francis Wayland, a Baptist minister and educator who became president of Brown University, provides us with an example of an evangelical father's approach to asserting his authority. In 1831, Wayland published an account of how he broke the will of his young son. Having noted that at fifteen months his son was "more than usually self willed," Wayland determined to subdue his temper. The opportunity came when the son, Heman, began to cry after being taken from his nurse. Wayland "resolved to seize" upon this opportunity to tame the child, and began withholding food and physical affection from his son. A two-day battle of wills ensued as Wayland enforced the fast and waited for the child to demonstrate contrition by voluntarily coming to him and taking food from his hand. "If a crumb was dropped on the floor he would eat it, but if *I* [italics in the original] offered him the piece of bread, he would push it away from him."[32] While the father was obviously going to win this contest, the hungry child resisted for close to forty hours before finally acknowledging his obeisance to paternal authority. There is much about this incident that seems bizarre to us, but apropos of the topic of authority and power, it is important to note that Wayland felt a fundamental duty to subdue the child's will. "There can be no greater cruelty than to suffer a child to grow up with an unsubdued temper."[33] To do so would be harmful to the child and to the family; thus, "seeking, therefore, his good, and the good of the family, I could do nothing else than I did."[34]

Wayland's account illustrates that some nineteenth-century fathers still felt a strong responsibility to subdue their children's early self assertions, particularly as evidenced in the writings of evangelicals. In 1846, Mary Richardson Walker recorded in her diary that both she and her husband used "the rod" on their two-year-old son to obtain his obedience. In a situation much like that described by Wayland, the Walkers withheld food but also beat the child when he refused to say "please" while asking for sugar. On this occasion the young Walker endured the punishment for two days before giving in to the wishes of his parents.[35] Such measures seem draconian and abusive to us today, yet these parents thought of themselves as loving and responsible caregivers. Indeed, as William McLoughlin has noted, Wayland exhibited considerable affection and tolerance for his children.[36]

An example from the other end of the spectrum comes from Bronson Alcott's journals. Alcott's transcendentalism led him to approach the inculcation of moral values much differently than Wayland and the Walkers. Indeed, at times he seems to have gloried in his children's abilities to make their will known. "The child must be treated as a free self-guiding, self-controlling being. He must be allowed to feel that he is under his own guidance, and that all external guidance is an injustice which is done to his nature unless his own will is intelligently submissive to it. . . . He must be free that he may be truly virtuous, for without freedom there is no such thing as virtue."[37] Alcott believed in a father's duty to oversee his children's moral development, but his definition of this was to see that his children kept themselves free from the bad influences of servants or low friends—so that their true and virtuous natures might flourish and dominate their characters. Thus he felt that children's wills, if left undefiled, would lead them to good. However, Alcott's high-minded ideals often fell short when faced with the realities of his children's behavior, and occasionally he even had to resort to spankings and other punishments. Indeed, in many ways, Alcott's approach emphasized control and manipulation of the child's environment even more than Wayland's.

Most middle-class fathers fell somewhere between Wayland and Alcott in their attitudes and responses to a child's assertive will. By the nineteenth century, most had rejected (or never held) Calvinist doctrines that condemned unbaptized children to Hell, and they no longer saw evil in each attempt of the child to assert itself. Even among some of the less conservative evangelicals these doctrines were losing favor.[38] But many of the parents in the North, coming from a Calvinistic New England heritage, still distrusted the will of their children. Ann North, wife of John Wesley North, wrote from her Minnesota home to her parents in New York, "Charlie is a beautiful boy—and generally, very 'pretty wayed[?],' but he has a very strong will and is very 'spunky' if he cannot have his own way. I do feel the need of help to train him, especially. I hope it will not be many weeks before his father will be here to attend to him."[39] The Norths felt that "careful management" of the child's will was the best means of teaching the child, and both parents did the managing. Speaking of their first child, Ann wrote, "We have three times been obliged to work a long time with her to make her mind. She showed considerable obstinacy, but we seem to have most perfect control of her now. She sometimes cries a little at being obliged to do what we tell her, but will do it, and we can immediately stop her crying."[40] Middle-class parents held to the innocence of their children, but most had a less sanguine view than did Alcott and his fellow transcendentalists of the benign nature of the child's will. They felt that bending the will toward a desire to follow Christian principles was the proper course, not allowing it to run free or breaking it.[41]

Fathers of this era, whatever their method or philosophy, did exercise considerable authority in the moral upbringing of their children. The approaches of Wayland and Alcott, located at opposite extremes of the childrearing spectrum, drew the ire of critics who questioned their ideas and methods, but not their right to govern their children. There was no cry for them and other self-appointed male experts like them to leave the rearing of children to women. Fathers, it seems, had a right to inculcate moral values in their children. Alcott and Wayland also drew from the dominant Protestant culture to buttress and define this active role. Obviously both felt strong obligations to shape their children's will—obligations stemming from their belief in God and the nature of man. As historian Phillip Greven notes concerning Protestant America, "Whether thought of in terms of breaking wills or shaping them, the obsession with authority, control, and obedience remains paramount."[42] The transcendentalist Bronson Alcott and the evangelical Francis Wayland, when examined alongside the "moderate" John Wesley North and strict evangelical Walkers, illustrate the way in which antebellum religious culture impressed upon a wide range of fathers the role and authority of moral educator.

While religion gave many fathers the responsibility and authority to teach morality, physical size and superior strength gave men the power to control in the early years. As long as fathers were larger and stronger than daughters and sons, they could use some form of corporal punishment or other physical means to discourage inappropriate behavior. The memory of this type of physical manipulation often stayed with a child in the form of fear. This fear of punishment, in turn, was used by fathers to habituate obedience in children. Unfortunately, determining the extent of the use of corporal punishment is problematic, for many antebellum Americans did not discuss the issue in their letters and diaries. One study of nineteenth-century diaries found it "not uncommon" for fathers to use the rod to discipline their children. According to the author, Paul C. Rosenblatt, "Even children under a year old might be beaten for some transgression. Some women diary keepers expressed disapproval of such whipping, although they seemed unable or unwilling to stop it, and engaged in the practice themselves."[43]

But Rosenblatt's assertion that it was common for fathers to use physical punishment, and even beatings, was not borne out in the sources used in this study—I found only three incidents of fathers using corporal punishment on their children.[44] Similarly, Stephen Frank's study of fathers during the nineteenth century found a similar low percentage of instances.[45] It is possible that these fathers merely did not record their use of spanking and whipping as punishment, but it is also possible that our perception of harshly punished children in the past may be exaggerated. Most middle-class parents no longer held to the practice of will-breaking by brute force, and it is telling that some who did, like Wayland, used means other than corporal punishment. Linda Pollock's study of American diaries found evidence that parents in early nineteenth-century America were somewhat more likely to record using physical punishment than in earlier centuries, but those that did were still in the minority.[46] Indeed, some fathers like Thomas Kilby Smith did not approve of whippings at all. "Kisses to the baby—don't, I pray you, whip her. The human family were [sic] not created to be beaten like dumb brutes— & nothing tends to mortify a child so much as stripes. Pray don't whip her."[47]

Whether Smith and men like him would have approved of spanking instead of whipping (or if they meant the same thing) is not known. The question is important, however, because there were different levels of the use of force by fathers. While some used corporal punishment, others withheld food or isolated the child. Each, however, is a physical manifestation of superior force used to manipulate the child. It seems that most men used a mixture of reason, affection, and force to control children; when an application to the developing reason of the young child did not work, or when fathers could not get children to obey by appealing to love, then men resorted to punishment. Some men undoubtedly used force more frequently and quickly than others, while some, like Bronson Alcott, rarely used force and felt that as a last resort it was virtually worthless. Still, while children were young, force in the form of corporal punishment or manipulation of the child's environment remained a powerful source of influence over children. The fact that men like Alcott, who vehemently opposed physical force in childrearing, still turned to it when they felt that all else failed shows its power for fathers.

Even the most affectionate and involved fathers found the threat of physical power useful. John Wesley North, despite all indications that he indeed was a loving father, controlled his son through manipulating fear. His wife wrote,

> It is a great help, as well as [a] great happiness, to me to have Mr. North at home. The children feel and do better. He has taken Charlie in hand, and is straightening him out as well as could be expected. He now puts him into his crib when it is time for him to go to sleep, and for him, he will lie there, and go to sleep without a word—but he will not for the rest of us. I think he will soon acquire the habit, and will then do for any one [sic]. He is afraid of his father.[48]

There is no evidence that North used corporal punishment with the child, but his ability to instill fear in young Charlie through whatever means enabled him to ensure obedience. Even long after children's reasoning and emotional capacity developed and fathers turned to more sophisticated means of control, the memory of physical force remained, buttressing power, but it most likely also added tension in the relationship.[49]

Whether or not physical punishment was one of the essential sources of nineteenth-century paternal power will probably never be adequately determined. While we can learn much about individual instances mentioned in the sources, as with other hidden behaviors, such as sexual abuse of children, there is no reliable way to determine frequency. Fortunately, not all fathering behaviors are so inaccessible. Particularly evident in the sources is men's appeal to two essential sources of paternal power—love and money. The growing importance of these two factors in the nineteenth century represents a significant change in the history of fatherhood. When men like Francis Wayland drew upon religious authority to break their children's will or used their physical size to force children into obedience, they were acting in ways consonant with older approaches to fathering. But when long-standing patriarchal structural supports based in law, church, and community began to erode under the pressure of nineteenth-century economic and social changes, fathers turned to newer means of control. Love, or rather the obligation that accompanies it, emerged as a powerful tool for fathers in the years following the Revolution. While families had always been a location of affection and love, in the end of the eighteenth and early nineteenth centuries, these emotions began to replace production as the primary purpose of the family unit. Family members came to expect emotional fulfillment from each other, and, not surprisingly, expressions of love increased in intensity and meaning during this time. Parents found this new intensity useful in inculcating obligation in children. And if love did not work, fathers could still rely on the power of the purse. Although property declined as a key source of fathers' power during these years, men still enjoyed economic power over their families. As sole breadwinners in the middle-class family of the nineteenth century, fathers controlled children's access to consumer items and to the schooling that had become essential to middle-class status. While fathers lost some of their traditional sources of patriarchal power in the antebellum period, they gained others.

Of these two newly important forms of influence, love seems to have been the most powerful and versatile. As long as parents cultivated emotional ties, fathers could tie obedience to children's sense of duty and guilt, allowing them to manipulate the behavior of young and old children even from a distance. In 1796, a Connecticut judge, William Edmond, promised his daughter Polly, "A good report of your conduct on my return would increase both my affection and esteem."[50] Even before the turn of the century, Edmond's manipulation of his daughter was typically straightforward and overt. Similarly, while in Congress in 1837, Thomas Lyon Hamer admonished his four-year-old son, "If you are kind to your brothers & sisters—obedient to your Mother and Miss Macbeth, & good to Miss Mary & John [servants]—then I shall love you very much and I will do almost anything for you which you may want done."[51] Hamer's implied threat that disobedience meant a withholding of his love indicates the high price he placed on control. Another father, also writing to his son in 1837, declared, "I have great confidence that you will be a good boy, and be an honor to your parents. You are my only son, and all my dependence; and as you love me, I hope you will do nothing but what is right."[52]

Fathers' use of the obligation of love was extensive, as indicated by the number of permutations of such appeals. For example, while away from home Judge William Edmond not only told Polly that her obedience would bring his love but also claimed, "My happiness on my return will much depend on the account given of your behavior."[53] Certainly Polly thought twice before committing some infraction while under the heavy burden of her father's happiness. John Milton Putnam, a New Hampshire minister and future father-in-law of Isaac Metcalf, also mentioned his own happiness when entreating his eleven-year-old daughter, Antoinette, to become truly converted to God. "Nothing would afford such joy to your parents' hearts, as to have evidence of your being truly a child of God." Then in the same letter, Putnam appealed to her sense of gratitude. "We are willing to make great sacrifices for your good; and we hope & trust you will avail yourself, to the best advantage, of your present peculiar privileges."[54]

Children generally responded positively to these appeals. An exchange between Jane Elfreth and her father Jacob, a Philadelphia Quaker, subtly illustrates how these interactions encouraged obligation in the child. After enjoying fresh oysters provided by her father, nine-year-old Jane wrote in a family book kept for practicing the art of letter-writing, "we were much obliged to thee for thee is very kind. I know for thee gives us a good many things we dont [sic] deserve."[55] Jane's conviction that she did not deserve her father's largess illustrates her sense of indebtedness in the relationship. Jacob Elfreth, as breadwinner, was able to foster this by giving gifts such as oysters, and Jane Elfreth responded by "improving" herself through practicing her letter-writing. Once established, these kinds of obligations could shape father-child relationships for years. Finding himself occupying the same room at Harvard that his father had lived in years earlier, one son wrote to his mother, "Surely a feeling of love for him who once dwelt where I dwell, will ally itself with conscience and restrain me from evil and wrong."[56]

Nineteenth-century culture taught that obedience accompanied love for one's parents, and fathers often played on children's developing sense of duty, guilt, or reason to get them to obey. "You know I have told you a hundred times," wrote William Edmond to Polly Edmond, "and written in your little books almost as often, 'to be good is the way to be happy'—be good, my dear, be amiable, and you shall be happy—happy as parents can make you."[57] He further cautioned ten-year-old Polly, who was away at school, "If you conduct yourself as you ought to do, I shall certainly know it, and it will give me pleasure. I shall see all your behavior in my magic looking-glass as plain as I used to discover what you had been doing by your eyes—this magic glass is fastened to a little Bell that rattles terribly whenever you sit crooked, laugh loud, look sullen, behave rudely, forget your courtesy, and the like."[58]

Fathers also occasionally appealed to children's love and reverence for deceased friends and relatives. Occasionally they reminded children of the last words of loved ones who had died, calculating that the admonitions of the dying would carry more weight. Jacob Elfreth even invoked this strategy well before his own death.

> Should my children read this after my head is laid in the silent grave, let them remember that it was their father's most anxious desire for them that they might look to Christ for their pattern and their guide, and endeavour to tread in his sacred steps; obey his precepts and commandments, and in all their actions do that which they think will be pleasing in his sight. Then, after they leave this world they will live with him forever.[59]

Appeals to the influence of friends, God, and the last words of loved ones, or even duty or high-minded ideals of morality, could be construed to mean that fathers' influence over children was weak, leading to a search for any and all sources that might stay the decline. Some historians have made this argument, suggesting that fathers, having lost much of their economic power, had to resort to these less concrete means of influence. Historian Altina Waller notes that since "patriarchal authority was solidly based in real economic power over the lives of children," when fathers' economic control declined, then paternal power declined.[60] While this argument may have some validity, a few unanswered questions make it apparent that it needs further study and refinement. For example, how are we to reconcile an idea of declining economic power with the reality that fathers' breadwinning role largely increased in these years, while women and children's producer roles declined? Certainly, this made children more dependent upon fathers while they lived at home.

Nor is it clear when and how men's economic power over children declined. We still have insufficient primary research on fathers and patriarchy in the colonial period to give us an accurate beginning point to use in charting change. The most common argument holds that as land declined in importance in the industrializing economy of the nineteenth century, fathers could no longer hold grown children under their sway through promise of inheritance when they died. Such an argument, however, neglects the history of land use and inheritance in America. Many fathers were having a hard time finding land enough to pass on to children long before the nineteenth century and industrialization.[61] Indeed, very few men through history have been fortunate enough to have holdings that could be divided up to provide dowries for all daughters and livelihoods for all sons.[62] The land argument, then, does not explain a decline in the father's status in the nineteenth century, nor does it explain how fathers with little land or those who practiced primogeniture maintained control over all their children before the alleged decline. Changes in inheritance patterns undoubtedly altered family authority structures, but the argument is too narrow to explain an across-the-board decline in fathers' power and authority in the nineteenth century.

A more complex view of paternal power allows us to see that men still used their economic position to influence children in the nineteenth century. Some fathers used their breadwinner status to promise children treats or favors if they would be good. While representing Ohio in Congress, Thomas Lyon Hamer used this method via his wife. "As to Mary, if she learns well I shall bring her a fine new book of some kind when I come home. . . . Does Washington try to talk any? . . . If he is a good boy I will bring him something too. Ophelia & Thomas shall have presents if they are good & so shall Clinton."[63] Similarly, Jane Elfreth's father brought home "a small box of paints" in reward for braving the extraction of two teeth.[64]

Petty bribery, however, was hardly a cornerstone of men's paternal power. Of far greater importance was fathers' control over the funds that paid for education. Since education in many respects replaced land as the prerequisite to male success in nineteenth-century America, fathers were able to influence preadult sons by controlling these opportunities. Not only could they use payment for college tuition, room, and board as incentives, but fathers also controlled the decision concerning the completion of secondary schooling. Apprenticeships and putting young children in other families to work were no longer the norm for the middling classes in the nineteenth century, but the labor of a son or daughter might be needed on the farm or in the family business. "Just as I was becoming deeply interested in my studies," wrote Thomas Carter years after his adolescence, "I was obliged to leave school and help my father on the farm and in the shop."[65] On-the-job training was an attractive option for fathers who saw little need to pay for a classical education when a practical one could come through work experience. Daughters' educational options particularly were subject to questions of utilitarianism. Although the ideal of republican motherhood espoused a well-rounded curriculum for young women, competence in the "domestic arts" as taught by their mothers was still the primary goal of female education. Thus, not all fathers believed that daughters and sons needed extensive schooling, and if children wanted to continue in their studies, they often had to present a persuasive case to the breadwinner.

For months after committing an undisclosed sin, William Eaton was required by his father to make a weekly account of his time and money while at school. "Agreeable to Yr instructions, I Send you the weekly return. And can confidently anticipate the satisfaction my course of conduct will afford my parents. And I am still firm in the purpose of endeavoring to redeem that lost reputation & secure their confiding affections. I act under the impression that a returning sense & correspondent discharge, of my duty on my part, will serve to reinstate me, and give you a degree of happiness."[66] Later in the letter, Eaton again tries to emphasize his willingness to bow to his father's authority, "But why is it I have not heard from . . . Father? Believe me when I say I intend to reform radically and shall treasure up all advice from such a source. Do write."[67] Eaton's bowing and scraping to his father was due, in part, to his dependence on him for funds to stay in school. Although during the antebellum era colleges began to open up to young men whose fathers could not afford to pay full tuition, for most sons, a father's assistance meant the difference between succeeding and failing in obtaining an advanced degree.[68] Eaton provides a good example of how sons on the verge of adulthood relied on their fathers' funds to gain access to the opportunities necessary for successful entry into the middle class. Even in the years after school, William remained in financial debt to his father, prompting him to write in 1842, "Towards you, My Dear Father, I feel the strongest obligations."[69] As we shall see in Chapter 6, many fathers used this economic power to their advantage.

By examining antebellum letters and journals, it is a relatively easy task to prove that men held power and authority in the nineteenth-century family. But trying to discern how that power and authority have changed over the course of history is another matter. We clearly need more studies that look at all sources of men's power before we can say with confidence that fathers in the nineteenth century held less power than colonial fathers and more power than twentieth-century fathers. When that research has been completed, historians will do well to remember several weaknesses of the nineteenth-century middle-class father's position. There were obvious limits to his power over the purse. Education was somewhat less important for a daughter's future, and thus fathers needed to use other means of influencing them, and once children finished school, the father no longer had that particular means of controlling the son or daughter. The ability to perform the breadwinner role could be disrupted by sickness, injury, or old age. For example, Sarah Cleveland's father grew old and feeble of mind and body and could no longer earn for the family while she was still living at home. After she committed some offense (which is not made clear in the letter) her father tried to beat her. Sarah wrote to her brother that their father came downstairs, yelling, "'I will give that Sal A flogin; if she crys [sic] don't you go near her, Ma.'" Her father's decrepitude reduced this threat to a chance for Sarah to ridicule him. "I wish you could have seen him chase me round the kitchen doors with a stick of wood in his hand. I was so full of laugh[ter] that I could hardly run."[70] Two months earlier, Sarah's family had been evicted from their home because the father was unable to make payments. It is possible that the father's position in the nineteenth century, with his reliance on a wage, was somewhat less secure than the colonial father who had property. The latter probably had a cushion that the former did not. Still, this is assuming that the colonial father owned land—colonial artisans, for instance, probably had an even smaller buffer against economic failure than did most nineteenth-century breadwinners.

If colonial fathers indeed possessed greater economic control over children, nineteenth-century fathers seem to have had a greater ability to draw upon affection. Yet here too, antebellum fathers' power had limitations—weaknesses that perhaps can give us insight into how twentieth-century fathers arrived at an even more limited position of power. The case of Benjamin Hodge provides an illustrative example. The owner of a successful plant nursery in Buffalo, New York, Hodge rarely asserted himself in his family. Many antebellum fathers dictated the educational plans of their children, but when Hodge and his son differed over schooling, the son's desires took precedence. And in the home he often deferred to his wife. When his daughter became excited about attending a nearby dance school, she approached her father first. "I asked Father if we could go, he seemed to like it very much, but Mother did not like it and of course we could not go."[71] Instances like these led Hodge's daughter to refer to her mother as "the head of the family."[72]

Why Benjamin Hodge deferred to his wife and children is not completely clear. Like other middle-class fathers, Hodge's position as breadwinner gave him considerable power, but unlike some fathers he did not use that relationship as leverage to gain control. Similarly, his deference to his wife in the home did not stem from unfamiliarity with the domestic sphere, for he was intimately involved in the daily affairs of the home. The only clues come from several traumatic experiences earlier in his life. Two years into his first marriage, his wife and only child died, and then ten years later his three oldest children by his second marriage died of scarlet fever within the space of days of each other. Each set of deaths profoundly affected Hodge and seem to be the most likely explanation of his mildness. As the breadwinner in the home Benjamin Hodge clearly had economic power to control his family, yet he seems to have cherished their wishes too much to say no. We can see then, that the affection of children for fathers provided the latter with a strong influence over children. But in turn, the affection fathers had for children mitigated paternal authority by increasing the obligation of the father to respect the child's wishes. So, as a means of controlling children, love had the problems of a two-edged sword. The case of Benjamin Hodge is an example of how one edge of the sword could become sharper than the other, nullifying much of his paternal power.

Benjamin Hodge's story illustrates the changing purposes of fathering in the past. The concerns of colonial fathers had to do with subsistence, order, and saving souls, and much of society was organized to control children and ensure that these ends were met. The Northern antebellum father, on the other hand, emphasized education, nurturing, love, and respect of the rights of children—goals that tended toward the very different end of freedom and independence. When the rights of children became paramount, men's power obviously declined. According to early historian of the family Arthur W. Calhoun, "Emerson quoted a man who said that it was a misfortune to have been born in an age when children were nothing and to have spent mature life in an age when children were everything."[73] Education became not a tool to ensure good behavior, but an obligation required of the father. By the end of the nineteenth century, few middle-class fathers considered keeping a son out of school for the purpose of exploiting his labor. A privilege had become a right. It is possible that as the rights of children expanded, men's authority waned.

My purpose has not been to determine the exact share of power that men possessed in childrearing, primarily because, as shown here, the family was an interactive and flexible institution at this time. The division of labor and power between a married man and woman often varied, suggesting, as Karen Lystra has, that nineteenth-century men and women "skillfully used their sex roles rather than slavishly followed them."[74] There is no easy separate spheres answer to the issue of domestic power. After boarding with the different families of the children that he taught, one New England teacher wrote in 1847:

> Some are very indulgent—their children have everything they want, others have no command at all—make commands and pour forth threats, but never expect to see them obeyed or executed. Some rule with a tyrant's rod, appeal to nothing but brute force, allowing no reasoning, no talking nor scarcely thinking. While others scold from morn till night, without even then being satisfied.[75]

Despite the complexity of family types in the antebellum period, we can say that men had the authority to participate in raising their own children. They may not have always exercised that authority, and undoubtedly shared it with women and teachers, but Northern middle-class men still had a right and an obligation to see that children were raised properly. Ultimately, the real test of fathers' power in the nineteenth century was the success or failure of their childrearing goals. In this men were largely successful, as they prepared children to maintain their class status and adhere to middle-class morality. As we will see, children often resented their fathers' control, but they rarely rebelled against the values that fathers taught them. Men's position was secure as a whole culture buttressed their efforts to see that children developed proper attitudes toward work, gender, marriage, and morality.

chapter five

Providing a Middle-Class Future

O n October 17, 1835, Jacob Elfreth, a Philadelphia bookkeeper and Quaker, placed his oldest son, ten-year-old Joseph, on a stagecoach and sent him off to boarding school. Some days later he wrote to his other children, "It was a trial to him to leave home but he went away like a man without crying any. I hope he will be a good boy, and then he will be happy and it will be a comfort to his father and mother." Elfreth ended his letter with the aside, "I sent him a quart of chestnuts yesterday & a volume of Parleys' magazine both of which I expect will be very acceptable to him."[1]

This brief account describes significant rites of passage for both Jacob and Joseph Elfreth. For the son it was perhaps his first significant step down the path that would lead to manhood and independence, while for the father it marked the beginning to the end of his childrearing years. Such junctures in the lives of individuals often reveal the nature of beliefs and attitudes that are shaping those lives, and from this passage we are given glimpses into men's childrearing role in nineteenth-century America. Jacob Elfreth's decision to send Joseph away to school indicates the desire of a father to provide a proper middle-class future for the child—boys attended school to train for a middle-class occupation, while girls prepared for a proper marriage within their class. Jacob's expressed hope that Joseph would be "good" represents a reminder of the many hours spent teaching strong moral values to Joseph. Jacob's emphasis on his son's going alone and not crying suggests instruction on proper attitudes toward masculinity. Central to each of these comments is a fatherly desire to shape his children. Not only can we guess the topics of discussion that probably dominated the departure scene, but we can also suppose that Elfreth used the event (through the letter) to instruct his younger children in the same values. Jacob Elfreth believed that his children needed a strong sense of morality and proper gender identity, along with the right secular knowledge, to succeed in the newly industrializing America, and thus, like most middle-class fathers during his day, he sought to teach these things to his children.

The passage, however, also illustrates the complex nature of men's childrearing role. By sending the gift of chestnuts and the magazine, Elfreth acknowledged Joseph's continuing emotional needs; it is clear that Jacob loved his son and cared for his happiness and comfort. But as we have seen, love and power were intertwined in antebellum families. The emotional tie fostered by the father enabled him to expect obedience from Joseph for the sake of parental "comfort." The chestnuts and the magazine were no doubt symbols to remind Joseph of this important relationship between love and obligation. The father's choice of *Parley's Magazine* is especially revealing. Like much of the juvenile miscellany of the time, this periodical contained a heavy dose of didacticism in its stories, fables, and games. Joseph could be entertained, while the father, from afar, could offer love and moral instruction through his gift. Children's love for their fathers was intimately intertwined with their obligation to obey and fathers' authority to teach them.

But children were not the only ones who felt obligation in the relationship; Elfreth's love for Joseph spurred him to provide a sound secular and spiritual education. Jacob would not have dreamed of sending Joseph off to school without a proper understanding of the rules of masculinity and morality any more than he would have seen him off without clothing or books. In a sense, Jacob Elfreth's instruction in these necessities represents the filling of the time-honored role of provider in a new, more modern way. Where colonial fathers worked to give their children the means to farm and the skills to perform a craft, along with a fear of God, middle-class antebellum fathers were more likely to see education, "proper" views on gender, and a strong moral compass as prerequisites to success and happiness. Ever since Mary P. Ryan's study of middle-class formation in Oneida County, New York, historians have understood that mothers played a key role in the transmission of class values in antebellum

America.[2] Unfortunately, Ryan's turn to the nineteenth-century proscriptive literature led her to ignore men's contributions to child-rearing. The advice-to-mothers literature, with its emphasis on separate spheres ideology, cannot take into account the realities of shared childrearing. In the sources that illuminate day-to-day life of middle-class families, we can see that the norms espoused by fathers served a key purpose in defining class boundaries. As the century progressed, the "respectable" middle class increasingly valued attributes that separated them from the "rougher" working classes and the "decadent" upper classes. By teaching these things, middle-class fathers hoped to provide children with the skills and knowledge needed to maintain class status in an increasingly turbulent world. Failing in this duty could mean jeopardizing their children's happiness in this life and the life after.

Men had other good reasons to be involved along with their wives in teaching children. Love certainly pushed fathers to instruct children on how to be successful, but by defining success according to the terms of middle-class culture, fathers were also protecting their own power and authority. For example, fathers had obvious motives when they instructed their children that obedience was a cardinal virtue, that girls were to be submissive, and that boys were to be industrious. Most of the values that defined the middle class tended to support or at least not threaten male patriarchal authority. But one cannot read this as merely a conservative ploy to preserve authority, for although much of men's childrearing perpetuated established norms, their efforts also sought eventually to instill a sense of independence in the child. Nineteenth-century fathers knew that while they would still have some influence over adult children, they were also training them to make their own decisions about marriage, work, religion, and family. Fathers' childrearing was composed of a complex mix of motivations: concern for the child's happiness, obligation to teach the child the skills necessary for independence, and a desire to keep power. Middle-class fathers were usually able to express love and fulfill their duty and at the same time buttress the structure of their authority.

This chapter looks at the themes of value inculcation and culture transmission in the lives of fathers of children approximately three years old through the first years of adolescence. This stage began as early as three years into the father's marriage and lasted until the youngest child reached the teenage years. Given the life expectancy of men in the nineteenth century, this period lasted virtually almost all of their adult life. The choice to cover this long period in one chapter reflects the continuity in the relationships between men and children during this stage. As fathers aged and children passed through the stages of preadolescence and adolescence, the relationship matured, but its structure remained basically unchanged throughout. In these years fathers were providers, as always, but they were also teachers. The purpose of their instruction was to provide a proper future for their children while at the same time maintaining established cultural norms. In the end, we have to remember that all of this was done in the context of love, hope, and obligation toward the child.

In colonial Puritan New England, and even the Mid-Atlantic colonies where religion had less of a hold on people's lives, the paternal teaching role was shaped by faith. For most fathers before the Revolution, no instruction was more important than guidance onto the path of salvation. In the minds of these religiously inclined fathers, the kingdom of God was the fundamental goal of all childrearing. Not surprisingly, in the nineteenth century, even though religion's influence was on the decline, many fathers still saw redemption as the ultimate goal of their childrearing endeavors. While Jacob Elfreth valued secular education, his "most anxious desire" was for his offspring to "look to Christ for their pattern and their guide."[3] John Putnam, a New Hampshire Congregationalist minister, had a similar hope for his eleven-year-old daughter. Writing to her he declared, "Nothing would afford such joy to your parents' hearts, as to have evidence of your being truly a child of God."[4] Six years later, after commending her scholarly work, he again reminded her, "But remember my dear—very dear child, that acquirements in religion are of all things most important."[5] To bring about these ends, religious fathers encouraged church attendance, held family prayer and hymn-singing in their homes, discussed gospel topics, and sometimes used the Bible as an early primer in childhood education.

But the reward of eternal life came not only through church attendance and prayer but also through right living in the secular world; thus, religious fathers sought to instill in children a desire to be righteous in all aspects of their life. Even among the men whose interest in organized religion had waned or was nonexistent, Protestant morality and terminology usually dominated their childrearing.[6] Mary Ryan has rightly called religion the "language and central ideological structure" of antebellum American society.[7] Teachings founded in the

Judeo-Christian culture permeated society, as men naturally turned to the Protestant religious culture to structure their childrearing. The injunction found in Ephesians, "And ye fathers, provoke not your children to wrath: but bring them up in the nurture and admonition of the Lord,"[8] was interpreted throughout middle-class culture as a general paternal obligation to instill moral values in children. Although women outnumbered men in churches throughout the nineteenth-century, middle-class fathers generally still believed that "proper" moral character and Christian conduct were necessary to function well in antebellum middle-class society.

Indeed, there were moral traits that fathers almost universally sought to instill in their children, regardless of religious persuasion. Invariably, when writing home, men admonished even the youngest of children to "be good." Fathers were usually quite vague as to the meaning of "good," perhaps because children knew what was expected of them. However, in most instances being "good" appeared to mean obedience to parental guidance, getting along with siblings, and diligence in studies. "I am very glad to hear that my little boys are good children," wrote Charles Rich while absent from home. "I hope they will always mind quick what their mother tells them and always be pleasant to each other & learn to read very well."[9]

Obedience was the cornerstone of paternal childrearing, just as it was in religion. If a father could not command it, he could do little with his child. Much of men's power and authority thus focused on instilling a desire in children to obey. Among the earliest methods that fathers turned to in their efforts to inculcate obedience was to control the child's environment. While en route to the gold fields of California, John Craven warned his wife to keep their young son "as much as you can from other Children, in particular those that are older than himself for he is a child that will learn any thing very quick, and it is a melancholy fact that children learn the evil first."[10] Other fathers generally were not as pessimistic about their children's capacity to mar their blank slate, but nonetheless tried to counter the potentially damaging influence of worldly evils by beginning instruction in religious and moral values while their daughters and sons were quite young.

As children's reasoning powers began to emerge, fathers could turn to more sophisticated methods of inculcating obedience. Many fathers followed the biblical advice to "train up a child in the way that he should go: and when he is old he will not depart from it."[11] In other words, fathers hoped to establish what historian Joseph F. Kett calls "an internal gyroscope, a self-activating, self-regulating, all-purpose inner control."[12] With this developed conscience, a child who reached the years of independence would still be guided by the values that parents had taught in the child's youth. This approach allowed parents to foster independence (a central goal of middle-class childrearing), while still maintaining a kind of control over a child's actions.

To facilitate the development of the conscience, fathers emphasized that obedience brought love, happiness, and virtue. While serving in the New York State Legislature in 1837, Daniel Dickson made it clear to his young son that obedience and happiness went hand in hand:

> Nothing is so attractive in a boy your age as obedience, kindness, and good-nature. If you have and practise [sic] these you will enjoy yourself much better than you otherwise can, and be beloved by all around you. God has wisely ordered that our happiness shall depend on our good conduct. If we pursue that path of virtue it will lead us to happiness; but if we indulge in vice of any kind, it destroys our enjoyment and will surely bring us to shame.[13]

This was not mere rhetoric masking a father's desire to buttress paternal authority; fathers like Dickson sincerely wanted their sons and daughters to be happy. However, the result was the same, for children seeking the proper path to happiness tended to internalize obedience to their fathers' wishes. In the view of nineteenth-century fathers, reinforcing their authority was synonymous with ensuring the happiness of their children. It was absolutely essential then that fathers teach children to obey.

By the time daughters and sons reached adolescence they had internalized basic morality, allowing men to expand their instruction into more complicated matters of sexual purity, moral propriety, and virtuous conduct. Puberty marked the point at which fathers began to differentiate between their sons and daughters when instilling moral values. Surprisingly, fathers were more likely to lecture their sons than their daughters on the importance of being virtuous. "Let your Conduct be such as will bear the strictest Scrutiny," wrote physician Nathaniel Saltonstall to his son at the turn of the nineteenth century, "and do not deviate from the Principle of Morality."[14] As during the preteen years, the admonition is given in general terms, but sons seem to have understood the warnings hidden behind the obscure rhetoric. Another Saltonstall son acknowledged his father's duty to monitor and govern his behavior: "I have lived long enough (although I have not lived long) to know the effects of Dissipation. And I shall forever blame you, if you ever hear of my inclining that way, and do not immediately take [me] from Boston."[15]

This special concern for the virtue of sons most likely reflects the greater degree of independence given to males in antebellum society. Adolescent sons had a higher rate of geographic mobility than teenage daughters did. Sons were more likely to work or attend school away from home and thus had greater access to the vices of the day. Drunkenness, gambling, and frequenting prostitutes were vices generally unavailable to middle-class daughters. The idea of a daughter frequenting a prostitute was absurd to antebellum Americans, for it violated fundamental views of middle-class womanhood. The few middle-class women who followed a path of prostitution or drunkenness essentially rejected middle class status and became part of the "base" lower classes. For the middle class, dissipation, the habitual participation in such vices, was primarily identified as a male sin. Aside from moral degradation, fathers feared "dissipation" because their economic obligations still extended to prodigal sons. Fathers were often expected to make good the debts of even mature sons. One father, for example, "made himself penniless to meet a $2500 embezzlement" of a son who had taken to drink and gambling.[16] It is no wonder then that men felt that their sons more than their daughters needed instruction on virtue.

Because the financial and emotional well-being of both son and father could rest on a son's actions, many fathers tried to maintain close control over their adolescent boys. As a son prepared for education or work, the reputation of the school or employer was scrupulously examined, and fathers often visited the place of study or employment to assess the child's situation. As mentioned in the previous chapter, Keith Spence went so far as to arrange to have his teenage son assigned to the same ship that he served on. He wrote to his wife, "[Y]ou may be assured, I shall let no opportunity escape of working upon him, and giving his mind that bent to knowledge, virtue & honor, to which it cannot but have a natural inclination, in spite of the slight impressions made upon it, by the vulgar souls with whom misfortune made him for a while associates."[17] Most fathers, however, did not work in situations that allowed such direct monitoring, so they had to hope that they had been effective in inculcating virtue during the child's earlier years.

With daughters, however, fathers sought to enforce propriety, or the outward display of virtue. This difference in counsel to sons and daughters has two probable explanations: Men may have felt that mothers were best suited to discuss issues of virtue with daughters, thus leaving that duty to their wives; or it could be that females were thought to be more inclined to be virtuous than males. Historians suggest that by the early part of the nineteenth century, popular writers and the general populace believed that females were morally superior to males.[18] Combined with the limits on female independence in the antebellum period, these factors led fathers to think that their daughters were less likely to need instruction on virtue. The emphasis on female propriety suggests that fathers feared more what might be done to their daughters than what their daughters might do. In 1806 Keith Spence wrote to his wife,

> Harriet you say is to carry her Aunt Whipple to Newbury & Salem! My God! can this be suitable employment for a young, delicate & beautiful girl! To me it appears masculine and improper in the highest degree; and I may add, vulgar. The Girls may be handsome & improved; but their behavior in several cases you have mentioned I am sorry to say cannot meet my approbation. But manners change, and my ideas of them may be antiquated.[19]

Spence was clearly out of touch with his daughters' development, but his response still illustrates a father's desire to protect his daughters. One way fathers enforced established gender roles was to restrict female movement within set social and geographical boundaries, as illustrated by the limitations on female travel. Respectable women (especially young, single women) usually traveled with an escort of some kind, either another woman or a trusted adult male. Even walks around town or in the countryside were conducted under chaperone. In 1856, Lincoln Clark encouraged his teenage daughter to walk for exercise, but cautioned her, "of course you would not take such walks without some safe and judicious companion."[20] A long-distance trip to visit friends or relatives by a teenage daughter meant coordinating the schedule of a traveling companion. As a minister, John Putnam was able to arrange for a deacon of his church to escort his daughter while she traveled by train and coach from Illinois to her home in Vermont. Part of the way she traveled alone, and Putnam's concern is evident in the advice he gave to her to protect herself and all her valuables. "Be careful of both yourself & baggage; & see that you are right whenever there is a change of cars. *Have all your thoughts about you.*"[21] By imposing such restrictions, men perpetuated gender conventions that emphasized female weakness and the need for male protection; but it must be noted that this was done in the context of genuine concern for the daughter.

Nor were fathers' concerns unfounded, since failure to adhere to certain norms could bring harsh censure from the community. According to Maris A. Vinovskis, "The notion of the 'fallen' woman became so prevalent, that any sexual experience prior to marriage contaminated a woman and made her a less desirable marriage partner."[22] In particular, premarital pregnancy, less stigmatized in colonial times, was a blight on the family of the middle-class woman in the antebellum period.[23] According to Lincoln Clark few things could be worse. "Miss Hyde is pregnant—Aweful! A living death for a whole family."[24] Reputation and family honor were to be cherished and protected, and men made sure that daughters understood the gravity of remaining virtuous according to the rules of the day.

Some historians suggest that in the nineteenth century mothers were society's repositories of virtue, given the responsibility of inculcating moral values in children. Yet the mistakes of a child—a son's excessive gambling or a daughter's sexual indiscretions—could have serious ramifications for an entire family. Men knew the importance of maintaining some control over this part of the childrearing process, for impropriety could undermine the important ties that maintained class status. Keith Spence wrote home to his wife about their daughters, "I pray them to remember that from their good or bad conduct, must spring our happiness or misery."[25] Marriage was the means by which women maintained their class status, and an unwed daughter's marriageability was damaged by public knowledge of sexual relations. A son, in turn, could damage his status not only by becoming encumbered with debt that a father had to pay, but also by demonstrating himself untrustworthy to friends, neighbors, and acquaintances who were the potential business contacts so important to success in nineteenth-century commerce. Fathers, by helping their children avoid such mistakes, were illustrating both their love and their support of established norms.

Fathers' childrearing role also encompassed such lesser matters as encouraging the observance of social conventions. As children grew and became more active members of the community, fathers provided advice concerning manners and public decorum. Predictably, fathers spent more effort instructing daughters than sons on manners. Proper social conduct was important for both sexes, but gender roles in society attributed greater importance to a daughter's manners. Women were expected to please others, and proper manners made this easier. Etiquette was primarily a female concern, as demonstrated by Thomas Lyon Hamer's purchase of a book on etiquette for his wife and daughters while serving in Congress.[26] Similarly, Simeon Baldwin, a Connecticut lawyer and Superior Court judge, counseled his daughter, who was on the verge of womanhood,

> Always observe the manners of the most accomplished & most pleasing—find out what it is that makes them so, not by a servile imitation which is also servile and disgusting, but by an insensible assimilation of manners which will always be acquired by frequenting good company with a resolution to endeavor always to your utmost to make yourself acceptable to them & to please them. To please requires a determination to please—& such determination with good sense & good breeding will never fail.[27]

The concern for manners and community approbation suggests fathers' respect for and desire to maintain the network of communal obligations in antebellum society. The argument that urbanization undermined community ties in nineteenth-century America, once an established truism among historians, has been challenged by recent work in urban history. Historians of immigration have found that family ties and some communal ties still played an important part in shaping urban immigrant life.[28] The sources used for this study show that regardless of environment (rural, small town, or urban), middle-class people, like working-class immigrants, lived and functioned within a network of communal ties.[29] The influence of the community, then, was present when fathers instructed children on social skills. Bernard Wishy has suggested that in the antebellum period "there was a universal belief that a disobedient child reflected in the worst possible way on his parents."[30] Along with honesty and obedience, fathers taught cheerfulness, amiability, and control over one's temper, all for the purpose of social acceptance and maintaining the good name of the family. When his ten-year-old daughter went away to school, Judge William Edmond encouraged her to "be complaisant and obliging to all—it is a tribute easily paid and they will reward you with their love."[31] Children who visited friends or relatives, or those who went to board with other families, were expected to get along with their hosts. After Joseph Elfreth requested to visit an uncle, his father wrote, "if I was sure the[e] would be a good boy, and not to be troublesome to thy uncle & aunt but would be better there than thee is at home I should be willing thee should go ... if thy uncle Samuel is willing to take thee."[32]

In 1850, while away at school, fourteen-year-old Lyman Hodge had a disagreement over table manners with the head of the household where he was boarding. The advice of Lyman's father, Benjamin Hodge, illustrates the extent to which fathers respected their neighbors. "Very possibly Mr. F may be sometimes too rigid in his rules; but you know in all well conducted families, that there are certain regulations that all should endeavor to see carried out."[33] Benjamin was unusually lenient with his children, so this was not a buttressing of his own paternal power, but a plea for Lyman to please Mr. F and to respect the hierarchy of his house. As important as the elder Hodge considered education, "deportment at the table and all the other matters connected with a well regulated family are just as important, and I have no doubt but you do esteem them as such."[34]

Further examination of the interaction between Lyman, his father, and Mr. F suggests, however, a subtle shift in men's instruction in this area. Benjamin did not command Lyman to respect the wishes of Mr. F at all costs as a father might have done during the colonial period. Although he counseled Lyman to remain at the house of Mr. F, admonishing him to "make it a study to gain the goodwill of all," Lyman found the situation unbearable and moved on his own initiative. Despite having advised Lyman to place communal obligations above his personal feelings, Benjamin Hodge's respect for his son's rights could only allow him to accept Lyman's decision.[35]

While maintaining face within the community remained important to fathers, the focus and purpose of inculcating good social skills in children shifted toward concern for the child's ability to function in society. This change in emphasis is significant, for it reveals how men's approach to childrearing could change over time. Most of the accounts of fathers who emphasized conforming to communal expectations came from the period 1800 to the 1820s. For example,

John Gilman wrote to his absent son in 1797, "Am glad you are pleased with your situation, [and] hope you will please all in turn."[36] Thomas Lyon Hamer's advice to a child in 1838, by comparison, focuses on the child as an individual rather than as a part of a community. "Above all things . . . cultivate your temper. Without this you will be unhappy all your days."[37] The first emphasizes pleasing others, while the second stresses the need for self-control to attain personal happiness.

A similar shift can be found in the contrast between two examples of paternal advice about etiquette and dress. The following accounts not only reveal that fathers concerned themselves with female fashion and clothing but also show the growing value of children relative to the community. In 1804, not long after finishing a stint as an American consul in Tunis, William Eaton wrote to his step-daughter from Washington, DC. "If nothing unforeseen impedes I shall take a pleasure in procuring for you, at Philad.a or N York, the articles you intimate will be suitable to the season and the fashion. Shall be particular in procuring the [desired] shades of chenelle [sic]."[38] Lincoln Clark, almost fifty years later from the same city, sent home cloth and patterns for silk dresses for his two daughters. "The figure is [to] my taste, is much worn here, and I hope will please my dear children."[39] Eaton's concern in 1804 was to obtain articles that were "suitable" to fashion, while a half a century later Clark hoped his choices pleased his daughters. The difference is subtle, but it illustrates a change. By teaching etiquette to children, middle-class fathers hoped to provide the skills children required to function well in society and to maintain status, all in hopes of obtaining happiness.

Most fathers could agree upon a lengthy list of attributes they felt were appropriate to the middle class. In addition to obedience, virtue, and propriety, fathers taught industry, patience, kindness, affection, diligence, helpfulness, unselfishness, duty, honesty, thrift, punctuality, cheerfulness, loyalty to country, courage, and perseverance, among others.[40] As historians have sought to understand the differences between the sexes in antebellum America, they have often followed the lead of nineteenth-century observers who divided these traits between male and female poles. Values such as honesty, duty, and thrift were appropriate to either sex, but courage, industry, loyalty, and perseverance were thought to be masculine, while patience, kindness, affection, and unselfishness were considered more feminine.

We must be wary of these designations, however, for fathers were not always so gender-specific in teaching these values. Men knew that if sons and daughters were to succeed in all aspects of life they would need a wide range of knowledge and skills. They realized that although kindness and affection were desired virtues for daughters, and industry and perseverance for sons, both sexes benefited through possession of most or all of these traits. An overly simplistic separate spheres model might claim that men, knowing only masculine things, had only the masculine store of values to draw from when teaching children, and thus taught boys and girls basically the same way—the male way. But such an argument ignores the long list of traits taught by fathers, which is too complex to be considered one-dimensionally. Fathers, it seems, did not hesitate to teach their sons as well as their daughters to develop the virtues of kindness, unselfishness, affection, and helpfulness as skills for success in family and other personal relationships. Honesty, thrift, punctuality, industry, and perseverance were virtues that sons might need more in the workplace, but fathers also taught them to daughters for use at home or in public life.

In a letter written on December 31, 1837, Jacob Elfreth told each of his five children what he hoped and expected of them for the coming year.

> For Joseph, I wish he may become more patient of things which cross his own will, more Careful in his personal appearance, more diligent in his studies. For Jane I wish she may become more patient in her disposition, more affectionate to her brothers and Sisters, and more helpful to her Mother. For Caleb I wish he may become more patient of contradiction, retain his love of reading, and by cultivating brotherly love get rid of selfishness. For Sarah, I wish she may become faster in her movements, fonder of her books, and continue her disposition to be kind to her brothers and sisters and domestic in her habits. For James, I wish he may learn to speak plainer and always be careful to speak the truth.[41]

What is significant about Elfreth's tailored advice is that it turned more on each child's individual needs and personality than to his or her gender. As Elfreth continued the letter, he wrote that he hoped all his children would grow in grace and be dutiful to their parents, kind to each other, affectionate to relatives and friends, benevolent, charitable, able to control their anger, and able to overcome evil with good so that "when we are done with the things of this world we may all meet together a happy family in the world which is to come."[42] The Christian requirements for heaven included traits often thought to be feminine as well as masculine. Thus, men's religious beliefs validated their teaching of such "feminine" traits as virtue, patience, kindness, charity, benevolence, affection, and brotherly love.

Recent research into the history of masculinity corroborates the idea that fathers were not limited to a single "sphere" of knowledge. Historians are finding that the cluster of traits recognized as "manhood" included a surprisingly wide variety of attributes from which men could draw in dealing with their world. A leading historian of American manhood, E. Anthony Rotundo, has shown how masculinity contained the restrained and compassionate attributes associated with home and religion, along with the active and forceful traits that were rooted in the world of male competition, and the vigor and strength believed to be part of man's primitive nature. Therefore, men not only possessed different traits from which to draw but also did not perceive many of these attributes to be gender-specific.[43] In the words of one pundit in 1796, "I confess myself decidedly of the opinion of those who would rather form the two sexes to a resemblance of character, than contrast them. Virtue, wisdom, presence of mind, patience, vigour, capacity, application, are not sexual qualities—they belong to mankind—to all who have duties to perform and evils to endure."[44]

What fathers did view as gender specific were not so much traits but sex roles, and herein men retained their conservatism. Sex roles are those actions that a society expects men or women to perform by reason of their gender.[45] So, while fathers felt that few qualities were exclusively male or female, they did feel that traits needed to be utilized in properly gendered activities. The different implications of industriousness for daughters and sons illustrate this. In the changing economy of the nineteenth century, success in society came not only through manners and morality but also through hard work. The value men placed on work can be seen in the almost religious powers with which they imbued industriousness. "Industry," according to one father, "will accomplish everything that can be desired."[46] Diligence in work, it was thought, could promote virtue, happiness, and even health.[47] Austin Dunham's father sent him to school where he boarded with a family that "allowed" the boarding scholars to "keep hens and have a garden." His father hoped that the work would help his frail constitution. It seemed to be effective—Dunham was able to spend a summer working on a farm and another in a cotton mill for the benefit of the curative powers of work.[48]

Even daughters, like Jane Elfreth, seven years old, were counseled in the benefits of the Protestant work ethic.

> I think it would be better for thee if thee had a little more useful employment than thee seems to have. Thee might dust off the chairs and settee in the nursery, and put things to rights, and beat up thy bolster in the morning. Thee sometimes helps to dress thy Sister Sarah and thy brother James, but is apt to get out of patience and seems to think it is a hardship, whereas thee ought to be willing to help thy Mother who has a great deal too much to do. I have heard thy Grandmother say thy mother used to iron when she was so little that she had to stand on a stool to reach up to the table. Now my dear little Jane do try to be more industrious and make thyself useful.[49]

Although fathers clearly felt it their right to instruct daughters to be industrious, various tasks in middle-class households were fairly strictly divided by gender. Daughters occasionally helped fathers with male work, such as harvesting and household repairs, but usually their work was domestic. Fathers did advise and direct daughters in some matters concerning female tasks. Judge William Edmond, for example, admonished his daughter Polly to watch over her sick little sister, "I am sure you will pity her, and do everything in your power to render her as comfortable & happy as possible. I am not anxious to have her go alone at my return or indeed before the weather grows warm. Such little creatures are so much exposed when they first begin to totter about, from the fire and a thousand other accidents that it is scarcely to be wished that they should walk before they begin to have some little reason to govern themselves. Give my love to her in a sisterly & affectionate manner & kiss her for me."[50] Edmond was not only teaching his daughter the role of the nurse but also caretaker. In general, however, daughters' work was directed by the mother, limiting fathers to the inculcation of work values. Eliza Dwight remembered sitting in the parlor with her mother and sister preparing to hem towels when her father entered the room. "Seeing us sitting unemployed when we should be industrious, he exclaimed, with some severity of tone, 'Why are you idle?'" The mother replied that the daughters were soon to be working and that the father should go talk to the male side of the family about being lazy. The father retreated, knowing he had overstepped his bounds.[51] The father could urge industriousness on daughters, but it was not typically his place to direct their domestic work.

Fathers obviously had no such barriers with sons. Since boys would eventually grow up to take on the role of provider, the trait of industry was particularly important for sons to acquire. Sons learned quite early on that they were destined to the world of male work. At haying time, three-year-old Charlie Rich rode on the hay wagon with his father, and according to his mother, could hardly wait "to grow big so he can help his father."[52] In most middle-class families, preadolescent sons performed chores under the assignment of their fathers. Sons chopped wood, helped start fires, ran errands, helped in the gardens, tended livestock, milked cows, assisted in harvesting, and occasionally watched younger children.[53] Thus, not only did they perform necessary mundane chores, but they also learned independent work habits that fathers felt were necessary for success in male occupations.

It is important to note, however, that the meaning of industry for male children was changing during this period. In the new middle-class family structure, children evolved from laborers to students, and sons were raised to obtain the kinds of occupations that would maintain family status. This meant that fathers often encouraged sons to look for an occupation in areas other than farming and the trades, preferably in the professions or in business. Even by 1800 fathers no longer gave priority to teaching sons skills like leatherworking, tool sharpening, animal husbandry, woodworking, glaziery, and horticulture, but instead emphasized reading, oratory, penmanship, algebra, and punctiliousness. Fathers came to associate industriousness with diligence in studies and the acquiring of business and professional skills. Keith Spence reprimanded his young son (through a letter to his wife) for liking "play so much, and his School so little. If he does not alter soon, it will be too late; and he will be ruined forever. Let him turn therefore from the company of his idle and vicious companions, and apply his whole mind to his learning so that he may be fit to go to . . . some good Merchant by the time he is 14 years old."[54] Among the better-off middle-class farming families, fathers hired laborers to work in the fields rather than keep sons home from school. This is not to say that hard physical work was no longer important in the panoply of middle-class virtues taught by men; rather, it shows the way in which people adapted values to fit changes in society. In small towns and even urban areas, vestiges of faith in physical labor con-

tinued in symbolic areas, as families grew gardens or maintained livestock for the purpose of teaching the value of work to children.
Charles Penniman Daniell, for example, complained that his father, a
hardware merchant, had the odd idea that working all day in the
garden constituted leisure.[55]

The methods by which successful middle-class fathers instilled
good work values in their sons are, of course, difficult to pin down
with any precision. The issue is an important one, for it can shed light
on the larger matter of how fathers perpetuated cultural norms. We
know that indolence, the companion of dissipation, was looked upon
as a sin. Although fathers were less likely to correspond with sons
who rejected middle-class values, the sources do reveal that some sons
used laziness as a means to challenge the authority of their fathers. But
most seem to have eventually internalized the values and skills taught
by their fathers, for these were essential in the increasingly commercialized and industrialized society.[56] New Hampshire minister John
Milton Putnam was pleased to read the letter of his oldest son to his
youngest son. "'I most guess you think it rather hard now to work,
but by & by you will thank father for keeping you at your work.'"[57]

This discussion of industriousness shows the complexity of
fathers' participation in the inculcation of traits and proper gender
attributes. Changes in work altered the meaning of industry and how
fathers taught it, but men still felt this particular trait was of value
to both daughters and sons. Fathers' prominence in both the public
and the domestic arenas allowed them to urge both sexes to appreci-
ate the value of industriousness, but the gendered division of work
meant that men were more likely to teach sons the application of
industriousness.

Fathers did view certain qualities as almost exclusively male or
female. Many fathers encouraged sons to procure the "manly arts"—
horseback riding, shooting, boxing, and hunting—in order to learn
courage and strength. Sons were expected to maintain their honor,
even, for some fathers, to the point of fighting; crying or showing fear
in the face of hardship or danger was discouraged. Daughters, on the
other hand, were encouraged by fathers to develop a docile, modest
temperament and to spend their time becoming accomplished in the
"domestic arts."

Thomas Lyon Hamer and Thomas Kilby Smith were both frontier
lawyers and politicians whose correspondence reveals this desire to

produce feminine daughters and manly sons. Hamer's correspondence comes from the 1830s and 1840s, and Smith's from twenty years later. Writing to his five-year-old son, Hamer declared, "One of the first things for a Western boy to learn is to ride a horse, the next is to shoot a gun. My boys must learn both these things whilst they are small."[58] Likewise, Smith wrote of his sons, both under ten years old,

> I want them to gain physical strength and an aptitude for all manly sports and exercises. They must learn to box and wrestle with each other, and take long walks. They could walk together out to Mr. Dicksons or any where else they please in the country four or five miles from home, take their dinner with them and eat it in the woods. That's what I used to delight in as a boy & then they shall be prepared to learn to hunt—next fall they shall each have a gun & learn to shoot.[59]

But some fathers were less sanguine about the value of these pursuits; as one father reminded his son, "such diversions must not interfere with . . . School hours."[60] Still, most fathers, regardless of rural or urban environment, advocated exercise for their children's constitutions, but sons were particularly encouraged to engage in outdoor sports.

The evidence that fathers supported male aggressiveness through fighting is less pervasive but still evident. In 1863, Thomas Kilby Smith wrote what he expected of his sons ages eleven and nine when it came to matters of honor.

> They must bear themselves upright, always tell the truth, look everybody square in the eye & never take an insult from any boy. When they go into a fight they must always get the first blow. I mean always deliver the first blow and follow that . . . one up fast, either of them can whip a boy twice his size if he is only ready & prompt with his fist. I don't want them to seek quarrels. I don't want them to quarrel at all with boys, but if one is forced upon them, fight it right out, don't stop to have any words about it one way or the other but pitch right in & if they are so unfortunate to get worsted try it again another time, but never stay whipped by any boy.[61]

E. Anthony Rotundo has charted the rise in the latter part of the nineteenth century of a new gender ideal, "the Masculine Primitive," which led some fathers to approve of fist fights between boys.[62] Prior to that time, fighting was probably less accepted. John Wesley North recalled his youth in the 1830s, "My father was quite stern and severe, as I used to think; and nothing would have brought me a surer punishment than to have been caught in a fight with another boy."[63]

Thomas Kilby Smith's pugnacious advice to his sons, however, was probably influenced by his martial frame of mind. The letter cited above was sent to his sons while he was on campaign during the Civil War. Military service and war usually had the effect of increasing a father's concern about matters of honor. At the outbreak of the Civil War, Charles Henry Ray, watching friends and neighbors go away to battle, wrote to his sons, "I hope my children will never have to fight; but if it is necessary, when they grow up to be men, & go to war, I want them to be willing to die for a good cause."[64] Ray had never broached the subject of honor to his children before 1861. While in the Army during the Mexican-American war, Thomas Lyon Hamer pleaded with his sixteen-year-old son to maintain the honor of the family.

> Oh Thomas, if I never see you again hear my last request. Curb your temper. Be a man. Be a gentleman. Be an honor to your parents—to your brother & sisters, to your friends, to your country, to yourself. Do not break my heart. Do not cover my face with blushes or send me down to the grave in sorrow for the conduct of my first born son. If you knew how well I love you, you would never do anything to offend me.[65]

In the military, fist fights between truculent boys were left behind for more lethal defenses of honor. General William Eaton's son followed his father's footsteps into the military, but was killed in 1808 in a duel with a fellow officer. The father's response was not to condemn dueling, but to sorrowfully wonder whether his son's differences with the other officer had really been worth the risk of life. Eaton could not blame his son, for the child was following in the father's footsteps perhaps too closely—the father had also challenged a fellow officer to a duel in his younger days.[66] The evidence is limited, but it seems likely that the exaggerated standards of personal honor that permeated the armed forces may have found their way into the childrearing practices of military fathers.

Courage, another martial virtue, was also considered a manly trait. In a letter to his to his seven-year-old son, Thomas Lyon Hamer made an explicit connection between masculinity and courage:

I hope you have quit fighting the children—& nearly quit crying; and that you are not afraid of the dark. If so then you can be the Pappa until I get home. But if you fight little girls; or a little boy much smaller than yourself; or if you cry every time you fall down or stump your toe; or when you can't get what you want; or if you are afraid in the dark—then you are not to be the Pappa, but must be still a little fellow; and your mother must nurse you when you cry—and go out with you at night—just before you go to bed! But I do not believe this is so; you are too much of a man now![67]

This passage gives tacit approval to fighting boys of equal or greater size, but fighting girls and smaller boys was unmanly. Fear of the dark, crying at pain and disappointment, and dependence on mother for comfort as well as protection during the nightly trip to the outhouse were all disparaged. The message is clear: Boys on the path to manhood were to strive to be condescending to the weak, courageous in the face of pain, and independent of females.

Fathers schooled their sons in male roles in many ways. Sons undoubtedly watched their fathers' interaction with women and other men and learned patterns of conduct by example. When Hamer wrote to his son: "She [the younger Hamer's mother] is a good woman to you & me; & we ought not to do anything to displease her. She makes our breeches—and gives us bread & butter," he was instructing his son in the male's dominant role in the family.[68] A true man did not mistreat the woman that served him. By emphasizing honor, courage, and proficiency in manly pursuits, fathers encouraged their sons to believe not only that men had different roles than women did, but also that in some things they were by nature different than women.

That fathers taught sons about gender ideals is not surprising. Most historians of children concede that fathers at the very least were involved in the development of adolescent sons' masculine identity, even if only by providing a behavioral example. What is surprising, however, is that fathers also sought to instill in daughters proper gendered characteristics. In 1850 Lincoln Clark was gratified to hear that his adolescent daughter, Catherine, was doing well in school, "But what pleased me more than anything else was to know that you were docile and yielding." He continued, "I know of nothing more repulsive than to see a lady contemptuous[?], always resisting, and having her mouth stereotyped to say no! tho' there are occasions when she ought to say it. It is true we do not account you a lady now; but as the girl, so the woman."[69] Docility was never advocated for sons. William Edmond also encouraged his daughter to develop characteristics he thought appropriate for young women, such as mild manners, modesty, tenderness, and politeness.[70] Fathers also encouraged their daughters' interest in the domestic arts, as in the following advice William Edmond gave to his daughter Polly in 1799: "As the necessary part of female education therefore I consider the art of the Distaff, the buzzing of the wheel & the tory reel together with the noble science of the Pancake and custards."[71]

This is not to say that fathers were always comfortable and proficient in teaching daughters feminine values and roles. Indeed, men exhibited their clumsiness by occasionally giving daughters conflicting advice. After an operation on his daughter's eye, Lincoln Clark in a 1847 letter to his wife praised the daughter for "her submission and courage. I think she has high moral qualities, and I love her for them." But then he felt he had to feminize the attribute of courage to fit the gender. "I hope that at the same time that she may grow up with the softness of her sex, [that] she may have the spirit of the heroine, and submit without murmuring to any thing that is necessary."[72] Another example comes from Simeon Baldwin in 1806, who approved of his daughter's equestrian talents but warned her: "while I have said so much in favor of this I know you have too much good sense to consider this among the first accomplishments to which a young lady should aspire. You can seldom exhibit yourself in that attitude—you will every day of your life be called to exhibit yourself in the social circle."[73]

What at first glance may seem like mere awkward parenting actually reveals a primary tension in father-daughter relationships. In almost all such relationships in the sources, there was a great deal of affection between daughters and fathers. Men often demonstrated this affection in the context of their role as an advisor on both moral and pragmatic matters. Fathers' instruction to their daughters generally fell within the approved boundaries of female gender roles, but occasionally they encouraged behavior that challenged (on the surface) gender conventions of the time. John Pintard, a New York insurance company officer, proudly recounted the following incident to one of his two daughters. "By the way yr sister bought a small key hole saw the other day to be independent in her carpentering, wh[ich] made the man smile who sold it & who gave her a handsome handle for it, observing that it was the first saw ever purchased from him by a young lady."[74] Pintard was clearly in favor of his daughter's independence in carpentry. Lincoln Clark was responding to his perception of shortcomings in female gender conventions when he told his daughter Catherine, "Now is the harvest time for you to gather knowledge, and to secure the improvement, which will make you more than a picture to be looked at."[75] Clark obviously wanted more for his daughter than what he felt convention dictated a young woman should be. Like Benjamin Rush, one of the leading education authorities of the day, Clark objected to the model of womanhood that pressed women into the role of a passive ornament to be observed.[76]

Tensions arose, however, because these mild challenges were usually accompanied by strong reinforcements of traditional gender roles. Clark expressed his desire that Catherine, just turned eighteen, be "a woman of character as well as accomplishments" with "matured & settled opinions upon all important subjects." But in the same letter he admonished her to cultivate an "amiable, yielding, Christian spirit."[77] Although Clark encouraged assertion and accomplishment, he also emphasized passivity. By doing so, he failed to provide Catherine with outlets for these more aggressive traits. Clark cautioned her, "a reasonable ambition is right—an excessive one tends to make us unhappy."[78] Catherine was to be "yielding" and "amiable" in the face of this restrictive contradiction.

What does this conflicting advice mean? It may reflect male antipathy, conscious or unconscious, toward female gender ideals. A prominent argument used by literary scholars suggests that nineteenth-century masculinity hid a deep abiding fear of women and a distrust of all things feminine.[79] Although in theory men placed the nineteenth-century woman on a moral pedestal, they also believed that men were physically and intellectually superior to women. So, while men may or may not have feared femininity, they certainly held some aspects of female gender ideals in low regard. When fathers included "masculine" traits in their instruction to daughters, they superficially communicated what they believed to be the best education possible. Thus, their affection led them to be occasionally subversive in their instructions. Love, however, did not undermine sex roles, since on the whole fathers did not firmly stand behind the real changes that could have improved the place of their daughters in society.

Advice about female education provides a good illustration of how fathers supported some improvements for their daughters, but ultimately desired to maintain the status quo. By the nineteenth century, opposition to female education was limited to an occasional anachronistic voice. Among the middle class, fathers supported elementary education for their daughters, and many provided the means for secondary education. By the second quarter of the nineteenth century, there was even a rationale among educators justifying the education of girls by arguing that they grew to be women who would influence the lives of sons and husbands. What has been called the "republican motherhood" argument in essence sanctioned the education of girls by appealing to their future roles as wives and mothers.[80]

Fathers themselves, however, rarely stated that the goal of their daughters' education was preparation for future service to husbands and children. Instead, fathers couched their support of their daughters' education in rhetoric of the daughter's self-improvement and personal happiness. After sending his student daughter money, John Putnam, a minister with a limited income, wrote in 1846 that the expense of educating her was "nothing compared with the benefit I hope it will be to you to cultivate yr. mind, & prepare you for increased happiness, influence & usefulness in future life."[81] William Edmond reminded Polly while she was away at school, "nothing but the most earnest desire to have you improve in whatever can make you worthy of love and esteem could reconcile your parents to an hour's absence."[82] Like the paternal advice on values, fathers' support of female education was an attempt to provide for a child's happiness and well-being.

While most middle-class fathers supported female education, there was no consensus on an appropriate curriculum for girls. A few fathers felt that daughters needed an education only in domestic knowledge, which they could receive at home, although this seems to have been an outdated attitude by 1800.[83] Almost all middle-class men agreed that in the early years reading, writing, and spelling were necessary topics. Literacy, after all, was one of the things that separated the middle class from the working classes. "The more I read," wrote Lavina Watson to her father, "the more I am led to think on the vast advantage we, who are educated, possess over the other class of our fellow beings. How poor and few must their ideas be, all they know is of the world around them, with other things they never trouble themselves."[84] Beyond literacy, however, opinion was divided as to what subjects were appropriate for girls' secondary education. Such "ornamental arts" as dancing, drawing, music, and singing were often taught, although some fathers, as we have seen, wanted more for their daughters. Literature, languages, and history generally formed the core subjects that fathers sanctioned for their daughters. Even here, however, certain kinds of literature were cautioned against. One Congregationalist minister allowed his daughter to read Byron, but only enough to give her "a general idea of the character of his poems, and to loathe their spirit as tending to evil." "True," he wrote, "some of his poems are good, just as there are some good traits in the vilest of men. But as we would not wish to make such men our associates, so we should not wish to make ourselves very familiar with Byron's poems."[85] Fathers also often disapproved of the popular literature of the day, encouraging their daughters to read "good" literature in their spare time. Math and science were the areas usually most restricted for reasons of gender. Career military man William Eaton, for example, believed that at an early age daughters were "too tender" to study arithmetic.[86] And Lincoln Clark believed that literature was "better for a lady than science."[87] Still, some fathers advised their daughters to pursue the study of astronomy, chemistry, philosophy, geography, and anatomy.[88]

Paternal encouragement of daughters to study subjects that only years before were considered exclusively male topics indicates that female sex roles were in transition in the nineteenth century. But the changes were limited. While many fathers encouraged the increased opportunities for education available to their daughters, they rejected almost all avenues for women to use their education for anything other than "self-improvement." Even school teaching was usually considered secondary to the real goal for almost all women—that of getting married and raising a family. The republican motherhood argument put forth by commentators in the nineteenth century may have even been a theoretical attempt to justify this disjunction between education and opportunity.

With sons, the objective of education was less contradictory and thus much clearer. Fathers provided educational opportunities to sons so that they too could develop as individuals and citizens, but more importantly so that they could learn to be successful providers themselves. Education among the middle-class was increasingly becoming utilitarian in its goals as sons went to school for the purpose of career preparation.[89] Because of this, the debates over a curriculum for boys varied greatly from those over female education. The debate centered on the choice of a practical course of study that might include a clerkship in business versus the traditional classical education that pre-pared scholars for the ministry, law, or medicine. Once a son was in school, a father had a limited influence over the child's set course of study, except when it came to the less pragmatic realm of the arts. Music, dancing, and painting lessons were more likely to be the sub-ject of negotiation between fathers and sons because they did little to prepare a son for the future world of work. Sheldon Colton of Milan, Ohio, for example, was surprised to discover that his merchant father approved of his paintings, having "never expected to get a word of approval from him on the subject."[90] Keith Spence, from his distant position as purser in the Navy, approved of dancing lessons for his children, but only so that they might not be embarrassed when the social situation demanded the ability to dance.[91]

As education for boys became indispensable as a means of main-taining or obtaining class status, the importance of providing an edu-cation increased for fathers. Some farming fathers resisted sending sons to school, seeing sons in the traditional terms of farm labor, but most middle-class men exerted considerable effort and resources to see their sons properly schooled.[92] George Templeton Strong's father, a successful New York lawyer, wrote in 1834, "I consider the educa-tion of children as of inconceivable importance."[93] Prior to entering school at age six, the younger Strong was taught by his mother at home, but as the son grew older the father became more involved with his education. When George was thirteen years old, his father began to spend his evenings tutoring the boy. "This is the first winter since I have been in business," wrote the father, "that I have omitted coming to the office in the evening. My labor on the whole is substantially increased by this course, but I consider George's education as of so much importance, and the present such an interesting part of his life, that I deem it my duty to make the sacrifice."[94]

On the other end of the economic scale, when Clemens Clendenen was a teenager living on his father's farm, his brother encouraged him to go to school, solemnly reminding him, "remember that Knowledge (Education) is power."[95] The lesson was not lost on Clemens. In 1864 while in the Union Army he was captured and sent to the infamous Andersonville prison camp in Georgia, and, knowing the likelihood of his death, he wrote to his wife on a page torn from a daybook. "If you get this don't grieve for me. We have plenty to eat. But you hold on to your property and do all you can to give the Boys a good edu-cation. If I live I will be home sometime, if I don't live to get home you will have to do the best you can in this world and be prepared for the next."[96] The last words his wife ever received from him expressed hope that his sons would be educated so that they might have opportunities beyond the farm.

The importance to fathers of providing a good education for children is evident in their willingness to fill in the gaps where public education failed. When the local school in William Sewall's rural neighborhood began to falter in 1842, Sewall, a farmer, took charge of it for "the benefit of my own children." He taught lessons for a time, then had his oldest daughter take over the teaching responsibilities.[97] Eliza Dwight's father, objecting to her "catching something of the school girls' slang," pulled her and her sister out of school in their early teens, teaching them at home and directing their reading for an unstated length of time.[98] Likewise, Lucy and Joseph Clark Allen disliked the bad behavior that their children were learning in the public school, so they opened their own school in their home. For a time, Joseph, a minister, taught lessons in the morning and Lucy taught in the afternoon.[99] For fathers like these, educating their children was important enough for them to do it themselves. However, becoming a teacher or opening a school were not common solutions to such problems. Each of the three men saw their teaching stints as temporary diversions from their primary occupations. Eventually, Sewall and Clark delegated the job to women—a daughter and wife. Few fathers had the kind of job flexibility that allowed them to take such an active role in their children's education. Clark, for example, remained involved with the school, but his wife Lucy did the bulk of the teaching because his ministerial duties often took him away.

Instead of teaching lessons, fathers' participation in their children's education usually took different forms. In an age when the local school often relied heavily on the initiative of the parents, fathers made important contributions. In most parts of the country it was customary for teachers to board with the families of students, and fathers contributed by taking their turn. And some fathers provided necessary services or supplies to local schools and teachers. The most common type of participation, however, was in the capacity of supplementary tutor, as in the case of George Templeton Strong's father. Before or after work many fathers took the time to hear recitations, assign and correct math problems, assist with penmanship, suggest and direct readings, or any number of activities to further a child's education. Jacob Elfreth, for example, took his children to lectures at the local lyceum.[100] Even the act of correspondence could become used to further a child's education. Fathers encouraged proper penmanship, spelling, and use of logic in letters. Benjamin Hodge even sent arithmetic problems to his son and received the answers in return letters.[101] Clearly, many fathers after providing money, encouragement, direction, and tutoring felt that they were the driving force in the education of their children. When Elijah Grant wrote of his son, "I intend to Educate him as highly as I can without Injury to his health," he was unconsciously illustrating his claim to a primary role in his son's education.[102]

Inevitably, this relationship put pressure on children, especially sons, to succeed in school. With the future riding on the son's performance, many fathers pushed their sons. While at Harvard in 1855, Nicholas Longworth Anderson wrote to his mother,

> Father says that I know what he expects of me, and knowing, will accomplish it. I do know what he expects of me, and he expects too much, far too much. It is not only improbable but it is impossible for me to keep my present rank, but I can accomplish all that he desires in every other particular. I often wish that you and he would not love me so much, and not treat me so kindly and affectionately, for then I would not blame myself so much for my few qualities and attainments. As it is, however, I deserve I know not what. The most extreme punishment would be too good for me. Don't smile! I am in earnest. I am unworthy to be the son of two such parents.[103]

Anderson's letter reveals some of the complexity and contradiction inherent in men's childrearing role. Obviously, in this case, the father had a great deal of emotional control over his son, enough for Nicholas to transfer his resentment against his father onto himself. Yet Nicholas' father seems to have exerted this pressure not through didactic lectures or overt pressures to succeed but through affection and kindness. In addition to providing education, fathers also gave friendship and companionship as they spent time playing with and amusing their children. These activities strengthened attachments between fathers and children, which in turn further engendered a sense of obligation in both parties to fulfill their duties to each other.

Not surprisingly, many fathers used leisure time with children to further the larger goals of childrearing. Men often combined play and education. As Susan Winslow Hodge, the editor of *The Elfreth Book of Letters*, notes, "learning during this period was not confined to classroom hours but was expected to continue through appropriate use of leisure time."[104] In the name of learning, fathers participated in a variety of pastimes with children. Often in the evenings after supper and schoolwork were finished families gathered together in a parlor or kitchen to discuss the day's events, sing, or hear fathers read a favorite book out loud.[105] Fathers also purchased toys or instruments that were designed to combine play and learning. John Wesley North, for example, bought blocks with an "alphabetical menagerie" on them to help his daughter learn her letters.[106] And Matthias Zahm, a lower middle-class entrepreneur, recorded renting a "pianna" for seven dollars a year in 1839 so that his children could learn to play.[107] One father hired a "professional microscopist" to come and show his children the microscopic world.[108] The lines dividing formal education and home life were not always distinct. Luther Trussell expressed this to his foster daughter: "No one should ever dream their education is finished when they stop going to school. Education ought to be long as life."[109] Many fathers were able to incorporate education into their children's leisure time.

Psychologist Erik Erikson has argued that one way parents come to accept children's play as worthwhile is to see it as work or the learning of work.[110] But some fathers also believed that children needed to play for no other reason than to be happy. "I do not expect you to take up much of your leisure time in writing to me," wrote Edward Everett to Anne, his daughter, "because I think it very necessary for the health and happiness of children, that they should have time enough, not merely for exercise, but for play."[111] Seeing play as promoting the well-being of a child may have helped fathers justify joining in with children in activities that had no other purpose than fun. With younger children, fathers gave rides on their backs, pushed them on swings, and sometimes could be found on the floor wrestling with sons or building houses out of blocks.[112] One father went with his daughter to the circus; "the chief object of going was to take Emma, who had never seen such a thing."[113] George Templeton Strong and his father shared the hobby of fire alarm chasers. Even in the middle of the night the two would leave their beds to watch a blaze together.[114] Such activities seem to have had no motive other than enjoyment and served to bring fathers and children closer together.

Men's participation in play could be quite spontaneous. On a cold New England morning in March, Lucy Clark Allen, the wife of a minister, wrote, "This morning all the boys were upon it [the pond], skating and sliding; and it was such a glorious morning, and they looked so pretty on the ice, that I could not help leaving my breakfast things to go out, too. Mr. Allen [her husband] and Mr. Clarke were there, skating with the rest."[115] At other times, the activities were planned. Orville Browning was an Illinois lawyer and eventual senator who liked to spend the day fishing with his son and friends. "At day break this morning Seaman, his son Jo: myself & boy William started to Sand Slough fishing. Caught minnows in a little creek South of Town & at 7 O'clock in the morning were fishing about 6 miles below Town. Returned in the afternoon with more than 60 fine bass, and had a fry at my house for supper."[116]

Historians have noted the rise of holiday observance in the nineteenth century, arguing that it reflects the growing emotional importance of children in the family.[117] The sources used in this study support this claim. Men's participation in holiday festivities seems to have been mostly for the sake of enjoying and giving pleasure to children. On Thanksgiving in 1856, Lincoln Clark wrote to his daughter who was at school, "At 2 o['] clock we had our thanksgiving dinner, plain, but good and nice—we missed you, we remembered you, and regretted that you were not with us."[118] Gift-giving at Christmas time, New Year's, or on birthdays also became popular. George Templeton Strong wrote in his journal in 1855, "Most of the morning spent in the active pursuit of Christmas presents; after dinner, in arranging Johnny's for his astonishment, on the table in the middle parlor—Napoleon's Old Guard, the elephant with the moveable head, and so on, the railroad train ('long cars') being deposited on the floor."[119] Some fathers played Santa Claus, while in other homes children were aware of who purchased the gifts. Jane Elfreth knew who to ask when she wrote to her father, "Sis Sarah and me have been talking about Cristmas [sic] things or toys I should say. And I will put down a list of the things we want thee to buy us If thee please."[120]

The involvement of men in gift-giving, holiday celebrations, and the play of children suggests that the relationships between fathers and children were more than utilitarian arrangements to reproduce culture or transfer class status. Fathers understood that the spirit of the child needed nurturing just as much as the mind and body. Men clearly valued time with their children because most loved their daughters and sons. Yet love and the transmission of values were closely linked.

Love and affection intensified and complicated most relationships in such a way that emotion has to be considered as one of the defining characteristics of middle-class father-child relationships. It compelled fathers to expend energy and resources in providing the right kind of upbringing for their children; fathers keenly felt their duty as providers and teachers to give to their children the means to enter the middle class. They provided instruction in moral virtues and manners to ensure that children knew how to remain in good standing among peers and other members of the community. They fostered in children the conscience as an internal compass to guide sons away from dissipation and daughters from scandal. They enforced gender roles to guarantee masculine boys and feminine girls. They pressed children to become educated in order to be literate, understand the world, and be competent in careers and work. They instructed children in the power of love, and its use in influencing others. All these things were important skills in the growing antebellum middle class.

But as in other areas of paternal education, the providing of emotional sustenance supported men's authority. The giving of love and affection, like the inculcation of values, had the double result of both providing for children and controlling them at the same time. By strengthening the ties between fathers and children, love placed children under a greater obligation to obey. Fathers, of course, saw nothing duplicitous with this arrangement, since obedience was a primary goal of childrearing, particularly in the early years of the child. Through love, fathers could influence their daughters and sons far into their adult lives.

chapter six

Fathers and Children's Transition to Adulthood

At the age of thirty-five, Daniel S. Dickson, a self-taught lawyer who later became a United States Senator from New York, found himself in the unusual position of experiencing the final phase of the fathering role much earlier than most fathers. The "caprice of fortune" had placed in his care a parentless niece considerably older than his own children, which meant that she came of age early in his fathering years. Dickson accepted this role dutifully, as a man of his class was expected to do in the antebellum era, and came to identify himself as Louise's father with an obligation to see her marry well. At times he felt the weight of this duty; a "father who has a daughter arrived at women's estate," he wrote to Louise, "has a fearful responsibility to discharge." And like most fathers he felt a twinge of sorrow at the prospect of losing his daughter to another man. "I shall soon cease to be your guide and counselor, or to number you with those that look up to me for protection; to wait your return to the domestic threshold with a solicitude so peculiar to my nature, or to direct your footsteps."[1] Although "not bound by ties of consanguinity," Dickson loved Louise and experienced many of the same feelings that biological fathers had for children who were taking the first steps into their adult years. More importantly, Louise's coming of age precipitated a shift in his fathering role. As sons and daughters made life-changing decisions about career and marriage, fathers like Dickson found themselves with less influence over them. Fathers had to become reconciled to the replacement of their governing role by the less authoritative positions of advisor and supporter. If men lived long enough, they faced the changes that invariably came with this stage in the fathering cycle.

Not surprisingly, middle-class fathers approached this transition with mixed feelings. Dickson's reluctance to see his adoptive daughter "direct" her own footsteps was a common response. Like most fathers, Dickson had grown accustomed to protecting, directing, and governing Louise. His role of guide and disciplinarian was so ingrained into his behavior that it formed an essential component of his view of himself and his family. Fathers who had governed and encouraged their children for so many years inherently understood that power and authority were the essence of nineteenth-century fatherhood. Without the right and ability to influence, fathers ceased to be fathers. Some men resisted this change in status by holding fast to any and all sources of authority. Many were successful in maintaining influence through the continued use of economic incentives and appeals to love and duty. In some cases, adult children, such as William Eaton, remained in financial debt to fathers, prompting William to write in 1842, "towards you, My Dear Father, I feel the strongest obligations."[2] Occasionally fathers and children clashed over this extended control. Indeed, it was during the stage of semidependence that both rebellion on the part of children and physical and mental abuse perpetrated by fathers on children becomes most evident in the correspondence and journals used in this study. Although few in number, these instances of rebellion and abuse show an obvious tension between fathers and their children who had reached the threshold of adulthood but had not yet stepped over.[3]

Historian Joseph F. Kett suggests that these last stages in children's development can be divided into the categories of "semidependency" and independence. The former ran anywhere from "10 to 21 in the early part of the 19th century."[4] Semidependent children were given freedoms and responsibilities not available to younger children, but they obviously were still subordinate to parents. Even if they lived away at school or were working in another town, their fathers still retained some kind of legal or economic claim over their actions. Children became completely independent from parents only when they no longer looked to fathers for their primary economic support. Young women generally reached this stage when they shifted their economic subordination from father to husband at the time of marriage. Young men did so when they entered a profession or began earning enough to support themselves. The act of moving away from home or marrying contributed to this transition—several paths led to independence, and the age at which a child traveled those paths could vary.

One of the ironies of parenting is that its primary goal is to work oneself out of a job. Like most fathers, Daniel Dickson did not desire to keep Louise in a dependent position forever despite his attachment to her, and thus hoped to assist her in attaining a level of independence from his influence and aid. To fathers like Dickson, this was "a fearful responsibility to discharge," for it was a process fraught with danger. An impetuous or injudicious choice by a child could result in exchanging the "benevolent" paternalism of the father's authority with the exploitative control of a less forgiving master or husband. To prevent such mistakes, fathers continued to exert what influence they could in the lives of older children, but they also hoped that children could rely on what they had been taught earlier to produce the desired results—middle-class success. Fathers hoped that their children would enjoy home ownership and the freedom from want that came with middle-class incomes, but they also wished to see their children adhering to middle-class morality and develop fulfilling family relationships. If fathers felt that children were on the path to obtaining these goals, it eased the process of granting their children more freedom.

Independence brought a major shift in the relationship. As children married and proved their willingness to practice middle-class values, tensions between children and fathers often eased. Participation in the rites of marriage and family-building raised children to adult status in their fathers' eyes. As a result, their interaction began to take on tones of equality and mutual respect as many fathers welcomed sons into the brotherhood of the politically enfranchised or commiserated with a daughter on the vicissitudes of childrearing. And many sons and daughters, valuing ties with parents, consented to their fathers' continued guidance, although this advice usually was given in more of a spirit of equality than in the past. Most men, even if reluctant to accept the maturation of a child, eventually came to terms with the smaller role they played and sometimes discovered a richer, less tension-filled relationship with their children.

Finally, for fathers who lived into old age, the family cycle traveled full circle, occasionally to the point of role reversal. Advanced years often enfeebled men, bringing the need for care and assistance. Aged fathers who found themselves infirm, impoverished, or in need usually turned first to children for help. Adult children gave financial help and in many cases provided a home to men no longer able to maintain their middle-class status by themselves. For men used to long years of self-sufficiency and control, this dependent role was frequently disquieting and often not accepted gracefully.

Here then is the "decline" of fatherhood in the antebellum period; it lies in the transition that naturally came as children passed into adulthood and fathers became less important in their lives. As men watched, assisted, or delayed their children's passage into the adult world, their paternal power waned. Fathers, accustomed to providing advice, instruction, love, and support, still continued to play these roles to an extent, allowing them to maintain a position of influence in the extended family. This new position, however, generally did not command the same level of authority that earlier stages of fatherhood mustered.

Until children reached independence and proved themselves capable of maintaining middle-class status on their own, fathers continued to give advice and instruction. However, men were playing a much more subtle game at this stage than they did in their efforts with younger children. Fathers wanted control, but they also sought to maintain a loving relationship; they realized through experience (their own years as teenagers and over time with their own children) that the two were not always compatible. These were years of compromise. To allow children to grow and become responsible, men knew they had to give freedoms, and children came to expect them. Yet too much autonomy could lead to deviations from the middle-class norm, and fathers used a wide range of strategies to maintain their influence, including persuasion, obligation, and reason. In the nineteenth century, middle-class fathers emphasized to children that conforming to the rules of society brought happiness and success—rules that they would have called natural or God-given laws. In their insistent efforts to continue to promote these norms, we can see the lines of continuity between this stage of fatherhood and earlier stages; paternal education was less fundamental and overt in the lives of older teenage children, but the primary goal of that education remained the same.

For daughters, the assumed components of a woman's life work were childbirth, childcare, housework, home management, and the task of assisting a husband. Occasionally, however, some fathers encouraged and assisted daughters to work for pay outside the home before marriage. In each of the cases found in this study, fathers maintained significant control over their daughters' work situation. When Mary Paul raised the issue of laboring in the Lowell textile mills ("I think it would be much better for me than to stay about here"), she left the choice up to her father. "I want you to think of it and make up your mind," she wrote home in 1845.[5] Likewise, when the textile mill where Jenny Putnam worked increased its workday from eleven to fourteen hours, she told her sister, "Father is not willing that I should work on the 14 hour system, nor do I want to."[6] Employers in the Lowell system, aware of this control, emphasized the ordered, moral environment of the mills to convince Yankee farmers to allow their daughters to work away from home.[7]

In addition to millwork, young, unmarried women increasingly found employment as school teachers as the century progressed. Like work in the textile factories, teaching was usually temporary and monitored closely by fathers. After instructing school for a year, nineteen-year-old Antoinette Putnam hoped to continue with her own education for one semester, but her father, a New Hampshire minister, felt she had better continue teaching. "All your expenses co[u]ld probably not come short of $30.00 for the short space of 10 weeks. It takes a little too long to earn 30 dollars to get rid of it quite so quick."[8] Although Antoinette worked and earned her own wages, her father still made the decisions about her money, her work, and her education. In addition, John Putnam gave extensive advice to Antoinette on the proper way to teach and conduct herself in the classroom. "At all events, be determined to have good order. This is the glory of a school. Be particular, in your exercises. Let every thing go like clock-work. Let nothing go on at loose ends. If you are only systematic & particular, we have no doubt you will govern well, because we know that yr. scholars always love you, and they will try to please you, of course."[9]

In some respects, outside work can be seen as an assertion of independence by the young women, but until marriage, daughters were subject to the authority of their fathers. Men particularly scrutinized any activity, such as work, that drew daughters into the public arena. Eventually, if the woman remained single, she might develop a certain amount of autonomy, but in the male-dominated economy of the nineteenth century, such independence was uncommon. A daughter's work outside the home was almost always considered a temporary diversion until the right opportunity for marriage developed. Most middle-class daughters and fathers agreed that a young woman's primary goal was to learn the roles of wife and mother. Thus as a daughter matured, her preparation for work consisted of domestic work performed under the tutelage of her mother. Fathers could advise and guide, but it was not men's place to teach daughters the domestic arts.

A son's career, however, was much more central to a father's concerns in the antebellum period. It is often thought that as the patriarchal family system deteriorated in the nineteenth century, fathers had less influence over their sons' careers. As Robert Griswold in his history of fatherhood suggests, sons became less likely to follow in their father's footsteps during this period; "In short, the occupational tie between father and son was gradually severed."[10] Fathers not only had less say over what career their sons selected but, generally, were also less able to provide their sons the means for a successful career. "A man's social position depended, in theory, upon his own efforts," writes E. Anthony Rotundo, not the status that his father's position and wealth could attain for him.[11] Thus, when young men entered the world of work, they "often felt as if an audience of friends and family watched their first efforts at success. One youth even imagined an arena full of 'spectators' waiting 'in expectation.'"[12]

Behind this myth of the self-made man, however, lies the mundane reality of family ties and other connections. Historians are finding that working-class and immigrant family ties retained a significant role in job selection and family economic success in the new industrial world of the nineteenth century.[13] It is not surprising, therefore, that family bonds also played an important part in the work and success of middle-class men. In the changing economy of the nineteenth-century North, fathers were less likely to use the transmission of property or skills to establish sons, but most still felt it their duty to provide some kind of assistance. One father, writing to his daughter, complained of his son's lassitude. "Charles is here Idle yet and I do not know what to do with him or for him."[14] Partly fueling this father's frustration was his own unfulfilled obligation; he wanted to make something of his son, even help him in a career, but the son's idleness was thwarting anything that could be done "with him or for him."

Just what fathers did for sons varied considerably. The most obvious kind of aid was money for education or early business or professional ventures. As we have already seen, fathers made important financial contributions to the education of their sons, often exerting great control over the process to ensure the development of the right kinds of skills and values. Oftentimes this financial support continued during college or specialized professional training. Nathaniel Salton-stall, a successful Massachusetts physician, "without reluctance" financially supported his son Levi's training to be a lawyer because he "ever suppos'd it was consonant with your Desires in Respect to Education."[15] Such assistance, however, was meted out judiciously, for it conflicted somewhat with the goal of developing independence in children. On the eve of his search for a job, Levi recorded in his diary, "I hope to become independent; for I have called on my father unceremoniously for supplies long enough, and he has supplied me most liberally."[16] His father concurred, "On reflection you cannot expect I can aid you much more. Your Exertion, and assiduity must in future be your chief Prop, on which to depend."[17] As we shall see, these conflicting paternal goals of support and independence led to significant tensions between fathers and sons in this transition. Financial assistance and aid to careers given by Nathaniel Saltonstall and fathers like him were significant, often providing the margin between success and failure, and sons and fathers knew this. Thus, many sons viewed their father as a bank of first resort, borrowing interest-free money when unable to meet expenses or when investment opportunities arose.

Fathers also provided nonpecuniary forms of assistance: Some wielded their influence to gain positions and opportunities for their sons, while others still took sons into their own offices or shops. This placed them in a strong position to influence their sons' careers—perhaps not as strong as in the old patriarchal system, where the father kept sons on the farm or placed them in apprenticeships of his choosing—but sons had to defer to their fathers enough to receive this kind of help. Paternal advice and direction were to be heeded and followed if sons wished to maintain the benefits of their fathers' money and influence.[18]

Fathers used this ability to influence their sons' career choices in different ways. On one level, many felt that if they were helping with money then it was only prudent and right that they have a say in how it was spent.[19] Most fathers who loaned money, for example, expected an accounting of how their funds were being used. John Wesley North, in debt to his father-in-law, sent a periodic accounting of his investments and business prospects.[20] Funds for school also often came with the same type of obligation. We have already seen how William P. Eaton was required by his father to send home a weekly account of not only his financial expenditures but also the use of his time.[21] Some of these fathers still influenced, and in some cases determined, career choice. As a young man, George Templeton Strong had interests in science, journalism, and teaching, but his father, nearing sixty years of age, wanted a family member to take over his law practice. He insisted that George try law. Since George clerked in his father's office, the elder Strong was also able to oversee the young man's law education and continue to exert considerable control over the process. Significantly, the father paid for the building of a new house for the son when he first married, George dutifully having fulfilled his father's wishes.[22]

While most fathers did not exert this extent of control over their sons' career choices, most seem to have had the right and the inclination to influence their sons' opportunities for education and work. For example, fathers occasionally kept sons from school to help in the family business. Benjamin Stanton, an Ohio doctor, wrote of his son, "Byron is not going to school this winter. I thought that he had better stay at home and help post up accts and make settlements and read in the shop in the meantime."[23] Similarly, Thomas Carter's father owned a farm and carriage-building shop, where Thomas frequently worked in his teenage years. "Just as I was becoming deeply interested in my studies," remembers Carter, "I was obliged to leave school and help my father on the farm and in the shop."[24] However, Carter's father had more in mind for the son than farming and making carriages in the family shop, and soon after sent Thomas to clerk in a store. Storekeeping, however, did not appeal to Thomas, and against the wishes of his father he left the job. The next summer, however, at his father's behest he was back working as a clerk again. "So after due consideration, it was thought best that I should go and 'tend store' again."[25] The passive voice phrase "it was thought best" says much about his father's influence over his work. Eventually, his father's persistence paid off, and Thomas chose to become a merchant.

For lower middle-class fathers, maintaining this level of control was difficult. The closer to working class or subsistence farming a father was, the less likely that he was able to aid his sons financially in building middle-class careers. "I do not know what assistance I can give thee during thy studies," wrote Benjamin Stanton to his son entering the study of law. "I sometimes feel as tho' the draughts made on my pecuniary resources were as great as I could conveniently sustain—yet it is probable if I live and keep my health I may be able to do something for thee."[26] Stanton was a country doctor with few financial resources, but his inability to significantly contribute to his son's studies does not hide the fact that he still felt a strong obligation to assist in some way.

Stanton's situation illustrates the hierarchy of duty for men at this particular stage in their lives. Fathers still had to remain financially solvent in order to provide for their wives and remaining dependent children. Benjamin wrote again to his son two years later, "I am willing to assist thee as far as I can consistently with regard to my own necessities and those of others equally dependent upon me with thyself."[27] The obligation to help sons succeed in their careers was consequential but still of secondary importance to the father's own economic survival. The son, after all, was expected to be on the road to independence and therefore able to take responsibility for his own support—especially in families of limited means.

Benjamin Stanton's inability to provide much financial assistance allowed his sons to make their own career choices. Hoping his two oldest sons would also become doctors, Stanton sought to cultivate an interest in medicine in them. He started them off studying medicine, laying on them the injunction to report to him their "cases," to "get into the habit of writing on medical subjects" and to lecture on medicine whenever possible.[28] But without significant economic inducements, Stanton was unable to do much more than persuade. When one son switched to engineering, Benjamin acquiesced, but asked him to continue to study in the medical field, perhaps hoping that the son would tire of the detour and return to medicine. The tactic failed, however, for the son eventually became a lawyer. Benjamin's other son also chose law over medicine, suggesting the weakness of mere persuasion unaccompanied by financial inducements.

It is not surprising, then, that fathers offering little economic help to their sons sometimes saw sons defy parental wishes concerning careers. Perhaps nothing illustrates this better than the plight of many New England farmers in the antebellum period. Most fathers, hoping for something better for their children, supported their sons' ambitions that would take them away from the small, rocky New England farms, but some tried to prevent sons from leaving. A few were successful, but time and again, throughout the Northeastern part of the country, sons abandoned their fathers' small farms for professional opportunities or business careers in the seaboard cities or in the West. Without a strong economic hold, fathers could do little to force sons to remain.[29]

William Potter and his son, William Jr., were constantly at odds during the son's teenage and young adult years over this very issue.

The father wanted the son to work their small Massachusetts farm, and the son wanted an education. The father could see little use for a college education behind a plow, and kept William from school after he had turned eighteen. But with nothing to offer besides "hard working early to late," William senior had little chance of keeping his son at home under his authority. The younger William eventually completed his college education and became a minister.[30] We should be careful, however, about assuming that men like William Potter, Sr., had no authority. Like most fathers of the time the senior Potter appealed to his son's loyalties and sense of obligation. The son wrote in 1847,

> I spoke to father today in relation to going to Bridgewater [the normal school]. He spoke very discouragingly and almost induced me to resolve to say no more about leaving the farm, but to content myself to remain upon it through life. He overcame my feelings by alluding to the probability that he would not dwell on earth much longer, and that there would then be no one to take his place. In the bitter thought of the moment, I believed that I had been doing wrong, and that it would be right for me to sacrifice all my plans of future life, and live at home as contented as possible. But I am myself again, and reason, and I think I may say conscience, tell me to still press forward, and press forward I must.[31]

William, the son, eventually chose his own path, but this appeal to his sense of duty was quite persuasive. Although William decided to teach school and eventually graduated from Harvard and became a Unitarian minister, anathema to his Quaker father, he still remained under considerable paternal influence. He frequently felt guilty about opposing his father, and in his diary looked for reasons to support his opposition.

> The question has often occurred to me, whether we should be directed entirely as to our employment by the choice of our parents. It seems to me that there is in each of us, something which to point out our allotment—the sphere in which it is designed for us to labor. . . . I would not, without reason, oppose my father's wishes. I exceedingly dislike to do so, even where there is reason for it. Almost gladly would I remain here, did I consider it, for my benefit, and perhaps it will not be too much to add, the benefit of my fellow men.[32]

Nine years later, in the letter written to inform his father of his desire to enter the Unitarian ministry, William again couched his choice in terms of duty. "I cannot, of course, expect that thy acquiescence will be without regret; and this thought causes me not a little anxiety and pain. To thee my course will seem wrong, but to me it seems the path of duty. That credit be given me for this is all I ask for, and this I believe I shall receive."[33] Finally, William's justification traveled full circle to the argument that the values his father wished him to have—chief among them a willingness to fulfill duty—required him to oppose his father's direction. "I could wish that duty pointed otherwise. But, on the other hand, I know that thou thyself would have me follow duty, rather than any such wish."[34] William Potter, Jr.'s, choice to challenge his father's authority was fraught with anxiety and guilt, suggesting that although his father's economic influence over him was minimal, the emotional constraints were still quite strong. Throughout a ten-year period of disagreement, the son still remained close enough to his father to be concerned about how his actions would affect his father's feelings.

Did William Potter, Sr., feel a reciprocating concern for his son's feelings? Unfortunately we do not have his return letters, but it is clear from the son's letters that the father was ambivalent in his response to his son's rebellion. For example, despite his disapproval, the father did give some financial aid to help pay for the son's college education. Also, although there is no indication that he supported William's bid to become a Unitarian minister, he did become reconciled to his son's earlier choice to be a teacher. William Potter, Sr., seems to have respected his son's decisions sufficiently to be willing to mitigate his demands somewhat and thus prevent a break in their relationship.

In his study of Victorian families, Steven Mintz has used the metaphor of a lightning rod to describe the father's place in the nineteenth-century home; because fathers were at the center of the family power structure, they seemed to attract conflict.[35] But fathers did not live in a vacuum; to attract conflict they had to stand in a charged atmosphere that produced it. And the dynamics of relationships with semi-dependent children naturally produced that atmosphere in antebellum America. Not only did fathers have qualms about giving up control of their children, but children also had their own difficulty restraining their desires for freedom, struggling with the mixed signals of freedom and subordination that they received from fathers during this stage.

Meanwhile, teenage children's psychological and physiological development pushed them to explore their world and develop their own independent view of it—no longer was it enough to accept the view dictated by their fathers. And in the end, a society influenced by Enlightenment ideas and industrialization loosened the patriarchal grip, increasingly validating semidependent children's choices. It became the right of children to have a say in their own education, marriage, and careers. In the public places and events increasingly open to teenagers—religious revivals, schools, lyceums, parties, counting houses, mills—young women and men found the spaces necessary to explore that freedom. Yet this process of becoming men and women occurred while still subordinate to their fathers. No wonder, then, that it was during this stage, more than any other, that children and fathers clashed.[36]

We should remember, however, that during the nineteenth century, most children were obedient to their fathers, while most fathers gave their children space to test their new freedoms. Today we assume that as a matter of course children will challenge their parents' authority sometime before they reach adulthood. In the antebellum North, however, the traditions and social supports that sustained the patriarchal family system of the past, although somewhat eroded, were still strong. Most antebellum middle-class children did not openly rebel against their fathers. But unthinking obedience, if it ever was a characteristic of children, certainly was not part of the equation in most families at this time either. Sons and daughters of the middle class, as part of their developing independence, at some point usually examined their fathers critically and questioned much of what they stood for.

The realization that fathers had many human frailties was an important and illuminating early step of this questioning. Sarah Connell, who had a close relationship with her father and often traveled with him on business trips, was indignantly surprised to discover that her father could be quite harsh to a young debtor. "Why will my Father for the trifling sum of 100 dolls. confine within the narrow walls of a prison, a young Man in the bloom of youth. . . . Is he capable of such inhumanity? Benevolence is a duty enjoined by God Himself."[37] The unconscious comparison of her father to "God Himself" shows her disillusionment and discomfort accompanying the revelation of her father's human imperfections. The realization that fathers made mistakes opened the door for a reexamination of their authority.

It is likely, however, that nineteen-year-old Sarah did not confront her father over the matter. Unmarried daughters, after all, were in a constrained position in both the family and society. Unlike sons, they would rarely strike out on their own—the opportunities were just too few. They knew that their place was to always live under the control of men, before and after their marriages.[38] Thus, with fewer options open to them, daughters tended to avoid potentially disruptive behaviors like direct confrontations and open rebellion. Instead, daughters were more likely to challenge fathers indirectly. Some retreated into what Carol Smith-Rosenberg calls "the female world of love and ritual"—the intimate, deeply felt emotional relationships between women that often developed during teenage years.[39] Independent of their fathers, young women in these relationships could find love and support, and even explore values separate from those given them by their parents. Many daughters also participated in the broader heterosexual youth culture that was developing among middle-class teenagers and young adults in the North. Diaries of young women written during this period record pages of religious feeling, friendships, and young loves, while often meticulously avoiding mention of the fathers that lived in the same house.

Other young women used the method of humor to indirectly question their father's authority. While visiting relatives, Elizabeth Babcock wrote to her father, "Just see if I don't give myself airs! If you put your knife into the butter, your gingerbread into your tea, or rap on the table when you want your cup filled—I shall change my boarding place at once."[40] Hidden behind the jocose threat was real tension. Elizabeth resented the imperious rapping for tea (which she probably supplied) as a symbol of the deference she was forced to show to her father. Elizabeth also chose politics to challenge her father, although again it was done with a touch of humor to mask and soften the conflict. "Your consolatory messages in relation to the result of the election, have been quite thrown away upon me. . . . You like to sit in the darkness, and call it light. It is a very sad thing that our house should be divided against itself."[41]

The stakes had to be high for a young woman to directly challenge the position of her father. Almira Bidamon was the illegitimate child of Lewis Bidamon, a Midwest merchant who is probably best known for having married Emma Smith, the widow of Joseph Smith, the Mormon prophet. Almira's mere existence represented a challenge to her father's reputation, yet she was willing to jeopardize his standing in the community by pursuing a relationship with him. "Some of your ennymes [enemies] though[t] they would k[e]ep me blinded so as not to Claim you as a Father but I was never so blinded but what I Could see a little Light on the dark side of the question. I always beleived [sic] you to be my Father. I never dere [sic] mention your name till since I was of age."[42] Almira's desire for recognition by her father was matched by her hope for love. "Dear F, the Love I have for the[e] I cannot express. That Love has ever remained in my bre[a]st from my childhood to the present day but [I] allways [sic] kept it secreted from my relatives."[43] Almira's gamble paid off. Lewis Bidamon, contrary to common practice, acknowledged Almira as his daughter despite the social and economic cost.

More commonly, when daughters directly challenged their father's authority it was through an unsanctioned love affair or marriage. Romantic love and the possible opportunity to free oneself from a father's control occasionally weighed more heavily for some young women than a father's authority and the community's disapproval. Delia Page went to Manchester, New Hampshire, to work in the textile mills in 1859 and there became interested in a male coworker. Her adopted father, through a friend, investigated the young man's background and found he was married and had a child and a reputation as drinker and philanderer.[44] Alarmed, he wrote to Delia, "A person is known by the company he keeps. Therefore avoid him and all like him as you would the Plague."[45] When his daughter continued her love affair he engaged in a rare caution against premarital sex. "Permit no familiarities. They will only lower you in his estimation. For however unprincipaled [sic] a man may be, he always wishes for a virtuous wife. And one whose principals [sic] are strong enough for him to trust. When he is at liberty to give you his hand with his heart will be soon enough for intimacy."[46] All his advice came to naught, however, for Delia lived for a time with her suitor. In the ensuing years, Delia and her adopted father continued to correspond in a relationship remarkably free of stress considering Delia's actions. Perhaps the adoption made their relationship unique. Certainly Delia's direct disobedience placed her in the minority of middle-class daughters.

Although sons who rebelled against their fathers' authority were also in the minority, they were more numerous than their sisters. The greater opportunities for geographical mobility open to sons allowed more of them to directly challenge their fathers' authority by leaving home. In nineteenth-century America it was more acceptable for a teenage boy to be on his own than even today. Without compulsory education or the restrictions on hiring underage workers, there were more options open to boys, although it usually meant a significant decline in class status. By trading the support system of the family for freedom and independence, these young men were in effect serving notice that they no longer considered themselves dependents in need of parental guidance. In some cases young men were merely trying to escape abusive fathers, but in most instances, running away was a statement of independence and willingness to meet the world on their own terms, not those of their fathers.

It also seems that sons were more likely to rebel against fathers than daughters because their relationship was laden with higher expectations, and thus more tension. As Stephen M. Frank notes, fathers' economic relationship with sons contributed to resentment. Rural sons often did not care for their fathers' exploitation of their labor, while urban sons sometimes resented the financial obligations that they incurred through their education.[47] Moreover, sons had the difficult task of trying to be like and yet unlike their fathers. As E. Anthony Rotundo has shown, middle-class men were supposed to develop an identity "founded on independent action, cool detachment, and sober responsibility. Men aimed to make themselves individual actors, differentiated and separate from all others in a middle-class workplace that was open and fluid. Adult male identity—so detached and independent—contrasted with that of adult females, which was built on interdependence and connection."[48] Therefore, as sons matured, society told them that they were supposed to be independent, yet at the same time they usually needed help in establishing themselves, and fathers felt a strong responsibility to see them successfully placed in a career. The irony and tension of this conflict are evinced in the following passage written by one young man to his brother: "Sometimes father talks of making a farmer of me, and sometimes a printer, and sometimes a revolutionary pensioner, don't know yet what he will do. Don't know but it is doubtful about his making anything of me."[49]

Quite often a son's rebellion was sparked by a dispute with the father over the future course of the son's life. In 1859, not long after Lester Burnett told his son, Edward, of his plans for Edward's education and working arrangements, the son left home in protest. This, however, was merely the culmination of some months of antagonism between the two. The son had come to resent his father's efforts to govern him, and prior to this crisis, Edward had been challenging

Lester's control in a less direct manner. He had often told his mother, Olive, that "he would leave his father," and while working away from home one summer had begun drinking, much to the disappointment of his parents.[50]

In the early stages of Edward's rebellion, Lester, like any good father, stepped up his efforts to put his son back on the right path. He emphasized the importance of following the proper middle-class avenues to success—perseverance, controlling one's passions, temperance, hard work—but he also appealed to any other hold he had on Edward. These included giving money and occasional small gifts and asking Edward's older brother to encourage good behaviors in his brother. Edward viewed this effort to direct his life as an intrusion, which contributed to his decision to leave home.[51] After Edward left, Lester, who believed that he was only trying to do his duty as a father, felt betrayed and vented some of his frustrations on his wife. Olive, who acted at times as a mediator and conciliator between her husband and son, recorded that when Lester packed up Edward's things (presumably to send them to wherever Edward went), he would not allow her to see them, nor read the letter he wrote to Edward. Lester clearly viewed the conflict as one exclusively between himself and Edward, and did not want Olive's interference.[52]

Lester Burnett's sense of betrayal was common for fathers whose sons left home prematurely. Not only was the action an affront to the father's authority, but it also frequently represented a rejection of the values held dear by the father. In most of the cases observed in the sources, the rebellious son abandoned the religious beliefs and practices of the father. Many also turned to acknowledged challenges to proper middle-class values, such as drinking and gambling. To deny the inherent value of the beliefs that the father lived by was to strike at the very identity of the man. Thus, some fathers initially responded by disinheriting or taking other drastic measures that broke the links between fathers and sons.

The evidence suggests, however, that after the heat of confrontation cooled, most fathers and sons sought some kind of reconciliation. In all but one instance of a son's rebellion in the sources, fathers and sons reestablished their relationship.[53] In some cases the son, like the prodigal, was eventually repentant. One rebellious son, for example, reported to his sister that he had turned over a new leaf—going to church and "attending to Father's business."[54] This did not mean that reconciliation always brought a fundamental change in the way father and son viewed each other. Edward Burnett moved to join his brother in California where he began to correspond again with his father, but tensions remained between them. Lester continued to give advice and try to shape his son from afar, and Edward still seemed reluctant to listen. However, the distance probably eased the conflict between them.

Rebellion usually illuminated for the father the growing independence of a son, and eventually most men had to acknowledge the son's right to run his own life. Levi Ray's relationship with his son Charles took just such a turn. Levi, the owner of a blacksmith shop and foundry in Norwich, New York, believed in involving himself heavily in his sons' affairs, but upon hearing that twenty-year-old Charles had left the study of medicine for a career at sea he had to admit he could no longer control his son's decisions. "I never dreamed of your going a voyage to sea [y]et I do not oppose it." Levi had no choice but to commit his son's safety to God and hope that he would return home again, "with improved health and with correct business habits."[55] Still, Levi hoped to retain some influence in Charles' life. Levi particularly feared his son's tractable nature, considering him "something of a Chamelion [sic], taking the hue of the objects nearest you or in other words assimilating yourself to the company you are in."[56] Fearing Charles would pick up the rough habits of fellow sailors, he tried to enlist the aid of one of Charles' friends, offering to pay his way to join Charles at sea to provide a good influence on Charles.[57] Levi also continued to advise his son to read the Bible, increase his store of knowledge, and practice perseverance, proper moral conduct, and economy.

It is clear, however, that Levi began to accept his son's right to make his own decisions. After two years abroad, Charles returned to the United States to resume his study of medicine. In his letters, Levi began to discuss politics with Charles, ask financial favors and advice of him, and appeal to him to give some "fatherly" advice to Charles' younger brother. "Show him the rock on which you split. . . . [H]e is out a good deal nights, and does not obey fully when I tell him to be in every night and in good season."[58] Levi still gave Charles pointed advice, but he also began to treat him like an adult.

For most fathers and sons, distance and the eventual acceptance of the son's statement of independence lessened the tension between them. But more significantly, most sons did not maintain a concerted challenge of middle-class values for very long. Rebellious sons often temporarily abandoned these values as symbols of their fathers' authority, but after separation the need to challenge no longer existed.

When faced with finding a place in the world, these young men usually returned to the established ideas of success, morality, and work with which they were familiar—those taught to them by their fathers and mothers. Culturally, these young men remained middle class. Drinking, gambling, and even sexual experimentation were becoming increasingly associated with working-class leisure patterns during the early industrial period. Thus, junior clerks, college students, and budding merchants dabbled and experimented with such behaviors, but they knew that their success ultimately depended on publicly renouncing them.[59]

If children still needed something to rebel against, religion, as some historians have pointed out, provided abundant opportunities to assert independence without rejecting middle-class values. Sons and daughters could, in opposition to their fathers, reject established religion in general, change sects, or participate in the evangelical revivals of the time and still find acceptance in the community as long as basic Christian morality was not challenged.[60] Benjamin Hodge, for example, reported that while newly married but still living with his father's family,

> a most animated dispute took place between my aged father & myself on the doctrine of Universlvation [sic]—he contended for that dangerous doctrine & myself opposed it on gospel grounds, the old gentleman contended with great earnestness & more than once tears came into his eyes & his speech almost failed him. We both felt unpleasant but far from being angry but pitied each other for blindness on gospel grounds.[61]

It is clear from Benjamin's journal that there were other problems in his relationship with his father, suggesting that tensions stemming from his semidependent status (living at home) exacerbated the religious conflict.

There were, however, important factors in a minority of father-child relationships that prevented easy reconciliation. For a few fathers and their children, the conflict ran deeper than religious difference or stresses over growing up. Occasionally children made choices in their adult lives that permanently incorporated their rebellion against paternal authority, such as William Potter's decision to abandon Quakerism and become a Unitarian minister and Delia Page's choice to live with her married lover. Such choices could per-

petuate tension for years. Other children held deep-seated psychological resentments against their fathers that prevented any significant
mitigation of strained relationships. William Brown, against the
advice of his family, left home to look for gold in California, but
despite the distance William's relationship with his father did not
improve. If anything, his independence and a successful express mail
business provided him with the means to continue to challenge his
father. Indeed, his satisfaction at succeeding while his father's business
was actually failing was part of a complex relationship that included
warring desires both to reconcile and also to usurp his father's place
in the family structure. In Brown's correspondence with his father he
occasionally expressed his filial piety, but in letters to his mother and
siblings he was openly critical of his father. With proceeds from his
new business, William purchased a home for his mother, refusing any
assistance from the father. "If Father has paid any money from his
pocket for the house &c he can present his bill & get the money
refunded," he wrote to his mother. "I wish the property to be yours &
not be mixed with any other business."[62] Ostensibly, he wished to
protect his mother against his father's potential business failure, but it
is clear that William enjoyed the idea of paying for the home independent of his father. William also gave advice to his sister on marriage and chided his father on "making my back black & blue" in
earlier years. He even condescendingly wished his father luck in his
business efforts, writing "hope you will not get discouraged if you fail
in your young days."[63] Brown never overcame the resentment he felt
toward his father. Three years after leaving home he was shot and
killed in Stockton, California, by the clerk of his own company.

One possible explanation of Brown's persistent resentment may lie
in the corporal punishment he received at the hands of his father.
Phillip Greven has suggested that "whippings" like those that produced bruises on William Brown's back often result in hate and rage
against the assailant that can shape the psyche of the child "long after
the original pain has subsided and been forgotten or denied."[64] While
most tension between fathers and children at this stage in the family
cycle seems to have been temporary and eventually overcome, some
relationships had this darker stain of abuse that was undoubtedly
more damaging. While it may be true that men were and are generally
more aggressive than women, thus partially explaining why fathers
were more likely to abuse children than mothers, this study agrees
with Linda Gordon's assessment that family violence should be under-

stood in terms of the struggle for power within the family.[65] Men may have been more disposed to abuse children, but their place as the dominant power in the home definitely gave them the opportunity to be the primary perpetrators of domestic abuse. When fathers abused semidependent children it was usually in the context of the tensions over the growing independence of the child and the father's desire to retain control.

David Garrett, a minor customs official in Cleveland, Ohio, verbally and psychologically abused his stepson, John, over disobedience to rules that were overly stringent. Patty Garret, John's mother, reported to a relative that her husband "grows worse & worse to live with, is more fractious & exacting, he controls all the means & is more indolent if possible than before he went into the custom house. Being a subordinate there, he has to control himself & his ill humor is all visited upon his family. John's situation here is worse than being in Catholic purgatory, indeed something must be done or he [John] will be ruined."[66] David Garrett's disposition did not improve, however. He locked John out of the house when the son came home after curfew and at one point called John "a poor miserable good for nothing dog" and wished him dead and out of his sight.[67] Not long after, John left home to live with his brother.

Unfortunately, it is almost impossible to determine how widespread abuse was in the nineteenth century. The fact that few middle-class children openly rebelled against their fathers does not necessarily indicate a low incidence of abuse. We know that not all abused children rebel against their abuser. Some sublimate, deny, or even turn on themselves the resulting feelings of anger and hatred, often experiencing ambivalence or even loyalty to the abuser.[68] For example, the harsh treatment of William Brown by his father seems to have contributed to a surprisingly ambivalent feeling toward his father. Recalling a specific beating, William Brown wrote, "I think that whipping did me more real good than all the schools could ever do."[69] But in the cases examined here of the Brown and Garrett families, as the abused child neared adulthood he actively endeavored to leave home, suggesting that some children departed from home not looking forward but backward, seeking freedom from a past of verbal, sexual, or physical abuse.

It is likely that the incidences of abuse and rebellion were more numerous than the correspondence records—families that fought would tend to correspond less than harmonious ones. But the middle-class family by its nature emphasized cooperation, love, and order. The intergenerational tensions that arose between fathers and semi-dependent children usually did not permanently tear the fabric of family connections. At the point of marriage, the final step in separating from father and family, most children were still in good standing with their fathers. For most, the occasion of marriage was remarkably free of overt conflict. Family historians have shown how in the eighteenth century the decline of marriage as a property transaction increasingly opened the way for the marriage decision to be determined on the basis of romantic love and compatibility. As marriage became less a financial transaction and more a union of individuals who made their own choice, there was less tension between fathers and children over the matter.[70]

By the antebellum period, the practice of allowing children to make their own choice in marriage was widespread and generally accepted by courting couples and their fathers. Upon receiving a letter from his twenty-four-year-old son stating his desire to marry, Henry Sewall, who practiced law in Maine, wrote back,

> Although this contemplated event is to me unexpected, yet I cannot find it in my heart on a consideration of all circumstances within my knowledge to disapprove. The parties being of age and competent to forming the marriage contract, and having pledged their hearts how can I object to the formal pledge of their hands? And being themselves the persons immediately concerned they doubtless ought to be the most competent judges in the case.[71]

Three years earlier, in 1818, Henry's son left his home in Augusta, Maine, to take a position as a school teacher in Boston. On his twenty-first birthday William Sewall wrote, "This day I am free from father's family. No more I consider myself dependent on him for sufficiency in life."[72] William's choice to marry was merely the final step in that process. William wanted his father's blessing, but even his father could see that this was a "transaction which it seems you have deliberately settled in your own mind."[73] Henry hoped that this "important decision" had been made with suitable caution and reflection, but also believed that William had the right to make the final decision.

There were limits, however, to the freedom given children in matters of marriage. Fathers frowned on early marriages. Daughters in their early teens and sons who had not yet started a career were considered too young. Fathers were usually able to exercise veto power when a child tried to marry too early. When Hamilton Colton's fourteen-year-old daughter had a suitor calling on her "two or three times a day," he noted, "considering her age, I felt called upon to check it. . . . I want very much to give Lina a chance to see something more of the world & its inhabitants before she makes any entangling alliances."[74] The two lovers obeyed his wishes and remained apart. Fathers also expected children to choose to marry within the proper racial and social group. An admonition of a father to his daughter found in an advice book published in 1806 articulates this position: "I could never pretend to advise whom you should marry; but I can with great confidence advise whom you should not marry."[75] Keith Spence, from his position as a distant father, informed his wife, "I am for letting Harriet & all of them have their own way in that important concern, (Matrimony) as far as is consistent with Virtue and Honor."[76] Because class identification was based as much on morality as economic status, "Virtue and Honor" required the choice of a middle-class spouse. Fathers commonly sought to influence their children's circle of friends of the opposite sex, and if necessary could use their veto power when they felt a child had begun showing interest in the wrong people.

Some fathers were pleased by their children's marriage choice. After doing all that they could do to influence the process—inculcating the desire in their children to find mates who conformed to middle-class standards and controlling courtship opportunities—their children chose spouses from the socially acceptable group. John Milton Putnam spoke glowingly to his daughter Antoinette of her new husband, Isaac Metcalf. "It is rare that a young lady gets a husband that can take them [sic] over the quagmire, & sloughs, & 'mud' of this world, as the children of Israel were taken over the red sea [sic], dry shod. What a delightful palanque you have to ride in, the arms of Isaac! What mandarin of the Celestial empire [sic] ever rode so beautifully, or in so finely constructed & costly a carriage? Well, I rejoice that you are so well provided for."[77]

When children contemplated marriage, fathers were generally more protective of their daughters than of their sons. In each instance in the sources where a father vetoed a marriage choice, it was in the case of a daughter. Whether this indicates a greater control over daughters than sons is not clear. It is possible that fathers felt that daughters needed more guidance—daughters made the choice earlier and usually were still living at home. John Putnam clearly did not trust his youngest daughter's judgment when he wrote his son-in-law Isaac concerning her suitor. "He is certainly a young man of good appearance, & I presume of very respectable talents. But he is supposed to want enterprise, & firmness of purpose, & I think Jenny is quite too young yet to engage herself to such a man, especially as he is destitute of piety, which, (as you suggest) is the most of all to be regretted."[78] A case can be made that antebellum fathers believed that women were more susceptible to the influences of the heart, and thus more likely to make a mistake in this decision. Fathers like John Putnam feared that daughters, basing their decision on their emotions, might make an irreparable mistake that would deprive them of a chance for happiness. As one father wrote, "That love is blind with one eye & sees but poorly with the other is undoubtedly true. We look upon the best side of those we love. And are apt to think that any little defect we cannot avoid seeing will easily be cured by our affection and wisdom."[79] Yet in middle-class society at this time sons' judgment was also questioned. As noted by the nineteenth-century author of a book entitled *Letters from a Father to His Son, On Various Topics Relative to Literature and the Conduct of Life*, the choice of a wife was the season when a father's advice "produces the least effect" because "passion commonly takes this affair under its management, and excludes reason from her share of the deliberation."[80] Fathers were aware that sons and daughters were making marriage choices based on an emerging ideal that emphasized emotion over reason. Most felt it their duty to see that reason tempered emotional enthusiasm.

Some paternal protectiveness toward daughters of a marriageable age seems to have been caused by the reluctance of fathers to see their daughters become independent of their control. Fathers hoped to have daughters marry well and be happy, but they were also reluctant to relinquish the provider and protector roles that defined their relationships with daughters. Sons at the time of marriage were usually well on that road to economic independence, meaning that they had already severed many of the ties between themselves and their fathers. But until the father gave away his daughter to another man, he was the authority figure and primary man in her life. The hesitation evident in Daniel Dickson's comments at the beginning of this chapter illustrates this concern. But Dickson's belief that marrying off a daughter was a "fearful responsibility to discharge" suggests a worry deeper than such selfish motives. Most likely, fathers' interest in controlling the marriage choice of their daughters stemmed from the assumption that a bad marriage was harder on a woman than a man. When Thomas Jefferson estimated that his daughter had a fourteen-to-one chance of drawing a "blockhead" for a husband, he understood that women were at the economic mercy of their husbands' willingness to fulfill the provider role.[81] Fathers knew that marriage was, in the words of one father, "an engagement for life," and that "a very large portion" of a child's future happiness depended on making a wise choice.[82] Delia Page's adoptive father, Luther Trussell, fearing that "a mistake made in a moment may be lamented a lifetime," wrote to her in 1860.

> You now feel & enjoy independence trusting to your own ability to procure whatever you want, leaning on no one[,] no one depending on you. Change your condition by uniting your destiny to another (however good and great he may be) and this feeling is gone—gone forever. Whether that which follows will be more or less agreeable depends entirely on the fitness of the union. And as this union is usually for life it is of the utmost consequence that we make a deliberate and wise choice.[83]

There is a hint of insincerity in Luther's plea. He would never advocate that Delia seek to enjoy the fruits of independence for the rest of her life. Luther was instead hoping to prevent her from making a choice that she would rue the rest of her life. Still, it was Delia's decision. Fathers like Luther Trussell had considerable influence through cajolery, appeals to duty, appeals to love, or restricting the arena of courting, but if the child was of age the choice was in most cases not the father's. The "fearful" responsibility of letting children make their own choices—even wrong choices—was one of the last great tasks of the father.

The marriage of a daughter or son marked the end of many of the duties and rights of fatherhood. But the marriage of a child also signaled the beginning of a new stage in the father's life. The relinquishment of most of their authority over their children, and the accompanying easing of tensions, created new opportunities for men in their relationships with their children. Once they accepted their daughters and sons as adults, they then could make business and political alliances with them, seek advice from them, and develop a different brand of love and companionship.

However, while independent in theory, many children still relied on periodic financial assistance from their fathers. This aid could be as trivial as the borrowing of a horse or something as important as the borrowing of hundreds of dollars for a business venture. The example of George Loomis illustrates the extent of this kind of arrangement. Loomis' daughter Ann married John Wesley North and moved from New York to Minnesota. As we have seen, during the 1850s, North speculated in land and railroad ventures, and at one time owned a sawmill. George Loomis was a frequent source of cash for these investments. In the transaction, the Norths had the advantage of low interest loans and a creditor who allowed them to be flexible in their payments. Ann North wrote,

> My kindest of Parents, I believe I fully appreciate your goodness to us, as does my husband—and you must know, now that you have helped us to independence of the people here, that we shall now devote our energies to paying our debts to you. I confess very frankly to you, that although our indebtedness is very great I feell [sic] much easier that it is all to you, although our haste to release ourselves, entirely, is not in the least diminished.[84]

Children often paid a nonfinancial price for this service. Debt to a father brought with it the obligation of deference to the creditor. John Wesley North chafed at times under this burden. After Loomis had mildly reprimanded him for a bad investment, John wrote back with a hint of sarcasm, "You may rest assured I shall follow your counsel and not 'get' myself 'into another such scrape.'"[85] Another time, Ann North admitted to her father that John felt dreadful about asking for money and "disliked very much to trouble you with this matter as he was, he said, already under so much obligation to you."[86] Although North regretted the necessity of borrowing from Loomis, and "resolutely determined to be independent," he still felt the advantages of the arrangement outweighed borrowing from another source or going without.[87]

As sons and sons-in-law became established, many became capable of giving advice or financial assistance to fathers. For example, John Wesley North repaid his father-in-law by offering investment opportunities in Minnesota land. Occasionally, fathers who learned their business skills in a less complicated age turned to their sons for guidance. After inheriting $25,000, a small fortune for the time, John

Taylor Gilman asked the advice of his son in "vesting" the money. "It is not earning anything and I am at a loss how or where to place it."[88] Fathers also occasionally borrowed money from sons, although this happened less often than the reverse. It is important to note that this economic cooperation between children and fathers differed from the support fathers gave dependent and semidependent children. In almost every case the assistance was considered a loan, and the transaction was conducted as a business proposition between equal parties, not as provider and dependent. There still existed ties of obligation unique to family relationships, but because the interaction was made along more egalitarian lines, its character was fundamentally different.

Children still owed fathers a certain amount of deference, but as daughters and sons married, moved out of their fathers' homes, and began families of their own, they began to interact more with their parents as equals. Sons shared with their fathers the responsibility of the provider role, but also the brotherhood of the political male. Sons could be found alongside fathers (both literally and metaphorically) in the ranks of local militias and political parties. Levi Saltonstall wrote to his daughter of the initiation of his son into the world of party politics. "Your brother to day for the first time exercised his right of voting and you may rest assured it was on the side of justice, decency and good government. Though the whole state shall change and meanly cringe at the feet of Jefferson, and bow at the alter of Jacobinism, one federalist, 'true to the core' shall remain in Your Brother."[89] Historian Jean Baker's argument that sons learned party allegiance at home is corroborated by the evidence found in the sources used for this study.[90] Like Levi Saltonstall's son, young men usually followed their fathers' political inclinations. Charles Daniell wrote to his father from California, "I heard a kind of rumor some years ago that you had so far fallen into the tide of those down East isues [sic] as to be rather tainted with the free-soilism doctrine, I hope it isn't so. You didn't bring me up to any outside doctrines of politics or anything else."[91]

Fathers occasionally discussed politics with their daughters, but such conversations were generally of a different tenor. In the father's eyes, once a daughter married she was first and foremost a wife and then, usually not long after that, a mother. Thus, when fathers interacted with married daughters it was often concerning these important new roles. Fathers encouraged their daughters to be good wives. "Be all that a wife can be, in ministering to his comfort, & adding to the amount of his genuine bliss," wrote one father to his newly married daughter.[92] Once grandchildren appeared on the scene, fathers sometimes gave advice to daughters on a range of domestic tasks, including childrearing, living arrangements, purchasing furniture, children's diet, and exercise needs.[93] These admonitions were suggestions and not commands, as they might have been construed under different circumstances. Indeed, although many fathers were still full of advice on how their children should live their lives, father's letters to married children tended to become less didactic and authoritative, more trusting and confident in their children's ability to make good choices.

It is difficult to generalize concerning the relationships of middle-class empty-nest fathers and their children. The amount of interaction and influence men had in their adult children's lives varied. Some maintained a sizeable amount of control through the same economic and psychological influences that they possessed over their children in earlier years. Others only gave occasional suggestions. Some lived great distances from children, while others lived next door; some fathers had to rely on the mail, others could visit daily. But it is clear that the last son or daughter leaving home usually marked the beginning of the last major change in the life course of the father. Given the late marriage patterns and the life expectancy of middle-class men in the antebellum North, most fathers were quite old when they entered this last stage.

For some fathers these twilight years were pleasant, while others experienced health problems and financial woes. Fathers who had governed households and dictated behavior sometimes found the tables turned as children became empowered. For both fathers and children, the experience could be unsettling. Thomas Kilby Smith's aging father began to exhibit signs of senility, and Smith's concern, although hidden behind humor, can be seen in the letter he wrote to his mother. "As for Father what new vagary has found its way into his head now? He has sent up for *military* pantaloons & a vast list of other garments sufficient to fit a man out for a California expedition. Tell him that now [that] he is out from under my care I hope he'll try & behave himself & not go to rigging himself out like a . . . Militia Captain. I shall send to day by the *Columbia* such articles as I think you *need*."[94] Behind the humor of Smith's exaggerations lies a real concern for his parents' finances; his father's inability to work meant that his parents could not afford frivolous and eccentric buying sprees. Smith's concern was exacerbated by his inability to provide much financial help.

Men like Smith and his father were caught in the middle of a major economic transformation that produced disparities between expectations and realities. In earlier times, aging fathers had strategies based on an agrarian economy to cope with old age. Members of the middling ranks had farms or shops that they could turn over to a son or relative on the condition that a portion of the income be set aside for their support. Aged men might also move in with a daughter, son, or other relative and contribute to the family economy by providing knowledge and limited labor. While not resembling anything like what we would call planned retirement, these strategies generally prevented older men from falling into abject poverty. As the American economy commercialized and fewer men worked as farmers and artisans, however, these kinds of coping methods became less effective. Wage labor gradually replaced property as the basis for middle-class status, making aged fathers more economically vulnerable, for they had little to offer a son or daughter's family economy. Their knowledge, skills, and labor were not marketable in the new economic environment. Even their property—usually a home or sometimes a small farm—could not provide a comfortable income as property once might have. These changes meant not only that aged fathers had fewer resources, but also that their children's ability to help them had declined.

Yet children like Thomas Kilby Smith still felt obligated to try, and recent research has shown that most aged parents in the nineteenth century ended up living with their children; either they moved in with a son or daughter or at least one child never left his or her father's home.[95] Family members were the first ones to turn to when need arose. James Bell's aged father was unable to work and support his family, prompting Bell to write to his fiancée, "Now I feal [sic] it my duty to take care of them [his parents] while they live. It will be a task, but I can do it cheerfully for them."[96] Lincoln Clark expressed a similar sentiment to his father: "I feel that a child can scarcely have any excuse for neglecting his parents in any way, especially when they are advanced in years."[97] At times, economic realities thwarted filial piety. Lincoln Clark sent his wife and children to live with his parents not long after the aforementioned letter, but the arrangement was only temporary. Living several days' journey away from his parents and having financial problems himself, Clark could offer little practical help. "I hope they will see the force of my views and not think me selfish," wrote Clark to his wife Julia, "nothing would afford me more pleasure more real satisfaction than to pass the remainder of their days with them and do them all the good in my power—but they will see and feel that it is right for me to provide for a growing family whose wants are fast increasing; and still I trust God will provide for them."[98] Despite a strong sense of duty toward his parents, Clark's obligation was first to his own wife and children.

In an age before welfare, however, families sometimes had no choice but to care for aged fathers. When poor health or limited finances made it impossible for men to continue to provide for themselves, most moved in with children. For those that did take this step, it was almost always a difficult transition. Often unable to discern the larger forces that made them vulnerable in the first place, they blamed themselves for their weakness or failure. And to compound matters, the reversal of roles that accompanied the change usually did not sit well with them; after years of independence and acting as provider and protector of their families, dependent status galled them. "It has always appeared to me to be very undesirable to outlive one's usefulness," wrote John Putnam to his daughter and son-in-law. "The idea of living on, without doing any good—a mere incumbrance [sic] upon society & burden to friends, is to me truly dreadful. When I cease to be useful, my prayer is, 'Lord, let thy servant depart in peace.'"[99]

Unfortunately for Putnam, he lived for many years unable to "be useful." Some years before his death, his eyesight began to fail, putting his livelihood as a minister in jeopardy. For a time his wife read to him and he preached from memory, but eventually he had to retire. On a minister's salary he was unable to save much for retirement, which meant that for the last years of their lives, he and his wife were financially dependent on their children. He wrote to his daughter of an offer made to him by his son.

> George has invited us to live with him. He said, the last time he was at home, to his parents—'I owe you a living, for the care of my childhood.' It was very pleasant to us to hear such an expression of filial gratitude. But we shall not accept of a living on any such score as this. We intend he shall never owe us any less than he does now. We do not calculate to draw our support from his salary; but think there may be mutual advantage from associating our families together, rather than keeping up two establishments with only two persons in each family.[100]

The arrangement, however, was not successful. John Putnam's wife died not long after moving in with George, exacerbating John's sense of worthlessness. George Putnam reported to his sister, "Since Mother's death he has been very discontented. He said himself, 'I feel like a wanderer. I do not know where to go—nor what to do with myself. It seem[s] as if there was no place for me.'"[101] John Milton Putnam left his son's house to go live with his daughter. George wrote, "I felt that I could not let him go. But of course it was my duty to yield. I am willing to submit to anything that will add to his comfort & happiness, but I am afraid he will not find much more real happiness this side of the grave."[102]

Fathers who lived with children sometimes expressed their discomfort by being fractious and uncooperative. After Sara Ayer's mother died, she invited her father to live with her so that she could keep house for him. Instead he hired a servant, maintaining his independence for several more years until a stroke forced him to turn to his daughter. He clearly resented his dependence. "My father is unwell and so childish and unreasonable," wrote Sarah, "that I know not how to act towards him, as it seems as though he is determined not to be pleased with anything I did for him." The father further vexed Sarah by being a bad example to her children. "He often utters sentiments before my children which it is improper for them to hear, and which grieves me to the heart. If I attempt to say anything to him on religious subjects, he is either irretated [sic], or laughs at me; so that I fear to say anything to him."[103] Sarah Ayer's father, in the last stage of his life, became a father in title only.

From the relationships that aging fathers had with their children, we get hints as to the depth and complexity of the antebellum father-child tie. The obligation to provide for a father in the last years of his life illustrates the persistence of duty and love, which were inseparable in this culture. The societal expectations that required children to care for their aged fathers illustrate that elements of a more traditional fatherhood persisted in antebellum society. Conflicts that arose in the course of these new arrangements show that the tie retained considerable psychological importance. Some tension undoubtedly stemmed from past difficulties, while others formed anew. But for many fathers and their children, this last stage culminated in a more mature relationship that developed between two adults.

Men who came to this final stage of life stood at the intersection of changes that they could not avoid—their own aging, the maturing of their children, and the growth of a society where conventions that had protected the aged in times past were being undermined. In the twentieth century, perhaps children like Sarah Ayer would have placed their irascible fathers in rest homes, arguing (with some justification in Sarah's case) that it would be in her father's best interests to retain some independence from her. Aged fathers' reticence to turn to their children for aid, and their unease when it was unavoidable, stemmed from long years of acting in the roles of governor, educator, and provider. To become a dependent seemed unnatural to them. Their discomfort was exacerbated since they had to turn to those whom they had once given nourishment, help, and guidance. Not all men lived long enough to go through this dependent stage, but for those that did, it marked the end of their fatherhood role. That it took some form of debilitation to bring about the end of this role suggests how essential fatherhood was to middle-class men's lives in the antebellum era.

Conclusion

A sa Bailey, a moderately prosperous New Hampshire farmer, owned two hundred acres of land and between forty and fifty head of cattle in 1788. In December, according to an account left to us by his wife Abigail, Asa Bailey began to try to seduce his teenage daughter. He spent his time "in telling idle stories, and foolish riddles, and singing songs to her . . . wishing to make her free and sociable, and to erase from her mind all that fear and reserve, which he had ever taught his children to feel toward him. He had ever been sovereign, severe and hard with his children, and they stood in the greatest fear of him." The daughter resisted his advances and tried to avoid his company, "But as his will had ever been the law of the family, she saw no way to deliver herself from her cruel father. Such were her fears of him that she did not dare to talk with me, or any other person, upon her situation."[1] Eventually the father turned to violence, beating his daughter "with a beach stick, large enough for the driving of a team."[2] Abigail Bailey never described the circumstances under which rape occurred, but later in the account she does confirm that her husband committed incest. Despite Abigail's pleadings to the daughter to stay and testify against her father, the daughter left home when she turned eighteen and took no action against Asa Bailey for his crimes.[3]

Eventually, Asa gave Abigail legal cause to divorce him, but the extent to which he could abuse his children and wife with impunity is truly disturbing. During the course of the narrative, Abigail records that Asa committed adultery with a servant, raped and savagely beat his daughter, abandoned his children, and kidnapped his wife, taking her from New Hampshire to New York against her will. Even after these gross violations of his paternal stewardship, society still empowered Asa Bailey. At one point in this bizarre story, while under arrest for his crimes, Asa sent all his children away in an attempt to keep them from Abigail. She appealed to a lawyer for legal recourse but was told "the law [gave] a man a right to move his children where he should think best, and the wife had no right by law to take them from him."[4]

There is no question that Asa Bailey represents the darkest side of the patriarchal family system. The latitude that he had to viciously abuse his family stemmed from the power given to men by pre-1800 traditions and institutions of society; the law gave Bailey legal control of his children and the right to inflict harsh punishment, religion and received morality emphasized family obedience to the patriarch, and societal expectations of female purity prevented a frightened daughter from publicly condemning him. Clearly he held considerable power in this society. If we use Bailey's story as a starting point, we can see how paternal authority has declined since the eighteenth century. Although disturbed men like Bailey still live among us today, their ability to harm is circumscribed by greater awareness and preventive resources. Today a teacher or neighbor might notify authorities after noticing a child's bruises, or the victim might turn to one of the various social agencies for help. Under our current legal system Abigail also would have found it easier to prosecute her husband or obtain a divorce. These checks upon arbitrary acts by abusive men clearly show that men's power in our society is no longer as unchallenged as it was in the early national period.

This study has emphasized how men held domestic power in the antebellum period, with an eye to overturning a widely accepted image of the distant and powerless nineteenth-century father. We have seen how these men wielded family income, used their superior physical size, and manipulated sentiment to influence children. We have seen them share with wives and children domestic power over both mundane decisions and life-changing choices. In the process of showing this persistence of power, however, we have touched upon changes that anticipate and even indicate the decline of paternal place and power. In concluding this study, we need to address how fathers' power waned over time.

Although men's domestic power was varied and complex in the nineteenth century, it can be grouped into two broad subcategories—

men's control over family members' access to society (the market, education, and community) and their direct influence through a physical and emotional relationship with the child. Asa Bailey's ability to terrorize his family resided within both of these categories. His legal and economic place as head of the family insulated him from societal censure for an amount of time that seems unfathomable by today's standards, while his superior physical strength and domineering nature emboldened him to commit his crimes in the first place. But this arbitrary power was being undermined long before Bailey's time. Even before 1788, legal, religious, and educational changes began to challenge men's insular position by limiting their control over family members' access to society. Men as a group maintained dominance over businesses, schools, and government, but individual fathers still lost power to these same institutions, as many of their duties and powers were taken up by them. Institutional patriarchy thus persisted and even expanded under the growth of the capitalist economy, but paternal patriarchy declined.[5] Likewise, men's power through their personal relationships changed as new ideas about love and the rights of children influenced father-child relationships.

When examining patriarchal decline, we need to keep the complexity of men's power in mind; not all changes reduced fathers' power and authority in the home. For example, we have seen how middle-class men used their new role as sole breadwinner in the nineteenth century to augment their domestic power. In a society where consumption was increasingly a measure of class status, wives and children were dependent upon men's access to the market. Sons particularly looked to their fathers' financial help for education and early business ventures. But at the same time that men came to control funds coming into the family, children were enjoying greater access to other parts of society. Young women and men flocked to the revivals of the antebellum period, often without their fathers, and began to experience intensely personal religious experiences on their own. Unlike the Puritan era, in which fathers were intermediaries between their children and the church, popular evangelical religion allowed teenagers direct access to God and religious experience. Moreover, as religious culture became further secularized in the nineteenth century, books and schools vied with parents for the job of teaching morality.

The rise of public education in the nineteenth century is usually cited as the primary contributor to fathers' declining control over children's access to society. The importance of paternal instruction in the lives of colonial children has probably been overstated in American historiography, but whatever role fathers filled as instructor of secular knowledge was largely taken over by schools in the nineteenth century. Antebellum fathers, as we have seen, imparted considerable advice on morality and religion, but their place as a secular tutor was limited for the most part to a part-time role. But here again the story is a bit more complex than this simple formulation. The rise in the significance of education also added to men's power by virtue of their control over funds for tuition, books, and room and board when schooling required the student to live away from home. Thus, while men's instruction probably declined, they still exercised considerable authority over access to education.

The one source of paternal power absent from much of this book's debate is men's connection to the polis. The sources used in this study were not conducive to an exploration of fathers' legal and political rights, but changes in law clearly played a part in the decline of unqualified patriarchal power. Anglo-American family law, which had been protective of patriarchal rights in the colonial period, began to emphasize the rights of individuals after the Revolution. Legal perceptions of the custody of children, for example, shifted from a view of the father as the "natural guardian" best suited to care for the child to one where judges decided the best interests of a child. In divorce cases, this meant that the custody of younger children and daughters usually went to the mother, while the custody of older boys usually was given to the father. In matters of parental consent for marriage, a similar decline occurred. By 1800, fathers had only limited influence over their children's matrimonial choices, but as the century progressed, the legal establishment began to take even more of the patriarch's power, overseeing decisions such as fitness to wed and age limitations. In general, this shift from patriarchal law to a more liberal, individualistic law represents fathers' reduced ability to decide the fate of their children.[6]

Men's influence engendered through physical affection and emotional bonding with their children also had a mixed record in the nineteenth century. The question of whether or not the rise of market capitalism reduced the amount of time fathers spent with their children has received considerable conjectural attention but still has not been adequately answered. To begin with, we still do not know whether colonial fathers actually spent more time with children than later generations, nor do we know if they followed the injunctions of ministers to use time with children for inculcating morality. To argue that fathers began to spend less time with children requires a clearer picture of the colonial era than we presently have. Nineteenth-century fathers obviously spent a great deal of time and energy on their careers, but many also seemed to have had time for children as well. Some new types of jobs that arose in the industrial economy did cause men to spend considerable time away from home, but their right to advise wives and children did not seem to diminish with this distance. Much of fathers' power appears not to have depended upon proximity. In light of the power that antebellum fathers did hold, and until we have more evidence showing colonial fathering behaviors, it is probably best to moderate the claim that men's power declined precipitously with the advent of an industrial economy. In a long-term sense it is most likely true that commercialization and industrialization helped undermine patriarchal power, but the change was far more complex and gradual than a simplistic time-away-from-home argument. Stephen M. Frank's reading of the advice literature leads him to suggest that "what nineteenth-century moralists lamented as the loss of fathers to the workplace was not so much a change in the amount of time men actually spent with their children as a shift in cultural emphasis, in the desire for greater family togetherness."[7] Perhaps future in-depth studies of fathers in these new careers will answer some of our questions about the connection of work and childrearing.

One evident change in the family life of the antebellum era was an increase in the importance of sentiment in shaping people's actions. As the century progressed, men more and more looked to emotional relationships with children as a means to instruct and control. Affection and love were important before 1800—obviously all men were not monsters like Asa Bailey—but for nineteenth-century middle-class Americans, these bonds formed the reason for family relationships. Men's romantic relationships with wives, their responses to the death of children, their increasing appeal to children's sense of duty based on love—such examples demonstrate that emotional ties played an essential role in antebellum middle-class families. Men could still use their physical dominance to guarantee obedience in children, but increasingly fathers preferred to rely on sentiment to foster obligation in their children. Fathers cultivated sincere attachments to young children through providing, care, and play, then they utilized these to instruct and instill middle-class values. Wielding authority through such bonds differed greatly from the untempered patriarchal authority of fathers like Asa Bailey: nonetheless it often proved just as effective in producing the desired results. The power of this method of fathering rested in its versatility; it was used to influence children from toilet training through courting and even after marriage. And it developed naturally in the course of an affective relationship.

Despite the effective way it fosters obligation, love has its weaknesses. Any overtly manipulative form of control can breed resentment, and fathers who frequently used this means often found children rebelling, particularly during adolescence. The limits of affectionate obligation can be seen in the sons who chose their own career paths and the occasional daughter who married against the will of a father. But perhaps more limiting in the long run was the two-edged nature of sentiment. Love can bring powerful pressures to bear on children, but relationships are usually reciprocal, and fathers frequently felt pressure to respect the desires of their children. Although this limited the arbitrary nature of men's power, it does not mean children's power in this relationship was on equal footing. Affectionate fathers wanted the best for their children, and middle-class culture dictated that self-control, moral living, and the Protestant work ethic were the keys to success. Thus, fathers had the task of convincing children to want to live by these guidelines. When faced with this challenge they often used reason to sway sons and daughters to their point of view, employing considerable space in letters to justify their decisions. Here again, the sources reveal the complexity of men's influence over children in the antebellum period.

Although outside of its formal scope, this study can give us some hints about father's power after 1860. We can agree with other historians who suggest that men's loss of authority to schools, judges, state agencies, and other societal institutions continued after the Civil War, perhaps even accelerated. Progressive era reforms, such as anti-child labor laws and compulsory schooling, chipped away at fathers' unmitigated right to direct the lives of their children. After 1900, what little authority men began to exert in the birthing room during the 1800s was largely lost when women started choosing to deliver their children at the hospital rather than at home.[8] Despite this declining trend, we can also assume that paternal power retained its complexity and that changes in the twentieth century were rarely simplistic in nature. For example, reciprocal affectionate relationships continued to shape father-children ties, and men relied even more on love as a means of influence; but the growth of leisure opportunities and a burgeoning youth culture meant that respecting the wishes of children entailed giving them freedom to pursue pleasure outside the home. Child-centered childrearing advice promoted a more permissive approach, giving children greater ability to make their own choices in a consumer society where choices were multiplying. Indeed, the power of youth culture grew as the century progressed, representing a new challenge to parental influence. Through several trends—an education system that gave children a physical and social space for their own expression, information from new forms of mass communication, and a consumer economy that trained children to become consumers—children became further empowered.

Fathers' ability to shape their children's lives has clearly been challenged by these changes. Although men retained control over much of the family income in most families throughout the century, the ability to use this power seems to have been limited by societal expectations and the expansion of children's rights. Compulsory secondary education and the availability of college to most Americans through school loans and assistance took away a great deal of men's ability to control access to schooling, education itself shifting over the course of a century-and-a-half from a privilege to a right. Similarly, the idea of an allowance, although monetarily of little impact upon family income, demonstrates that children increasingly were thought to have a right to a portion of family income in middle-class households. While fathers occasionally manipulate funds that give children mobility and access to consumer goods, societal mores generally prevent them from arbitrarily using these methods as extensive measures of control over children.

Along with the rise in status of children in families, the change that has probably most affected men in the twentieth century is their loss of the sole breadwinner status. The gradual increase in the number and percentage of women working outside the home has long-reaching effects that we are only beginning to understand. Men still earned more than women, and in many families they even controlled the money their wives made, but clearly this development undermined their monopoly on economic power. Children could now turn to another source for income, and women did not need to remain married to abusive husbands in order to provide for themselves and their children.

The growing availability of divorce and leisure opportunities also contributed to the decline in paternal authority after the Civil War. Divorced men often faced barriers of distance or legal restrictions on the amount of time they could spend with their children. Unlike work-related absences, separation caused by divorce often resulted in a real decline in fathers' status, as disgruntled former wives frequently pursued strategies that undermined their former husbands' authority. Because judges during much of the century tended to give preference to mothers in custody cases, men saw their influence over children wane.

Leisure activities could also be a significant distraction. Fathers could spend their evenings and weekends at sporting events, fraternal lodges, saloons, nightclubs, or civic meetings. They could golf, cycle, see a show, or go shopping in the stores of the vastly expanded consumer economy. The commercialization of leisure increased the number of activities that vied with their fathering duties. In the new industrialized America there were myriad potential challenges to fathers' place in families.

While these social and economic changes undoubtedly had a significant impact upon fatherhood, we must take care not to exaggerate their effects. Our tendency to build on popular images rather than on the safer ground of sound historical research makes one wonder if fatherhood in other times is as misperceived as nineteenth-century fatherhood. Have the changes to twentieth-century fatherhood been exaggerated? Have we obscured its complexity? In a path-breaking book on myth and families, John Gillis points out that there are two kinds of families—those that we live by and those that we live with.[9] The first represents our perceptions of how families should be; the second, the way that they are. Often our ideals about how families should function and be structured bear limited resemblance to how they actually are. The mythic families that we try to live by do influence us, but they are an ideal, not an indicator of behavior. We rarely measure up to these lofty paragons.

In arguing that the historical profession has relied too heavily upon the sources that illuminate Gillis' first category, this study has of course generalized and in doing so has slighted the works of historians who have used a variety of means to study the realities behind the myths. Unfortunately, because historians in general do not carefully differentiate between the ideal and actual behavior, historical findings are often an incongruous mixture of both. And, because of the persistence of ideal forms (separate spheres and domesticity), new findings that challenge them are often ignored or, at best, grafted onto these established patterns. There is much to be learned from studies of the first type of family, but we should not mistake the ideal for behavior. If the distinction is not understood and maintained, we will perpetuate myths and confusion about families both in the past and today.[10]

In light of what we have learned about nineteenth-century father-hood, and drawing upon Gillis' findings, this study proposes three ana-lytical categories for families. The first is the societal "ideal" promoted by contemporary politicians, observers, and "experts." Most histories of the family tend to be about this category, probably because the sources that show the ideal, such as the nineteenth-century advice lit-erature, are plentiful and filled with generalizations that are conducive to synthesis. The second category arises from family members' interac-tion with these cultural images. Interpreting them through the lenses of their own family needs and culture, family members produce their own views of the ideal family by which they feel they should live. Sources illuminating this category are harder to find, but can be found in col-lections where individuals, in the context of daily family life, write about their attitudes concerning childrearing, marriage, and gender relations. Often their reading of literature from the first category spurs them to articulate their own views of what a family should be. Finally, the third category is the actual lived experience of families, which is perhaps the most elusive for historians to capture, for people in the past often neglected to leave a record of everyday behavior. In short, to borrow from Gillis, there are families that "experts" publicly promote, families that family members feel they should live by, and families that members actually live with.

This common cultural disjunction in the popular mind between what families are supposed to be like and what they are contributes to unrealistic expectations even today. Historians have recently begun to question our tendency to see a golden age of family life in the past.[11] Indeed, each generation seems to have its own view of a golden age. As John Gillis notes, "For the Victorians, the traditional family, imagined to be rooted and extended, was located sometime before industrializa-tion and urbanization, but for those who came of age during the First World War, tradition was associated with the Victorians themselves; today we think of the 1950s and early 1960s as the location of the fam-ily and community life we imagine to have lost."[12] Thus, when we read observers in any age decrying the deterioration of fathers' power and place in the home, we should wonder if these earlier fathers really were as ideal as they imply. We share with our ancestors a tendency to think that family life was better before our parents' time, a perception often divorced from historical evidence. We should be cautious when inter-preting jeremiads of the past; they usually exaggerate change and rarely provide an accurate view of the past.

What about our other biases that we are reluctant to acknowledge? It is common for historians before they address an issue to let readers know where they stand; Marxists who study capitalism or feminists who look at gender relations will often inform the reader of their viewpoints before beginning their analysis. Should historians of the family admit that they are parent, sibling, or child? Is it possible that the complex psychological relationships that we have with our own fathers shape our perceptions of fathers in the past? How much of historians' focus on issues of paternal decline, absence, and incompetence is a product of psychology? Answers to these questions are beyond this study, but it is logical to assume that our relationships with our fathers (and other family members) affect the family history we write. We cannot avoid the fact that most modern Westerners feel some resentment toward their fathers often long into their adult lives. Nor can we rule out the possibility that both the public's and the historical profession's focus on paternal decline and absence could be explained partly by tensions they feel within their own father-child relationships.

That we need to account for such fundamental biases illuminates the important and complex place fathers still hold in our society. Is it possible that the public has overplayed the current theme of paternal powerlessness? Have we overemphasized what fathers should be and slighted what fathers do? Nineteenth-century observers accused men of abandoning their families for the lure of the business world, leaving them bereft of moral guidance, yet we have seen how middle-class fathers retained an active and crucial place in families throughout the entire antebellum era. When we remember that there are psychological and cultural factors that predispose us to focus on how fathers do not measure up to ideal images of fatherhood, then we can become more cautious as we interpret these accusations in any time period. Studies by Gillis and Stephanie Coontz illustrate that it would be wise to look beyond such stereotypes as the ineffective twentieth-century father.[13] Fortunately, men no longer have the kind of arbitrary patriarchal power exhibited by Asa Bailey, but many structures in American society, within and outside the family, still have patriarchal elements that give men advantages over other family members. Fathers in this country still shape the lives of their children and in turn are shaped by fatherhood.

Note on Sources

To understand the fathers behind the stereotypes, I turned to sources that illuminate both behavior and attitudes. Letters, diaries, journals, autobiographies, and wills, if used properly, tell us a great deal about actions and beliefs in private life. Letters are among the most productive sources because they give pictures of everyday life and often provide a record of emotional expression. I purposely avoided using the prescriptive literature written during the early nineteenth century because of its propensity for dividing the world into separate spheres and its uncertain relation to the lived lives of common Americans. This literature accepts an idealized view of marriage and family that was not often found in the realities of daily living in the antebellum era. While the advice literature that proliferated after 1830 can perhaps tell us something about public perceptions of societal conventions, it is not a reliable source for understanding actual behavior or even private beliefs.

My pool of sources includes documents from the private collections of over ninety families whose papers are found in the Huntington Library in San Marino, California; the Newberry Library in Chicago, Illinois; and some published sources. Approximately one-quarter of these families lived in large cities such as New York, Philadelphia, and Chicago. One-quarter lived in rural areas, and the remaining half came from town environments. These collections contain information on over 110 fathers, but I have focused on twenty men and their families who left especially detailed records of their lives.

One advantage of these sources is their organization by family. In most collections, the letters and journals of fathers are interspersed with documents written by wives, daughters, sons, mothers, and other relatives. To guard against an overemphasis of the father's role in the home, I used these other letters to show other family members' perceptions of fathers and how they interacted with them. These sources reveal that men's lives were intertwined with the lives of wives, children, and parents in complex patterns of authority, love, responsibility, and tension. Even where the father was physically absent, these records show that all family members usually regarded him as an integral part of the family. Thus, in many respects, this study of the father is also a study of the family.

While personal correspondence and private writings provide an invaluable source for understanding the private lives of individuals, they have their limitations. Perhaps the most difficult problem is the anecdotal nature of the evidence. To avoid overemphasizing isolated behaviors or aberrant values, I have tried to identify trends that were evident in several collections and also use representative passages to illustrate those trends. However, issues such as sexuality, birth, and birth control were so rarely discussed in the nineteenth century that it is very difficult to find evidence of attitudes and behaviors associated with them. Where I have broached such topics, I have noted the sources that I have used to form my conclusions. However, I have elected to include this material, despite its limitations, because of the opportunity to learn about important private matters.

Family papers, of course, have built-in biases. The kinds of people whose papers end up in historical repositories tend to be well-known men from the upper and upper middle-class echelons of society. Thus, my pool of individuals includes some fathers who, although middle class, became known for their part in wars, politics, and so on. These include military generals, state and national politicians, judges, a well-known writer, and several prominent lawyers and ministers. But I also have more information on lesser-known individuals—farmers, small-town ministers and lawyers, clerks, and their wives and children—people that form the bulk of the middle class in the first half of the nineteenth century. A second bias of these sources is that the families who corresponded tended to remain intact. Since I found correspondence to be particularly rich in information about fathering, I relied on letters more than any other single source. Unfortunately, fathers and children who are not on good terms with each other generally do not correspond. To at least partially offset this bias, where possible I used the journals and diaries of children and fathers who no longer communicated to explore some of the tensions in their relationship.

Identifying the socioeconomic status of these middle-class fathers has been another significant challenge of this study. My working definition of middle class is best characterized by what it is not. The fathers I studied were not the rich, the working class, nor the poor, but those in the middle ranks of society. This group did not necessarily perceive themselves as a unified group. Thus, my use of the term "class" does not necessarily require class consciousness. Middle-class fathers generally held occupations in the professions or business—the kind of jobs that generated enough income for home-owning and educating their children. Some farm owners are included in this study because they held cultural attitudes generally found among the middle class and because they were wealthy enough to employ servants or hired hands. Occupational information was available for 90 of the 113 fathers used. Because some men had more than one occupation during the period covered by the collection, there are a total of 135 occupations listed.

Occupations of Men In Sample

Occupation	Number	Percent
Merchant/Store Owner	21	15.6
Lawyer	20	14.8
Farmer	19	14.1
Politician	14	10.4
Boat Captain	6	4.4
Land Speculator	6	4.4
Miner*	6	4.4
Minister	6	4.4
School Teacher	6	4.4
Clerk/Bookkeeper	5	3.7
Judge	5	3.7
Military Officer	5	3.7
Physician	5	3.7
Bank/Insurance Officer	3	2.2
Engineer/Surveyor	3	2.2
Editor/Publisher	2	1.5
Factory Owner	2	1.5
Toll Road Official	1	0.7
Totals	135	99.8

*These miners were all men who left middle-class lifestyles temporarily to hunt for gold in California.

While income sufficient to support a middle-class way of life was indicative of middle-class status, other traits had little to do with income. Some fathers whose occupations were not readily apparent from the sources were included here because of the social traits they exhibited. Middle-class fathers tended to support involvement in civic organizations, public education programs, and religion. If not church-goers themselves, much of their value system was essentially Protestant in nature. Thus, I have used a definition of middle class that incorporates both economic status and cultural traits.

Some of the fathers were much closer to the upper class than others, while others bordered on working-class status. I have included these fathers because they tell us something about fathers who were perhaps in transition from one level to another. Also, the boundaries of the middle class were not hard and distinct at this time in American history. Leaving out these transitional fathers would deprive us of a critical component of the middling ranks of American society. One exception to this rule of vague class boundaries, however, was race. All fathers in this study are white. In the country at large, very few nonwhite Americans were able to overcome the barriers of economic discrimination and racism that permeated American society in the nineteenth century to become members of the middle class. Most found themselves locked into working-class status or worse. Thus, race was one of the factors that whites often used in defining themselves as middle class. A few African Americans were able to gain a foothold in their ranks, but they still faced racial attitudes that kept them separated from white Americans.

Manuscripts and Published Collections

AND THE FATHER(S) IN EACH COLLECTION

AT THE HUNTINGTON LIBRARY, SAN MARINO, CALIFORNIA

Abbot, George Jacob, Collection
John Taylor Gilman, Sr.
Jacob Abbot
George Jacob Abbot
Nicholas Emery

Adams, Phinehas, Collection
Phinehas Adams

Allen, William Henry, Collection
William Allen

Appleton-Foster Collection
Nathaniel Appleton
John W. Foster

Baldwin Family Collection

Bell, James Alvin, Collection

Bidamon, Lewis, Collection
Lewis Bidamon

Bissell, Mary Eleanor, Collection
Roswell Mills
Thomas Bissell
Elijah Grant

Bouvier, John, Collection
John Bouvier

Brown, William, Collection
Joseph Brown

Burnett, Wellington Cleveland, Collection
Lester Burnett
Wellington Cleveland Burnett
Charles Cleveland

California File
John Joseph Craven
Solomon A. Gorges
Jonathan Heros
John Hyde
Crawford Medorem
Farnham Plummer
Gregory Yale

Clark, Lincoln, Collection
Lincoln Clark
Erastus Smith
William Williams
Elisha Clark

Clendenen, Clemens, Collection
James Clendenen
Clemens Clendenen

Colton, Sheldon, Collection
Hamilton Colton

Curtis, Samuel Ryan, Collection
Samuel Ryan Curtis

Daniell, Charles Penniman,
  Collection
Josiah Newell Daniell

Dartt Family Collection
Robert Mitchell
John Mitchell

Eaton, William, Collection
William Eaton

Eaton, William P., Collection
Joseph Eaton
William P. Eaton

Edwards, Pierpont, Collection
Pierpont Edwards

Fairbanks-Judson Collection
Everett Judson

Gardner, William Bunker, Collection
William Bunker Gardner

Hamer, Thomas Lyon, Collection
Thomas Lyon Hamer

Hodge, Benjamin, Collection
Benjamin Hodge, Sr.
Benjamin Hodge, Jr.

Huntington, Ebenezer, Collection
Samuel Huntington

Lake, Ann Getz Hutchinson Leech,
  Collection
John Getz
Andrew Leech

Moore, John, Collection
George Borrowe
John Moore

Newcomb-Johnson Collection
Daniel Newcomb
David Garrett

Nichols, Samuel, Collection
John Coleman
Samuel Nichols
George Taylor

North, John Wesley, Collection
George Loomis
John Wesley North

Parker, Lucien B., Collection

Phillips, George S., Collection
George S. Phillips
Daniel J. Phillips

Potter, William James, Collection
William James Potter, Sr.
Spooner Babcock

Ray, Charles Henry, Collection
Levi Ray
Charles Henry Ray

Smith, Samuel Francis, Collection
Samuel Francis Smith

Smith, Thomas Kilby, Collection
Thomas Kilby Smith

Spence-Lowell Collection
Keith Spence

Stanton, William, Collection
Benjamin Stanton

Walker, Elkanah, Collection
Elkanah Walker

Warren Family Collection
Alexander Horn

Watson, John Fanning, Collection
John Fanning Watson

AT THE NEWBERRY LIBRARY, CHICAGO, ILLINOIS

Brown, Edward Eagle,
  Family Papers
William Brown

Carter, Thomas Butler, Collection
Thomas Butler Carter

Everett, Robert, Collection
Robert Everett

Pearce, Christopher Gardner,
  Collection
Christopher Gardner Pearce

Metcalf Family Papers
Isaac Metcalf
Charles Rich
John Milton Putnam

PUBLISHED PRIMARY SOURCES

Larz Anderson
Anderson, Isabell, ed. *The Letters and Journals of General Nicholas Long-worth Anderson, 1854–1892*. New York: Flemin H. Revell Company, 1942.

Samuel Ayer
Ayer, Sarah Connell. *Diary of Sarah Connell Ayer, 1805–1835*. Portland, ME: Lefavor-Tower Co., 1910.

Asa Bailey
Bailey, Abigail. *Memoirs of Mrs. Abigail Bailey*. Boston: Samuel T. Armstrong, publisher, 1815. Reprint. Edited by Ethan Smith. New York: Arno Press, 1980.

Simeon Baldwin
Baldwin, Simeon E., ed. *Life and Letters of Simeon Baldwin*. New Haven, CT: The Tuttle, Morehouse & Taylor Co., 1919.

Orville Hickman Browning
Browning, Orville Hickman. *The Diary of Orville Hickman Browning: Volume I, 1850–1864*, vol. 20. Edited by Theodore Calvin Pease and James G. Randall. *Collections of the Illinois State Historical Library*. Springfield, IL: Illinois State Historical Library, 1925.

Edward Everett
Bush, Phillipa Call, ed. *Memoir of Anne Gorham Everett; With Extracts from Her Correspondence and Journal*. Boston: n.p., 1857.

William Edmond
Curtis, Elizabeth, ed. *Letters and Journals: Judge William Edmond, 1755–1838; Judge Holbrook Curtis, 1787–1858; Judge William Edmond Curtis, 1823–1880; William Edmond Curtis, 1855–1923; Dr. Holbrook Curtis, 1856–1920*. Hartford, CT: The Case, Lockwood & Brainard Co., 1926.

Richard Henry Dana, Jr.
Dana, Richard Henry, Jr. *The Journal of Richard Henry Dana, Jr.*, vol. I. Edited by Robert F. Lucid. Cambridge, MA: Belknap Press, 1968.

James Colles
Deforest, Emily Johnston, ed. *James Colles, 1788–1883: Life and Letters.* New York: n.p., 1926.

Daniel S. Dickson
Dickinson, John R., ed. *Speeches, Correspondence, etc., of the Late Daniel S. Dickson, of New York,* 2 vols. New York: G. P. Putnam & Son, 1867.

Bela Paul, Abner Hodgen, and Luther Trussell
Dublin, Thomas, ed. *Farm to Factory: Women's Letters, 1830–1860.* New York: Columbia University Press, 1981.

Austin C. Dunham
Dunham, Austin C. *Reminiscences of Austin C. Dunham.* Hartford, CT: The Case, Lockwood & Brainard Co., n.d.

Elijah Cobb
Elijah Cobb, 1768–1848: A Cape Cod Skipper. New Haven, CT: Yale University Press, 1925.

Jacob Elfreth
Hodge, Susan Winslow, ed. *The Elfreth Book of Letters.* Philadelphia: University of Pennsylvania Press, 1985.

Almon Danforth Hodges
Hodges, Almon Danforth, Jr., ed. *Almon Danforth Hodges and His Neighbors.* Boston: n.p., 1909.

William Swain
Holliday, J. S. *The World Rushed In: The California Gold Rush Experience.* New York: Simon and Schuster, 1981.

Jonathan Larcom
Larcom, Jonathan. "Diary," in *The Essex Institute Historical Collections* 87 (1951), 65–95.

Nathaniel Saltonstall
Massachusetts Historical Society, *The Saltonstall Papers, 1607–1815.* Edited by Robert E. Moody. Boston: Massachusetts Historical Society, 1974.

Joseph Allen
Memorial of Joseph and Lucy Clark Allen. Boston: George H. Ellis, Printer, 1891.

William Lloyd Garrison

Merrill, Walter, ed. *The Letters of William Lloyd Garrison: No Union with Slave-Holders, 1841–1849*. Cambridge, MA: Belknap Press, 1973.

Samuel Cormany and Benjamin Bowman

Mohr, James C., ed. *The Cormany Diaries: A Northern Family in the Civil War*. Pittsburgh: University of Pittsburgh Press, 1982.

Zenas Cowles

Mosely, Laura Hadley, ed. *The Diaries of Julia Cowles*. New Haven, CT: Yale University Press, 1931.

John Pintard

The New York Historical Society. *Letters from John Pintard to His Daughter Eliza Pintard Noel Davidson, 1816–1833*, 2 vols. *Collections of The New York Historical Society for the Year of 1937*. New York: J. J. Little & Ives Co., 1944.

James Parker

Parker, James. "Extracts from the Diary of James Parker of Shirley, Massachusetts," in *New England Historical and Genealogical Register* 69 (1915) and 70 (1916).

William Eaton

Prentiss, Charles, ed. *The Life of the Late Gen. William Eaton*. Brookfield, MA: E. Merriam & Co., 1813.

S. S. Prentiss

Prentiss, George Lewis, ed. *A Memoir of S. S. Prentiss*, vol. 1. New York: Charles Scribner, 1853.

James Savage

Rogers, Emma Savage, ed. *Letters of James Savage to His Family*. Boston: n.p., 1906.

Henry Sewall and William Sewall

Sewall, William. *Diary of William Sewall, 1797–1846, Formerly of Augusta Maine, Maryland, Virginia and Pioneer in Illinois*. Edited by John C. E. Goodall. Beardstown, IL: Hartman Printing Co., 1930.

George Templeton Strong and Samuel Ruggles

Strong, George Templeton. *The Diary of George Templeton Strong: Young Man in New York, 1835–1849*, vol. I. Edited by Allan Nevins and Milton Halsey Thomas. New York: The Macmillan Co., 1952.

———. *The Diary of George Templeton Strong: The Turbulent Fifties, 1850–1859*, vol. II. Edited by Allan Nevins and Milton Halsey Thomas. New York: The Macmillan Co., 1952.

Daniel Appleton White and Caleb Foote

Tileston, Mary Wilder, ed. *Caleb and Mary Wilder Foote: Reminiscences and Letters*. Boston: Houghton Mifflin Co., 1918.

Calvin Fletcher

Thornbrough, Gayle, ed. *The Diary of Calvin Fletcher, Vol. 1, 1817–1838: Including Letters of Calvin Fletcher and Diaries and Letters of His Wife Sarah Hill Fletcher*. Indianapolis: Indiana Historical Society, 1972.

Matthias Zahm

Zahm, Matthias. "Matthias Zahm's Diary," Robert H. Goodall, ed., in *Papers Read Before the Lancaster County Historical Society* 47 (no. 4, 1947): 61–92.

Notes

INTRODUCTION

1. For a good overview of the decline of American fatherhood, see John Demos, "The Changing Faces of Fatherhood," in Demos, *Past, Present, and Personal: The Family and Life Course in American History* (New York: Oxford University Press, 1986), 61. For fathers in nineteenth-century literature, see Charles Strickland, *Victorian Domesticity: Families in the Life and Art of Louisa May Alcott* (Tuscaloosa, AL: University of Alabama Press, 1985), 118. For a look at more recent views of fatherhood, see R. LaRossa et al., "The Fluctuating Image of the 20th Century American Father," *Journal of Marriage and the Family* 53 (1991): 987–97.
2. Stephanie Coontz, *The Way We Never Were: American Families and the Nostalgia Trap* (New York: Basic Books, 1992), 23–25.
3. For a description of sources and methodology, see "Note on Sources."
4. Anne L. Kuhn, *The Mother's Role in Childhood Education: New England Concepts, 1830–1860* (New Haven, CT: Yale University Press, 1947); Robert Sunley, "Early Nineteenth-Century American Literature on Child Rearing," in *Childhood in Contemporary Cultures*, ed. Margaret Mead and Martha Wolfenstein (Chicago: University of Chicago Press, 1955), 150–67; Barbara Welter, "The Cult of True Womanhood: 1820–1860," *American Quarterly* 18 (summer 1966): 151–74; Carl N. Degler, *At Odds: Women and the Family in America from the Revolution to the Present* (New York: Oxford University Press, 1980); Mary P. Ryan, *The Empire of the Mother: American Writing about Domesticity 1830–1860* (New York: Institute for Research in History and Haworth Press, 1982); Mary P. Ryan, *Cradle of the Middle Class: The Family in Oneida County, New York, 1790–1865* (Cambridge, England: Cambridge University Press, 1981).
5. Ryan, *Cradle of the Middle Class*, 232.
6. For the father's place in the colonial family, see Edmund Morgan, *The Puritan Family: Religion & Domestic Relations in Seventeenth-Century New England*, rev. ed. (New York: Harper & Row, 1966); John Demos, *A Little*

Commonwealth: Family Life in Plymouth Colony (London: Oxford University Press, 1970); Phillip Greven, *Four Generations: Population, Land, and Family in Andover, Massachusetts* (Ithaca, NY: Cornell University Press, 1970). Almost every historian who has touched on the subject agrees that the father's role declined sometime during the eighteenth and nineteenth centuries. Some, like Greven, *Four Generations*, and Richard Sennett, *Families against the City: Middle Class Homes of Industrial Chicago, 1872–1890* (Cambridge, MA: Harvard University Press, 1970), focus on declining economic power over children. Others, especially Michael Grossberg, *Governing the Hearth: Law and the Family in Nineteenth-Century America* (Chapel Hill: University of North Carolina Press, 1985), chart a decline in legal power. The largest body of work comes from the history of women and motherhood, which argues that men's childrearing role in the home declined. See, for example, Carl N. Degler, *At Odds*; Catherine M. Scholten, *Childbearing in American Society: 1650–1850*, ed. with preface and introduction by Lynne Withey (New York: New York University, 1985); Ryan, *Cradle of the Middle Class*; Linda Kerber, "The Republican Mother: Women and the Enlightenment—An American Perspective," *American Quarterly* 28 (summer 1976): 187–205. The first works written specifically on fatherhood were largely overview essays showing the opportunity for research on the subject. See John Demos, "The Changing Faces of Fatherhood"; E. Anthony Rotundo, "American Fatherhood: A Historical Perspective," *American Behavioral Scientist* 29 (September/October 1985): 7–25; Maris A. Vinovskis, "Young Fathers and Their Children: Some Historical and Policy Perspectives," in Vinovskis, *An "Epidemic" of Adolescent Pregnancy? Some Historical and Policy Considerations* (New York: Oxford University Press, 1988). Several historians, however, are rectifying the neglect of the topic. See Stephen M. Frank, *Life with Father: Parenthood and Masculinity in the Nineteenth-Century American North* (Baltimore: Johns Hopkins University Press, 1998); Stephen M. Frank, "'Rendering Aid and Comfort': Images of Fatherhood in the Letters of Civil War Soldiers from Massachusetts and Michigan," *Journal of Social History* 26 (fall 1992): 7–31; Robert L. Griswold, *Fatherhood in America: A History* (New York: Basic Books, 1993); E. Anthony Rotundo, *American Manhood: Transformations in Masculinity from the Revolution to the Modern Era* (New York: Basic Books, 1993); Steven Mintz, *A Prison of Expectations: The Family in Victorian Culture* (New York: New York University Press, 1983); John R. Gillis, *A World of Their Own Making: Myth, Ritual, and the Quest for Family Values* (New York: Basic Books, 1996), ch. 9. These studies, however, begin with many of the assumptions that have shaped the history of fatherhood to this point, and thus most emphasize decline. Even Frank's work, which goes the furthest toward challenging the declension idea, is still heavily influenced by sources and views that emphasize a loss of paternal place.

7.   The first and most influential study to address colonial fatherhood was Morgan, *The Puritan Family*. For syntheses of historians' views on colonial fatherhood, see Frank, *Life with Father*, 9–15; Demos, "Changing Faces of Fatherhood"; Steven Mintz and Susan Kellogg, *Domestic Revolutions: A Social History of the American Family* (New York: The Free Press, 1988), ch. 1.

8. Mary Beth Norton, *Founding Mothers and Fathers: Gendered Power and the Forming of American Society* (New York: Vintage Books, 1997), 69, 127–30; Vinovskis, *An "Epidemic" of Adolescent Pregnancy?*

9. Greven, *Four Generations.*

10. Cotton Mather, *A Family Well Ordered, or an Essay to Render Parents and Children Happy in One Another* (Boston: B. Green & J. Allen, for Michael Perry . . . & Benjamin Eliot . . . , 1699), 26, 36–37. There are a few works that have looked at colonial men's fathering behaviors. See Daniel Vickers, *Farmers and Fishermen: Two Centuries of Work in Essex County, Massachusetts, 1630–1850* (Chapel Hill: University of North Carolina Press, 1994); Anne S. Lombard, "Manliness, Rationality, and Parenting in Anglo American New England before 1750," unpublished paper.

11. Alan MacFarlane, *The Origins of English Individualism: The Family, Property and Social Transition* (New York: Cambridge University Press, 1978); Lawrence Stone, *The Family, Sex and Marriage in England, 1500–1800* (New York: Harper & Row, 1977).

12. Jay Mechling, "Advice to Historians on Advice to Mothers," *Journal of Social History* 9 (fall 1975): 44–63. Italics in original.

13. Linda Kerber, *Women of the Republic: Intellect and Ideology in Revolutionary America* (Chapel Hill: University of North Carolina Press, 1980), 11, 199–200; Kuhn, *The Mother's Role*, 73–74; Altina Waller, *Reverend Beecher and Mrs. Tilton: Sex and Class in Victorian America* (Amherst: University of Massachusetts Press, 1982), ch. 4; Welter, "The Cult of True Womanhood."

14. Linda K. Kerber, "Separate Spheres, Female Worlds, Woman's Place: The Rhetoric of Women's History," *Journal of American History* 75 (June 1988): 9–39.

15. See Christina Hardyment, *Dream Babies: Three Centuries of Good Advice on Child Care* (New York: Harper & Row, 1983), 38–78; Linda Kerber, *Women of the Republic: Intellect and Ideology in Revolutionary America* (Chapel Hill: University of North Carolina Press, 1980); Sunley, "Early Nineteenth-Century American Literature on Child Rearing"; Ryan, *Empire of the Mother*; Kuhn, *The Mother's Role*; Welter, "The Cult of True Womanhood"; Marilyn Dell Brady, "The New Model Middle-Class Family (1815–1930)," in *American Families: A Research Guide and Historical Handbook*, ed. Joseph M. Hawes and Elizabeth I. Nybakken (New York: Greenwood Press, 1991), 92–94.

16. Talcott Parsons et al., *Family, Socialization and Interaction Process* (Glencoe, IL: The Free Press, 1955).

17. Barrie Thorne, "Feminist Rethinking of the Family," in *Rethinking the Family: Some Feminist Questions*, ed. Barrie Thorne and Marilyn Yalom (London: Longman, 1982), 7, 15. See also Mintz and Kellogg, *Domestic Revolutions*, 246, 249; Mintz, *A Prison of Expectations*, conclusion; D. H. J. Morgan, *Social Theory and Family* (London: Routledge & Kegan Paul, 1975), 25–48; Glen H. Elder, "Approaches to Social Change and the Family," in *Turning Points*, ed. John Demos and Sarane Spence Boocock (Chicago: University of Chicago Press, 1978), S6; Tim Carrigan, Bob Connell, and John Lee, "Toward a New Sociology of Masculinity," in *The Making of Masculinities: The New Men's Studies*, ed. Harry Brod (Boston:

Allen & Unwin, 1987), 66–68; Elizabeth Pleck, "Two Worlds in One: Work and Family," *Journal of Social History* 10 (1979): 178–95.

18. Ryan, *Cradle of the Middle Class*, 232.

19. Demos, "The Changing Faces of Fatherhood," 50.

20. Griswold, *Fatherhood in America*; Frank, *Life with Father*.

21. Demos, "The Changing Faces of Fatherhood."

22. Jay Fliegelman, *Prodigals and Pilgrims: The American Revolution against Patriarchal Authority, 1750–1800* (Cambridge, England: Cambridge University Press, 1982), 168–69; Ryan, *Cradle of the Middle Class*, 67–71; Charles Strickland, "A Transcendentalist Father: The Child-Rearing Practices of Bronson Alcott," *Perspectives in American History* 3 (1969): 5–76; Bernard Wishy, *The Child and the Republic: The Dawn of Modern American Child Nurture* (Philadelphia: University of Pennsylvania Press, 1968), 4; Mary Lynn Stevens Heininger et al., *A Century of Childhood, 1820–1920* (Rochester, NY: Margaret Woodbury Strong Museum, 1984), 2–4; Kathryn Kish Sklar, *Catherine Beecher: A Study in American Domesticity* (New Haven, CT: Yale University Press, 1973), ch. 1.

23. Pleck, "Two Worlds in One," 178–95; Griswold, *American Fatherhood*, ch. 2; Mintz and Kellogg, *Domestic Revolutions*, ch. 3.

24. Linda Gordon, *Heroes of Their Own Lives: The Politics and History of Family Violence, Boston 1880–1960* (New York: Viking, 1988), preface.

25. Fathers usually acted as providers for their children, but not all providers were fathers. Interested friends and relatives could act as fathers. The only requirements were a willingness to provide for the nurture of the child and the compliance or absence of the biological father. Sometimes these provisions were supplementary to the biological father's participation, but most often in such a situation the biological father was deceased or the child had moved from home. Mothers also acted as a type of provider, supplying love, education, care, and nurturing to children. Providing, in this sense then, is much the same as parenting. This complementarity of the terms "providing" and "parenting" reveals that the roles of mothers and fathers overlapped a great deal. Still, many aspects of fathers' parenting were distinct from those of mothers because of elements of masculinity, labor division, and patriarchal power that shaped men's lives during the antebellum period. See Fliegelman, *Prodigals and Pilgrims*, ch. 7.

26. Degler, *At Odds*, 8–9; See also Ryan, *Empire of the Mother*; Ryan, *Cradle of the Middle Class*.

27. Philippe Ariés, *Western Attitudes Toward DEATH: From the Middle Ages to the Present* (Baltimore: Johns Hopkins University Press, 1974), 1. See also Phillip Greven, *The Protestant Temperament: Patterns of Child-Rearing, Religious Experience, and the Self in Early America* (New York: Knopf, 1977), 16.

28. Some men started out in these states but moved their families to Western or Southern states during the course of their lives. A few also lived for a time in California. These migrating fathers were included, with the understanding that the moves and new homes often influenced their fathering.

29. Historians that have applied the life course model to family history have observed that the economic fortunes of the family could change over the

course of its existence. In the early stages, when men were just starting their careers, family income was often considerably less than when men were established. Thus, it was common for a family's class status to change in the course of a man's fathering years. Tamara K. Hareven, "The History of the Family and the Complexity of Social Change," *American Historical Review* 96 (February 1991): 106; Tamara K. Hareven, "Cycles, Courses, and Cohorts: Reflections on the Theoretical and Methodological Approaches to the Historical Study of Family Development," *Journal of Social History* 12 (1978): 97–109.

CHAPTER ONE

1. Lincoln Clark to Julia Clark, 27 September 1845, Lincoln Clark Collection, Huntington Library.
2. Lincoln Clark to Julia Clark, 28 March 1847, Clark Collection.
3. John Demos, "The Changing Faces of Fatherhood," reprinted in Demos, *Past, Present and Personal: The Family and Life Course in American History* (New York: Oxford University Press, 1986), 55.
4. Mary P. Ryan, *Cradle of the Middle Class: The Family in Oneida County, New York, 1790–1865* (Cambridge, England: Cambridge University Press, 1981), 101.
5. Nancy F. Cott, *The Bonds of Womanhood: Woman's Sphere in New England, 1780–1835* (New Haven, CT: Yale University Press, 1977), 20; Robert L. Griswold, *Fatherhood in America: A History* (New York: Basic Books, 1993); Daniel T. Rodgers, *The Work Ethic in Industrial America, 1850–1920* (Chicago: University of Chicago Press, 1974); E. Anthony Rotundo, *American Manhood: Transformations in Masculinity from the Revolution to the Modern Era* (New York: Basic Books, 1993).
6. Stuart M. Blumin, *The Emergence of the Middle Class: Social Experience in the American City, 1760–1900* (Ithaca, NY: Cornell University Press, 1989), 78–83; Glenn Porter and Harold C. Livesay, *Merchants and Manufacturers: Studies in the Changing Structure of Nineteenth-Century Marketing* (Baltimore: Johns Hopkins University Press, 1971), 5–10; Alfred D. Chandler, Jr., *The Visible Hand: The Managerial Revolution in American Business* (Cambridge, MA: Belknap Press, 1977), 15.
7. George Templeton Strong, *The Diary of George Templeton Strong: The Turbulent Fifties, 1850–1859*, vol. 2, ed. Allan Nevins and Milton Halsey Thomas (New York: The Macmillan Co., 1952), 228.
8. John Pintard to Eliza Pintard Davidson, 24 May 1819, in *Letters from John Pintard to His Daughter Eliza Pintard Noel Davidson, 1816–1833*, vol. 1, *Collections of The New York Historical Society for the Year of 1937* (New York: J. J. Little & Ives Co., 1944), 193–94.
9. William A. Alcott, *The Young Wife, or Duties of Woman in the Marriage Relation* (1837; reprint, New York: Arno Press & The New York Times, 1972), 361.
10. Strong, *Diary*, vol. 2, 120.
11. Rinaldo Parker to Eunice Parker, 24 September and 22 October 1837, Lucien B. Parker Collection, Huntington Library.
12. Rodgers, *Work Ethic in Industrial America*, 125.

13. Ibid., 125.
14. William James Potter to William Potter, 6 April 1856, William James Potter Collection, Huntington Library. See also William James Potter to William Potter, 6 July 1855.
15. William James Potter to William Potter, 8 July 1855, Potter Collection.
16. Thomas Kilby Smith to Elizabeth Smith, probably 29 June 1852, Thomas Kilby Smith Collection, Huntington Library.
17. Robert L. Griswold, *Family and Divorce in California, 1850–1890: Victorian Illusions and Everyday Realities* (Albany: State University of New York Press, 1982), 101.
18. For a differing viewpoint, see Hans Medick and David Warren Sabean, "Interest and Emotion in Family and Kinship Studies: A Critique of Social History and Anthropology," in *Interest and Emotion: Essays on the Study of Family and Kinship*, ed. Hans Medick and David Warren Sabean (Cambridge, England: Cambridge University Press, 1984).
19. Peter N. Stearns, *Be a Man!: Males in Modern Society* (New York: Holmes & Meier Publishers, Inc., 1979), 85.
20. Sarah Connell Ayer, *Diary of Sarah Connell Ayer, 1805–1835* (Portland, ME: Lefavor-Tower Co., 1910), 342–69.
21. Griswold, *Fatherhood in America*, 13–14.
22. Keith Spence to Mary Spence, 10 January 1801, Spence-Lowell Collection, Huntington Library.
23. Keith Spence to Mary Spence, 13 June 1799, Spence-Lowell Collection.
24. William P. Eaton to Joseph Eaton, 25 November 1853, William P. Eaton Collection, Huntington Library.
25. Rotundo, *American Manhood*, 169.
26. John Pintard to Eliza Pintard Davidson, 17–18 August 1818, in *Letters from John Pintard*, vol. 1, 139. Pintard was economically middle class with upper-class aspirations and connections, and thus perhaps more prone to view his lack of wealth as an obstacle to his daughter's marriage.
27. James Alvin Bell to Augusta Anna Halleck, 2 May 1858, James Alvin Bell Collection, Huntington Library.
28. John Pintard to Eliza Pintard Davidson, 4 May 1818, in *Letters from John Pintard*, vol. 1, 120.
29. Charles Henry Ray to Jane Ray, 24 June 1855, Charles Henry Ray Collection, Huntington Library.
30. William P. Eaton to his mother, 17 February 1851, Eaton Collection.
31. Lincoln Clark to Julia Clark (sister), 10 June 1829, Clark Collection. His parents lived in Hadley, Massachusetts.
32. Aaron Burr to Pierpont Edwards, 27 March 1801, Pierpont Edwards Collection, Huntington Library.
33. Johnny Faragher and Christine Stansell, "Women and Their Families on the Overland Trail to California and Oregon, 1842–1867," *Feminist Studies* 2 (no. 2/3, 1975): 150–66.
34. Isaac Metcalf to Antoinette Putnam Metcalf, 22 June 1855, Metcalf Family Papers, Newberry Library.
35. John Wesley North to Ann North, 30 May 1861, John Wesley North Collection, Huntington Library.

36. See Karen Lystra, *Searching the Heart: Women, Men, and Romantic Love in Nineteenth-Century America* (New York: Oxford University Press, 1989), 131–34.

37. Carl N. Degler, *At Odds: Women and the Family in America from the Revolution to the Present* (New York: Oxford University Press, 1980), 41, 75.

38. Degler, *At Odds*; Anne L. Kuhn, *The Mother's Role in Childhood Education: New England Concepts, 1830–1860* (New Haven, CT: Yale University Press, 1947); Robert Sunley, "Early Nineteenth-Century American Literature on Child Rearing," in *Childhood in Contemporary Cultures*, ed. Margaret Mead and Martha Wolfenstein (Chicago: University of Chicago Press, 1955), 150–67; Barbara Welter, "The Cult of True Womanhood, 1820–1860," *American Quarterly* 18 (summer 1966): 151–74. For exceptions to this argument in a rural context, see Nancy Grey Osterud, *Bonds of Community: The Lives of Farm Women in Nineteenth-Century New York* (Ithaca, NY: Cornell University Press, 1991); Joan M. Jensen, *Loosening the Bonds: Mid-Atlantic Farm Women, 1750–1850* (New Haven, CT: Yale University Press, 1986).

39. For examples of collections that show a range of male domestic work, see the Metcalf Family Papers, Newberry Library; John Wesley North Collection, Huntington Library; William Bunker Gardner Collection, Huntington Library; *Letters from John Pintard*.

40. Samuel Cormany, *The Cormany Diaries: A Northern Family in the Civil War*, ed. James C. Mohr (Pittsburgh, PA: University of Pittsburgh Press, 1982), 181.

41. Isaac Metcalf to Antoinette Putnam Metcalf, 1 February 1859, Metcalf Family Papers.

42. See for example, Alcott, *The Young Wife*, 262.

43. Journal kept by Isaac and Antoinette Metcalf, Metcalf Family Papers, entry by Antoinette, 7 October 1856, 251.

44. Ibid., 253.

45. Jane Elfreth to Jacob Elfreth, 27 October 1836, in *The Elfreth Book of Letters*, ed. Susan Winslow Hodge (Philadelphia: University of Pennsylvania Press, 1985), 121.

46. Stephen M. Frank argues that men usually did not get involved until sicknesses became serious enough to warrant the attention of a doctor. While serious illnesses were more likely to spur men's involvement, I found fathers nursing children who were ill with common colds, teething, and other nonthreatening illnesses. Stephen M. Frank, *Life with Father: Parenthood and Masculinity in the Nineteenth-Century American North* (Baltimore: Johns Hopkins University Press, 1998), 76–80.

47. Faye E. Dudden, *Serving Women: Household Service in Nineteenth-Century America* (Middletown, CT: Wesleyan University Press, 1983), 136–37. Gunther Barth has argued that "Shopping . . . reinforced the separation between the two spheres of life, leaving the acquisition of the funds for shopping to man while making the task itself a woman's affair" (Gunther Barth, *City People: The Rise of Modern City Culture in Nineteenth-Century America* [New York: Oxford University Press, 1980], 146).

48. George Templeton Strong, *The Diary of George Templeton Strong: Young*

Man in New York, 1835–1849, vol. 1, ed. Allan Nevins and Milton Halsey Thomas (New York: The Macmillan Co., 1952), 331.

49. John Pintard to Eliza Pintard Noel Davidson, 11–14 November 1816, in *Letters from John Pintard*, vol. 1, 35.

50. John Pintard to Eliza Pintard Noel Davidson, 26 August 1820, in Ibid., vol. 1, 317.

51. Blumin, *Emergence of the Middle Class*, 185.

52. Alcott, *The Young Wife*, 247–48.

53. Laurel Thatcher Ulrich, *Good Wives: Image and Reality in the Lives of Women in Northern New England, 1650–1750* (New York: Knopf, 1980), ch. 2.

54. Griswold, *Fatherhood in America*.

55. Ibid., 14. Griswold's portrayal of this aspect of nineteenth-century fatherhood is more sympathetic than most, but he still comes to the same conclusion. See also Mary P. Ryan, *The Empire of the Mother: American Writing about Domesticity 1830–1860* (New York: Institute for Research in History and Haworth Press, 1982); Bernard Wishy, *The Child and the Republic: The Dawn of Modern American Child Nurture* (Philadelphia: University of Pennsylvania Press, 1968), ch. 3; Kuhn, *Childhood Education*, 4–5; Welter, "Cult of True Womanhood."

56. Benjamin Franklin, *The Autobiography of Benjamin Franklin: A Restoration of a "Fair Copy,"* ed. Max Farrand (San Marino, CA: The Huntington Library, 1964), 11–16.

57. Benjamin Hodge, Sr., account book for years 1795–1798, Benjamin Hodge Collection, Huntington Library; Diary of Clemens Clendenen, Clendenen Collection, Huntington Library. Hodge spent 99 days away from the farm. He also spent 51 days logging or gathering wood, 29 harvesting, 23 fencing, and 20 making shoes (his trade). Clendenen spent 102 days away, and an additional 34 working on others' farms, 25 hauling wood, 21 harvesting, and 19 planting.

58. John S. C. Abott, "Paternal Neglect," *Parents Magazine* 2 (March 1842): 148.

59. Griswold, *Fatherhood in America*, 14. See also Ryan, *Empire of the Mother*; Wishy, *Child and the Republic*, ch. 3; Kuhn, *Childhood Education*, 4–5.

60. *Elfreth Book of Letters*, 42, 51, 76, 78, 82.

61. Jacob Elfreth to Jane Elfreth, 2 November 1836, Ibid., 122.

62. Frances Hodge to Lyman Hodge, 6 February 1852, Hodge Collection.

63. Isaac Metcalf to Antoinette Putnam Metcalf, 22 May 1856, Metcalf Family Papers.

64. Ayer, *Diary*, 279.

65. *Memorial of Joseph and Lucy Clark Allen* (Boston: George H. Ellis, Printer, 1891), 207. See also Strong, *Diary*, vol. 1, Introduction.

66. John Pintard to Eliza Pintard Noel Davidson, 2 May 1820, in *Letters from John Pintard*, vol. 1, 286.

67. See John Wesley North to George Loomis, 9–10 February 1851, North Collection.

68. Sam B. Warner, Jr., *Streetcar Suburbs: The Progress of Growth in Boston, 1870–1900* (Cambridge, MA: Harvard University Press, 1962). For a view that finds the origins of the suburb in a slightly earlier period, see Kenneth T. Jackson, *Crabgrass Frontier: The Suburbanization of the United States* (New York: Oxford University Press, 1985).

69. Theodore Hershberg, Harold E. Cox, Dale B. Light, Jr., and Richard R. Greenfield, "'The Journey to Work': An Empirical Investigation of Work, Residence and Transportation, Philadelphia, 1850 and 1880," in *Philadelphia: Work, Space, Family, and Group Experience in the 19th Century: Essays Toward an Interdisciplinary History of the City*, ed. Theodore Hershberg (New York: Oxford University Press, 1981), 134–54.

70. Albina Rich to Charles Rich, 31 December 1853–January 2, 1854, Metcalf Family Papers.

71. Albina Rich to Charles Rich, 8–9 January 1854, Metcalf Family Papers.

72. Elizabeth Haven Thacher to Mary Appleton Foster, 26 June 1836, Appleton-Foster Collection, Huntington Library. It is not clear from the collection whether Elizabeth was widowed or her husband was working away from the family.

73. Christopher Gardner Pearce to Jane Ann Pearce, 10 March 1843, Christopher Gardner Pearce Collection, Newberry Library. This section of the letter was damaged when unsealed.

74. Thomas Lyon Hamer to Lydia Bruce Hamer, 9 September 1837, Thomas Lyon Hamer Collection, Huntington Library.

75. Thomas Lyon Hamer to Lydia Bruce Hamer, 15 December 1829, Hamer Collection. Hamer probably spent his voluntary two years at home (there are no letters to his wife during the next two years), but was soon back in politics.

76. Lincoln Clark to Julia Clark, 19 October 1845, Clark Collection.

77. Daniel S. Dickson to Lydia Dickson, 5 January 1837, in *Speeches, Correspondence, Etc., of the Late Daniel S. Dickson, of New York*, vol. 2, ed. John R. Dickson (New York: G. P. Putnam & Sons, 1867), 334.

78. William Swain to Sabrina and Patience Swain, 15 April 1850, in *The World Rushed In: The California Gold Rush Experience*, ed. J. S. Holliday (New York: Simon and Schuster, 1981), 360.

79. Ibid., 360.

80. Keith Spence to Mary Traill Spence, 12 December 1805 and 21 December 1805, Spence-Lowell Collection. It is not fully evident from the record why Keith Spence left his home in Portsmouth, New Hampshire, and why he stayed away, although from hints in the collection it was most likely debt. He did have chronic economic problems and seems to have been an unlucky businessman. In 1799 he lost all of his money in a failed shipping venture and then in 1803 was captured by Barbary pirates and spent over a year as a prisoner in Tripoli. Still, there is some unexplained tension not evident from the sources that kept Keith Spence apart from his family.

81. Keith Spence to Mary Traill Spence, 30 January 1801, Spence-Lowell Collection. See also Keith Spence to Mary Traill Spence, 10 January 1801 and

Mary Traill Spence to Rebecca Lowell, 7 March 1801, Spence-Lowell Collection.

82. Keith Spence to Mary Traill Spence, 21 November 1797, Spence-Lowell Collection.

83. Keith Spence to Mary Traill Spence, 25 July 1797, Spence-Lowell Collection.

84. Keith Spence to Mary Traill Spence, 10 January 1801, Spence-Lowell Collection.

85. Keith Spence to Mary Traill Spence, 13 June 1799 and 26 December 1799, Spence-Lowell Collection.

86. Keith Spence to Mary Traill Spence, 30 April 1802, Spence-Lowell Collection.

87. Ryan, *Cradle of the Middle Class*, 101.

CHAPTER TWO

1. Isaac Chauncy Haight, facsimile of journal, entry for 1 October 1846, Mormon Collection, Huntington Library.

2. George Templeton Strong, *The Diary of George Templeton Strong: Young Man in New York, 1835–1849*, vol. 1, ed. Allan Nevins and Milton Halsey Thomas (New York: The Macmillan Co., 1952), 348–49.

3. Ibid., 349.

4. George Templeton Strong, *The Diary of George Templeton Strong: The Turbulent Fifties, 1850–1859*, vol. 2, ed. Allan Nevins and Milton Halsey Thomas (New York: The Macmillan Co., 1952), 42.

5. Catharine M. Scholten, *Childbearing in American Society: 1650–1850* (New York: New York University Press, 1985), 9; Richard and Dorothy C. Wertz, *Lying-In: A History of Childbirth in America* (New York: The Free Press, 1977), 1.

6. Cotton Mather, "Elizabeth in Her Holy Retirement: An Essay to Prepare a Pious Woman for Her Lying In," in *The Colonial American Family: Collected Essays* (New York: Arno Press, 1972), 30.

7. John Demos, *A Little Commonwealth: Family Life in Plymouth Colony* (London: Oxford University Press, 1970); John Demos, *Past, Present and Personal: The Family and Life Course in American History* (New York: Oxford University Press, 1986), 43–48; Mary Beth Norton, *Liberty's Daughters: The Revolutionary Experience of Women, 1750–1800* (Boston: Little, Brown and Co., 1980), ch. 3; E. Anthony Rotundo, "American Fatherhood: A Historical Perspective," *American Behavioral Scientist* 29 (September/October 1985): 8–10. For a differing view of colonial parenting, see Linda A. Pollock, *Forgotten Children: Parent-Child Relations from 1500–1900* (Cambridge, England: Cambridge University Press, 1983).

8. George S. Phillips, journal entry for 23 December 1844, George S. Phillips Collection, Huntington Library.

9. Karen Lystra, *Searching the Heart: Women, Men, and Romantic Love in Nineteenth-Century America* (New York: Oxford University Press, 1989), 42. See also Ellen K. Rothman, *Hands and Hearts: A History of Courtship in America* (Cambridge, MA: Harvard University Press, 1987).

10. Samuel Francis Smith to Mary White Smith, 16 September 1834, Samuel Francis Smith Collection, Huntington Library.

11. Isaac Metcalf to Antoinette Putnam, ca. March 1850, in Isaac Metcalf's letterbook, Metcalf Family Papers, Newberry Library. See also Levi Ray to Charles Henry Ray, 17 June 1847, Charles Henry Ray Collection, Huntington Library.

12. Nathaniel Hawthorne to Sophia Peabody, 21 April 1840, Nathaniel Hawthorne Collection, Huntington Library.

13. Stephen Mintz and Susan Kellogg, *Domestic Revolutions: A Social History of American Family Life* (New York: The Free Press, 1988), 51–52; James Reed, *From Private Vice to Public Virtue: The Birth Control Movement and American Society since 1830* (New York: Basic Books, 1978), ch. 1; Jan Lewis and Kenneth A. Lockridge, "'Sally Has Been Sick': Pregnancy and Family Limitation among Virginia Gentry Women, 1780–1830," *Journal of Social History* 22 (fall 1988): 5–20.

14. Daniel Scott Smith, "Family Limitation, Sexual Control, and Domestic Feminism in Victorian America," *Feminist Studies* 1 (1973): 40–57. For a revision of the arguments made in this article, see Daniel Scott Smith, "'Early' Fertility Decline in America: A Problem in Family History," *Journal of Family History* 12 (1987): 73–84.

15. See Richard A. Easterlin, "Population Change and Farm Settlement in the Northern United States," *Journal of Economic History* 36 (1976): 45–75; Morton Owen Shapiro, *Filling Up America: An Economic-Demographic Model of Population Growth and Distribution in the Nineteenth-Century United States* (Greenwich, CT: JAI Press, 1986); Mintz and Kellogg, *Domestic Revolutions*, 51–52; Reed, *From Private Vice*, 22–27, 55.

16. William Lloyd Garrison, *The Letters of William Lloyd Garrison: No Union with Slave-Holders, 1841–1849*, ed. Walter Merrill (Cambridge, MA: Belknap Press, 1973), 462.

17. Although only 4 of the 110 men studied wrote about taking steps to limit the size of their families, from the overwhelming number of small families in the sample, it is evident that some kind of family limitation was practiced by many more.

18. Scholten, *Childbearing in American Society*, 100–102.

19. Thomas Lyon Hamer to Lydia Bruce Higgins Hamer, 18 April 1838, Thomas Lyon Hamer Collection, Huntington Library.

20. Thomas Lyon Hamer to Lydia Bruce Higgins Hamer, 4 May 1838, Hamer Collection.

21. Henry F. Hitch to Elizabeth Babcock, 7 September 1863, William James Potter Collection, Huntington Library.

22. Richard Henry Dana, Jr., *The Journal of Richard Henry Dana, Jr.*, vol. 1, ed. Robert F. Lucid (Cambridge, MA: Belknap Press, 1968), 267.

23. Samuel Cormany, *The Cormany Diaries: A Northern Family in the Civil War*, ed. James C. Mohr (Pittsburgh, PA: University of Pittsburgh Press, 1982), 183.

24. E. Anthony Rotundo, *American Manhood: Transformations in Masculinity from the Revolution to the Modern Era* (New York: Basic Books, 1993),

122. See also Charles Rosenberg, "Sexuality, Class and Role in Nineteenth-Century America," *American Quarterly* 35 (1973): 150.

25. Linda Gordon, *Woman's Body, Woman's Right: A Social History of Birth Control in America* (New York: Grossman Publishers, 1976), 41, 62; Rotundo, *American Manhood*, 157–63; Carl N. Degler, *At Odds: Women and the Family in America from the Revolution to the Present* (New York: Oxford University Press, 1980), 184, 211; Smith, "Family Limitation," 123.

26. Strong, *Diary*, vol. 2, 3.

27. Calvin Fletcher, *The Diary of Calvin Fletcher, 1817–1838, Including Letters of Calvin Fletcher and Diaries and Letters of His Wife Sarah Hill Fletcher*, vol. 1, ed. Gayle Thornbrough (Indianapolis: Indiana Historical Society, 1972), 258, 453. See Sylvia D. Hoffert, *Private Matters: American Attitudes toward Childbearing and Infant Nurture in the Urban North, 1800–1860* (Urbana: University of Illinois Press, 1989), 17.

28. Tench Fairchild to Charles Henry Ray, 17 March 1845, Ray Collection. See also Hoffert, *Private Matters*, 17; Mary P. Ryan, *Cradle of the Middle Class: The Family in Oneida County, New York, 1790–1865* (Cambridge, England: Cambridge University Press, 1981), 157.

29. Charles Henry Ray to Jane Ray, 16 February 1855, Ray Collection.

30. Lincoln Clark to Sarah Smith, 27 February 1838, Lincoln Clark Collection, Huntington Library.

31. Lincoln Clark to Julia Clark, 21 December 1851, Clark Collection.

32. Nancy Osterud and John Fulton, "Family Limitation and Age at Marriage: Fertility Decline in Sturbridge, Massachusetts, 1730–1850," *Population Studies* 30 (1976): 481–94; Robert V. Wells, "Family Size and Fertility Control in Eighteenth-Century America: A Study of Quaker Families," *Population Studies* 25 (1971): 73–82; Robert V. Wells, *Revolutions in Americans' Lives: A Demographic Perspective on the History of Americans, Their Families, and Their Society* (Westport, CT: Greenwood Press, 1982), 95.

33. Carl Degler makes the point that knowing which form of fertility curtailment was used would enable historians to tell which sex was primarily responsible for the reduction in family size. Abortion and douching would indicate that women controlled limitation, while coitus interruptus and use of condoms would argue for men. Abstinence might suggest either sex. However, in the marriages described here, spouses felt a great deal of obligation to respect the wishes of the other, thus conceivably one sex might influence the other to use a form of contraception. The question is moot, however, because we still cannot say with any accuracy which form of birth control was the most widely used to bring about the reduction in family size. Degler, *At Odds*, 184.

34. Judith Walzer Leavitt, *Brought to Bed: Childbearing in America, 1750–1950* (New York: Oxford University Press, 1986), 87–115.

35. Ibid., 90–97.

36. E. Anthony Rotundo, "Learning about Manhood: Gender Ideals and the Middle-Class Family in Nineteenth-Century America," in *Manliness and Morality: Middle-Class Masculinity in Britain and America, 1800–1940*,

ed. J. A. Mangan and James Walvin (New York: St. Martin's Press, 1987), 37.

37. The fact that it was the second pregnancy, not the first, may have contributed to Metcalf's nonchalance.

38. Antoinette Putnam Metcalf, journal entry for 29 March 1855, manuscript journal kept jointly by Isaac and Antoinette Metcalf, Metcalf Family Papers. See also journal entries by Isaac Metcalf for 22 March 1855 and 6 September 1855.

39. Isaac Metcalf, in ibid., entry for 31 March 1855.

40. Isaac Metcalf, in ibid., entries for 6 September 1855 and 10 September 1855. It is possible that the twins came early, since three days before the birth Isaac took Antoinette fishing in a nearby brook.

41. Hoffert, *Private Matters*, 2; Lystra, *Searching the Heart*, 77.

42. Cormany, *Cormany Diaries*, 180.

43. Stephen M. Frank, *Life with Father: Parenthood and Masculinity in the Nineteenth-Century American North* (Baltimore: Johns Hopkins University Press, 1998), 100.

44. Mary White Smith to Samuel Francis Smith, 5 April 1835, Smith Collection.

45. Ann North to Ann Lewis, 1 July 1860, John Wesley North Collection, Huntington Library; See also Mary White Smith to Samuel Francis Smith, 5 April 1835, Smith Collection; Lendal G. Boyd to George J. Abbot, 20 September 1844, George Jacob Abbot Collection, Huntington Library; Cormany, *Cormany Diaries*, 180; Ann North to Mary Ann Loomis, 15 April 1860, North Collection.

46. Jane Ann Pearce to Christopher Gardner Pearce, 14 September 1843, Christopher Gardner Pearce Collection, Newberry Library.

47. Strong, *Diary*, vol. 1, 343.

48. Lincoln Clark to Julia Clark, 5 July 1852, Clark Collection. It is not clear if Lincoln knew of Julia's pregnancy at this point.

49. Lincoln Clark to Julia Clark, 2 February 1847, Clark Collection.

50. George S. Phillips, manuscript journal entry for 20 December 1844, Phillips Collection.

51. Charlotte Gardner, manuscript copy of journal, entries for April through 11 August 1854, William Bunker Gardner Collection, Huntington Library.

52. Gregory Yale to Fanny Yale, 28 April 1850, California File, Huntington Library.

53. Cormany, *Cormany Diaries*, 192–93.

54. J. Jill Suitor, "Husbands' Participation in Childbirth: A Nineteenth-Century Phenomenon," *Journal of Family History* 6 (1981): 283.

55. Horton Howard, *A Treatise on the Complaints Peculiar to Females* (Columbus, OH: Howard Pub., 1832), 129, as quoted in Suitor, "Husbands' Participation in Childbirth," 284.

56. Suitor, "Husbands' Participation in Childbirth," 285–87.

57. Strong, *Diary*, vol. 2, 70.

58. Wertz, *Lying-In*, 14; Leavitt, *Brought to Bed*, 105; Suitor, "Husbands' Participation in Childbirth," 285–86.

59. Hoffert, *Private Matters*, 76; Scholten, *Childbearing in American Society*, 46–48; Wertz, *Lying-In*, ch. 3.
60. Frank, *Life with Father*, 104.
61. Dana, *Journal*, vol. 1, 68–69.
62. Lincoln Clark to Sarah Smith, 27 February 1838, Clark Collection.
63. Leavitt, *Brought to Bed*, 21. See also Hoffert, *Private Matters*, 38; Degler, *At Odds*, 225.
64. John Wesley North to George and Mary Ann Loomis, 3 March 1852, North Collection. See also Hoffert, *Private Matters*, 80.
65. Cormany, *Cormany Diaries*, 192.
66. Ibid., 192–94.
67. Leavitt, *Brought to Bed*, 87–115.
68. Sarah Robinson to Catherine Jones, 1 February 1840, Clark Collection.
69. Lincoln Clark to Julia White, 25 December 1839, Clark Collection. For other examples, see Samuel Francis Smith to Susan Eleanor Parker, 17 September 1837, Smith Collection; John Wesley North to George and Mary Ann Loomis, 15, 17 September 1850, North Collection; Abigail Bailey, *Memoirs of Mrs. Abigail Bailey*, ed. Ethan Smith (1815; reprint, New York: Arno Press, 1980), 42.
70. Lendal G. Boyd to George Jacob Abbot, 20 September 1844, Abbot Collection.
71. Samuel Furber to Isaac Metcalf, 16 August 1856; see also 6 August 1856, Metcalf Collection.

CHAPTER THREE

1. Catharine M. Scholten, *Childbearing in American Society, 1650–1850* (New York: New York University Press, 1985), 71–73; Carl N. Degler, *At Odds: Women and the Family in America from the Revolution to the Present* (New York: Oxford University Press, 1980), 79–81.
2. Scholten, *Childbearing in American Society*, 73.
3. Anne L. Kuhn, *The Mother's Role in Childhood Education: New England Concepts, 1830–1860* (New Haven, CT: Yale University Press, 1947); Robert Sunley, "Early Nineteenth-Century American Literature on Child Rearing," in *Childhood in Contemporary Cultures*, ed. Margaret Mead and Martha Wolfenstein (Chicago: University of Chicago Press, 1955), 150–67; Barbara Welter, "The Cult of True Womanhood, 1820–1860," *American Quarterly* 18 (summer 1966): 151–74.
4. Lorna McKee and Margaret O'Brien, *The Father Figure* (London: Tavistock Publications, 1982), 8.
5. Wellington Burnett to Jane Cleveland Burnett, 9 June 1857, Wellington Cleveland Burnett Collection, Huntington Library.
6. George Templeton Strong, *The Diary of George Templeton Strong: The Turbulent Fifties, 1850–1859*, vol. 2, ed. Allan Nevins and Milton Halsey Thomas (New York: The Macmillan Co., 1952), 71. See also John North to George S. Loomis, 7 March 1852, John Wesley North Collection, Huntington Library.
7. William Stanton to David Stanton, 5 March 1858, William Stanton Collection, Huntington Library; Samuel Francis Smith to Sarah Bryant Smith, 28

October 1835, Samuel Francis Smith Collection, Huntington Library. For a differing viewpoint, see Lewis O. Saum, "Death in the Popular Mind of Pre-Civil War America," *American Quarterly* 26 (December 1974), 485–86.

8. Strong, *Diary*, vol. 2, 74–75.

9. Scholten, *Childbearing in American Society*, 73; John D'Emilio and Estelle B. Freedman, *Intimate Matters: A History of Sexuality in America*, 2nd ed. (Chicago: University of Chicago Press, 1997), 26; Christina Hardyment, *Dream Babies: Three Centuries of Good Advice on Childcare* (New York: Harper & Row, 1983), 4.

10. Samuel Cormany, *The Cormany Diaries: A Northern Family in the Civil War*, ed. James C. Mohr (Pittsburgh, PA: University of Pittsburgh Press, 1982), 193–94. This was a common belief during colonial times as well. See Sylvia D. Hoffert, *Private Matters: American Attitudes toward Childbearing and Infant Nurture in the Urban North, 1800–1860* (Urbana: University of Illinois Press, 1989), 148; Hardyment, *Dream Babies*, 47–48.

11. Samuel Cormany, *Cormany Diaries*, 214.

12. Daniel Scott Smith, "Family Limitation, Sexual Control, and Domestic Feminism in Victorian America," in *Clio's Consciousness Raised: New Perspectives on the History of Women*, ed. Mary Harman and Lois W. Banner (New York: Harper & Row Publishers, 1974), 127–28; Stephen M. Frank, *Life with Father: Parenthood and Masculinity in the Nineteenth-Century American North* (Baltimore: Johns Hopkins University Press, 1998), 97. Sylvia Hoffert is probably right when she claims that "men sometimes but not always hoped for sons." (Hoffert, *Private Matters*, 16).

13. Erastus Smith, Last Will and Testament, Hadley, Mass., 25 November 1829, Lincoln Clark Collection, Huntington Library.

14. Lincoln Clark to Sarah Smith, 27 February 1838, Clark Collection. It should be noted that Clark was writing to a woman who had given birth to six daughters.

15. Gregory Yale to Fanny Yale, 28 April 1850, California File, Huntington Library.

16. Preference for boys did not disappear with the family farm—Americans even in the twentieth century still hope more often for a son than a daughter. As long as a society remains patriarchal, it continues to encourage preference for sons over daughters. See Smith, "Family Limitation," 127.

17. Alan MacFarlane, *The Family Life of Ralph Josselin: A Seventeenth-Century Clergyman* (London: Cambridge University Press, 1970), 88. See also Mary Beth Norton, *Liberty's Daughters: The Revolutionary Experience of American Women, 1750–1800* (Boston: Little, Brown and Company, 1980), 85–87; Daniel Scott Smith, "Child-Naming Practices, Kinship Ties, and Change in Family Attitudes in Hingham, Massachusetts, 1640–1880," *Journal of Social History* 18 (summer 1985): 546, 555–57; Scholten, *Childbearing in American Society*, 61; Bertram Wyatt-Brown, *Honor and Violence in the Old South* (New York: Oxford University Press, 1986), 65–70.

18. Samuel Francis Smith to Sarah Bryant Smith, 28 October 1835, Smith Collection.

19. Ammi Brown to William Brown, 1 June 1821, William Brown Collection, Newberry Library.

20. Sarah Connell Ayer, *Diary of Sarah Connell Ayer* (Portland, ME: Lefavor-Tower Co., 1910), 237.

21. William Sewall, *Diary of William Sewall, 1797–1846: Formerly of Augusta, Maine, Maryland, Virginia, and Pioneer in Illinois*, ed. John Goodell (Beardstown, IL: Hartman Printing Co., 1930), 92.

22. Typescript copy of letter from Charles Henry Ray to Dear Sir, (probably E. B. Washburne), 24 December 1854, Charles Henry Ray Collection, Huntington Library.

23. Charles Henry Ray to Jane Ray, 18 February 1854, Ray Collection.

24. Charles Henry Ray to Jane Ray, 17 June 1855, Ray Collection.

25. Manuscript Journal of George S. Phillips, entry for 19 June 1845, George S. Phillips Collection, Huntington Library; Samuel Francis Smith to Susan Eleanor Parker, 14 March 1836, Smith Collection; Wellington Burnett to Jane Burnett, 12 January 1857, Burnett Collection; Lincoln Clark to Julia Clark, 24 July 1838 and 26 October 1839, Clark Collection; Thomas Carter to Aaron Carter, 25 July 1842, Thomas Carter Collection, Newberry Library; George W. Borrowe to John Moore, October 1822, John Moore Collection, Huntington Library; Sabrina Swain to William Swain, 15 April 1849, in *The World Rushed In: The California Gold Rush Experience*, ed. J. S. Holliday (New York: Simon and Schuster, 1981), 80.

26. Strong, *Diary*, vol. 2, 80; Thomas Carter to Aaron Carter, 25 July 1842, Carter Collection; Thomas Kilby Smith to Elizabeth Smith, 22 December 1854, Thomas Kilby Smith Collection, Huntington Library.

27. Joel Richman, "Men's Experiences of Pregnancy and Childbirth," in *The Father Figure*; Shirly M. H. Hanson and Fredrick W. Bozett, *Dimensions of Fatherhood* (Beverly Hills, CA: Sage Publications, 1985), chs. 3, 4; Samuel Osherson, *Finding Our Fathers: The Unfinished Business of Manhood* (New York: The Free Press, 1986), 36–37.

28. Thomas Kilby Smith to Elizabeth Smith, 22 December 1854, Thomas Kilby Smith Collection.

29. Strong, *Diary*, vol. 2, 74–75.

30. Ibid., 71–72.

31. Ibid., 85, 97.

32. Isaac Metcalf to Antoinette Putnam Metcalf, 5 August 1854, Metcalf Family Papers, Newberry Library; see also Elizabeth Phillips to George S. Phillips, 3 July 1847, Phillips Collection; Jane Elfreth to Jacob Elfreth, 22 January 1835, in *The Elfreth Book of Letters*, ed. Susan Winslow Hodge (Philadelphia: University of Pennsylvania, 1985), 38.

33. Ann North to George and Mary Ann Loomis, 29 January 1853, North Collection.

34. Charles Henry Ray to Jane Ray, 29 September 1855, Ray Collection.

35. Isaac Metcalf to Antoinette Putnam Metcalf, 20 February 1857, Metcalf Family Papers.

36. Mary White Smith to Samuel Francis Smith, 5 April 1835, Smith Collection.

37. Dorcas Brown to William Brown, 22 June 1821, Edward Eagle Brown Family Papers, Newberry Library.
38. Dorcas Brown to William Brown, 8 July 1821, Brown Family Papers.
39. Charles Henry Ray to Jane Ray, 24 June 1855, Ray Collection; Antoinette Putnam Metcalf, entry in journal kept jointly by Isaac and Antoinette Metcalf, 2 August 1855, Metcalf Family Papers; Ann North to Ann Lewis, 24 October 1852, North Collection.
40. John Wesley North to George Loomis, 1 January 1854, North Collection.
41. Christopher Gardner Pearce to Jane Ann Pearce, 10 August 1842, Christopher Gardner Pearce Collection, Newberry Library.
42. Lincoln Clark to Julia Clark, 26 October 1839, Clark Collection; see also Charles Rich to Albina Rich, 5 February 1854, Metcalf Family Papers.
43. Antoinette Putnam Metcalf, Journal kept jointly by Isaac Metcalf and Antoinette Putnam Metcalf, entry for 16 February 1855, Metcalf Family Papers.
44. Thomas Carter to Aaron Carter, 8 November 1842, Thomas Butler Carter Collection, Newberry Library.
45. Ettie Elliot to Augusta Halleck, 30 December 1860, James Alvin Bell Collection, Huntington Library.
46. Ann North to Ann Lewis, 7 August 1855, and Ann North to George and Mary Ann Loomis, 26 December 1852, North Collection.
47. John Wesley North to George Loomis, 19 December 1859, North Collection.
48. Lincoln Clark to Julia Clark, 24 July 1838, and Lincoln to Julia, 26 October 1839, Clark Collection.
49. William Swain to Sabrina Swain, 15 April 1850, in *The World Rushed In*, 360.
50. Most interchanges between husbands and wives during the early years of their family contained one or more of these topics. For good examples in the Huntington Library, see Ray Collection; Thomas Lyon Hamer Collection; Thomas Kilby Smith Collection; George Jacob Abbot Collection; North Collection; Clark Collection; and Wellington Cleveland Burnett Collection. In the Newberry Library, see the Metcalf Family Papers. See also *Cormany Diaries* and *The World Rushed In*.
51. George Swain to William Swain, 9 February 1850, in *The World Rushed In*, 345–46.
52. Ann North to Ann Hendrix Lewis, 3 October 1852, North Collection.
53. Ann North to George and Mary Ann Loomis, 25, 26 June 1854, North Collection.
54. Samuel Cormany, *Cormany Diaries*, 220.
55. Thomas Carter to Aaron Carter, 8 November 1842, Carter Collection.
56. Eleanor E. Maccoby, *Social Development: Psychological Growth and the Parent-Child Relationship* (New York: Harcourt, Brace Jovanovich, Inc., 1980), 46–62.
57. George W. Borrowe to John Moore, October 1822, John Moore Collection, Huntington Library.
58. Albina Rich to Antoinette Putnam Metcalf, ca. 1853, Metcalf Family Papers.

59. Jane Burnett to Wellington Burnett, 25 April 1857, Burnett Collection.

60. Sabrina Swain to William Swain, 15 April 1849, in *The World Rushed In*, 80.

61. Sabrina Swain to William Swain, 27 May 1849, in ibid., 138.

62. George Swain to William Swain, 26 July 1849, in ibid., 194–95.

63. For examples, see the manuscript journal of George Phillips, entries for 19 June 1845 and 16 April 1847, Phillips Collection; Isaac Metcalf in manuscript journal kept jointly by Isaac and Antoinette Metcalf, entries for 5–14 September 1856, Metcalf Family Papers; Ann North to George and Mary Ann Loomis, 21–24 September 1850, North Collection. Stephen M. Frank has found that during the Civil War fathers traveled to the battlefield to care for their wounded or ill adult sons. Stephen M. Frank, "'Rendering Aid and Comfort': Images of Fatherhood in the Letters of Civil War Soldiers from Massachusetts and Michigan," *Journal of Social History* 26 (fall 1992): 15.

64. Charles Rich to Albina Rich, 1 January 1854, Metcalf Family Papers. See also the letter dated 15 January 1854.

65. Antoinette Metcalf, in manuscript journal, 7 October 1856, Metcalf Family Papers.

66. Strong, *Diary*, vol. 2, 72.

67. Peter G. Slater, "'From the Cradle to the Coffin': Parental Bereavement and the Shadow of Infant Damnation in Puritan Society," in *Growing Up in America: Children in Historical Perspective*, ed. N. Ray Hiner and Joseph M. Hawes (Urbana: University of Illinois Press, 1985), 28–29.

68. George W. Borrowe to John Moore, October 1822, Moore Collection.

69. Hoffert, *Private Matters*, 171.

70. Samuel Cormany, *Cormany Diaries*, 211.

71. Slater, "'Cradle to the Coffin,'" 33–34; Paul C. Rosenblatt, *Bitter, Bitter Tears: Nineteenth-Century Diarists and Twentieth-Century Grief Theories* (Minneapolis: University of Minnesota Press, 1983), ch. 4.

72. George S. Phillips, journal entry for 19 June 1845, Phillips Collection.

73. Lincoln Clark to Julia Clark, 30 November 1851, Clark Collection.

74. Philippe Ariés, *Centuries of Childhood: A Social History of Family Life*, trans. Robert Baldick (New York: Vintage, 1962), 38–39; Edward Shorter, *The Making of the Modern Family* (New York: Basic Books, 1975), 169–75; Lewis O. Saum, "Death in the Popular Mind of Pre-Civil War America," *American Quarterly* 26 (December 1974): 484–86; David E. Stannard, *The Puritan Way of Death: A Study in Religion, Culture, and Social Change* (New York: Oxford University Press, 1977), 58–59.

75. Slater, "'Cradle to the Coffin,'" 30.

76. Linda A. Pollock, *Forgotten Children: Parent-Child Relations from 1500–1900* (Cambridge, England: Cambridge University Press, 1983), 124–38.

77. Lincoln Clark to Julia Clark, 30 November 1851, Clark Collection.

78. Thomas Carter to Aaron Carter, 8 November 1842, Carter Papers.

79. Erastus Smith to Ashley Williams, 28 January 1810, Clark Collection.

80. Philippe Ariés, *Western Attitudes toward DEATH: From the Middle Ages to the Present* (Baltimore: Johns Hopkins University Press, 1974), 67–68.

CHAPTER FOUR

1. George Swain to William Swain, 9 February 1850, in *The World Rushed In: The California Gold Rush Experience*, ed. J. S. Holliday (New York: Simon and Schuster, 1981), 345–46.

2. Sabrina Swain to William Swain, 7 December 1849, in ibid., 339.

3. William Swain to Sabrina and Patience Swain, 15 April 1850, in ibid., 360.

4. Carl N. Degler, *At Odds: Women and the Family in America from the Revolution to the Present* (New York: Oxford University Press, 1980), ch. 4; Linda Kerber, "The Republican Mother: Women and the Enlightenment—An American Perspective," *American Quarterly* 28 (summer 1976): 187–205; Anne L. Kuhn, *The Mother's Role in Childhood Education: New England Concepts 1830–1860* (New Haven, CT: Yale University Press, 1947).

5. Mary Beth Norton, *Founding Mothers and Fathers: Gendered Power and the Forming of American Society* (New York: Vintage Books, 1996), ch. 2; John Demos, "The Changing Face of Fatherhood," in Demos, *Past, Present and Personal: The Family and Life Course in American History* (New York: Oxford University Press, 1986), 45–46; Edmund Morgan, *The Puritan Family: Religion & Domestic Relations in Seventeenth-Century New England*, rev. ed. (New York: Harper & Row, 1966); John Demos, *A Little Commonwealth: Family Life in Plymouth Colony* (London: Oxford University Press, 1970), 128–44; David E. Stannard, "Death and the Puritan Child," *American Quarterly* 26 (December 1974): 467; John Robinson, "Of Children and Their Education," in *Child-Rearing Concepts, 1628–1861: Historical Sources*, ed. Phillip J. Greven (Itasca, IL: F. E. Peacock Publishers, Inc., 1973), 11.

6. For a good introduction to this view, see Steven Mintz and Susan Kellogg, *Domestic Revolutions: A Social History of American Family Life* (New York: The Free Press, 1988), ch. 3.

7. Ibid.; Barbara Welter, "The Cult of True Womanhood: 1820–1860," *American Quarterly* 18 (summer 1966): 151–74; Kuhn, *The Mother's Role in Childhood Education*; Mary P. Ryan, *The Empire of the Mother: American Writing about Domesticity 1830–1860* (New York: Institute for Research in History and Haworth Press, 1982); Mary P. Ryan, *Cradle of the Middle Class: The Family in Oneida County, New York, 1790–1865* (Cambridge, England: Cambridge University Press, 1981).

8. *Nauvoo Times and Seasons*, 1 March 1844.

9. Kerber, "The Republican Mother."

10. Ryan, *Empire of the Mother*; Ryan, *Cradle of the Middle Class*; Nancy F. Cott, *The Bonds of Womanhood: 'Woman's Sphere' in New England, 1780–1835* (New Haven, CT: Yale University Press, 1977), ch. 2.

11. William Swain to Sabrina and Patience Swain, 15 April 1850, in *The World Rushed In*, 345.

12. William Edmond to Polly Edmond, 17 February 1799, in *Letters and Journals: Judge William Edmond, 1755–1838; Judge Holbrook Curtis, 1787–1858; Judge William Edmond Curtis, 1823–1880; William Edmond Curtis, 1855–1923; Dr. Holbrook Curtis, 1856–1920*, ed. Elizabeth Curtis (Hartford, CT: The Case, Lockwood & Brainard Co., 1926), 23–24.

13. Christopher Gardner Pearce to Jane Ann Pearce, 28 January 1846, Christopher Gardner Pearce Collection, Newberry Library.

14. Antoinette Metcalf, manuscript journal for the years 1853–1854, entry for 5 July 1853, Metcalf Family Papers, Newberry Library.

15. Ann Brown to William Brown, 25 May 1825, Edward Eagle Brown Family Papers, Newberry Library.

16. Thomas Kilby Smith to Elizabeth Smith, 30 October 1851, Thomas Kilby Smith Collection, Huntington Library.

17. Christopher Gardner Pearce to Jane Ann Pearce, 11 August 1846, Pearce Collection.

18. Charles Rich to Albina Rich, 5 March 1854, Metcalf Family Papers.

19. William Swain to Sabrina Swain, 5 May 1849, in *The World Rushed In*, 100.

20. Bronson Alcott, "Observations on the Spiritual Nurture of My Children," manuscript journal written between October 1834 and February 1835, p. 112, as quoted in Charles Strickland, "A Transcendentalist Father: The Child-Rearing Practices of Bronson Alcott," *Perspectives in American History* 3 (1969): 51.

21. Abigail Alcott to Samuel and Lucretia May, 22 June 1833, as quoted in Strickland, "A Transcendentalist Father," 35.

22. Ibid., 35, 48.

23. See endnote 80 in Chapter 1.

24. Keith Spence to Mary Traill Spence, 10 January 1801, Spence-Lowell Collection, Huntington Library.

25. Keith Spence to Mary Traill Spence, 26 July 1803, Spence-Lowell Collection.

26. Keith Spence to Mary Traill Spence, 23 December 1801, Spence-Lowell Collection. Unfortunately, we do not have Mary's letters to help us see how she responded to his criticism and advice.

27. Keith Spence to Mary Traill Spence, 22 June 1802, Spence-Lowell Collection.

28. See Horace Bushnell, "Christian Nurture," in Greven, ed., *Child-Rearing Concepts*, 162; Demos, *A Little Commonwealth*, 135; William G. McLoughlin, "Evangelical Childrearing in the Age of Jackson: Francis Wayland's View on When and How to Subdue the Willfulness of Children," *Journal of Social History* 9 (fall 1975): 23.

29. Demos, *A Little Commonwealth*, 134–39; William G. McLoughlin, *Revivals, Awakenings, and Reform: An Essay on Religion and Social Change in America, 1607–1977* (Chicago: University of Chicago Press, 1978), 116–17; Mintz and Kellogg, *Domestic Revolutions*, 14–15; McLoughlin, "Evangelical Childrearing."

30. Peter G. Slater, *Children in the New England Mind in Death and in Life* (Hamden, CT: Archon Books, 1977), 143–48.

31. McLoughlin, "Evangelical Childrearing"; Strickland, "A Transcendentalist Father," 16–17; Joseph Smith, *The Pearl of Great Price*, rev. ed. (Salt Lake City, UT: The Church of Jesus Christ of Latter-day Saints, 1987), 37–38; Phillip J. Greven, *The Protestant Temperament: Patterns of Child-Rearing*,

Religious Experience, and the Self in Early America (New York: Knopf, 1977).

32. McLoughlin, "Evangelical Childrearing." Wayland's account of this incident is reprinted on pp. 35–39.

33. Ibid., 36.

34. Ibid., 38.

35. Mary Walker, manuscript journal, entries for 31 March and 2 April 1846, Elkanah Walker Collection, Huntington Library.

36. McLoughlin, "Evangelical Childrearing," 32.

37. Bronson Alcott, "Observations on the Life of My First Child during Her First Year," 45–46, Alcott Family Manuscripts, Houghton Library, Harvard University, as quoted in Strickland, "A Transcendentalist Father," 22.

38. Slater, *Children in the New England Mind*, ch. 2.

39. Ann North to Mary Ann Loomis, 15 April 1860, John Wesley North Collection, Huntington Library.

40. Ann North to George and Ann Loomis, 25, 26 June 1854, North Collection.

41. Greven, *The Protestant Temperament*, 28, 29, 156. Greven argues that the emerging middle class generally fell into this moderate category of childrearing. See also Mary Lynn Heininger et al., *A Century of Childhood, 1820–1920* (Rochester, NY: Margaret Woodbury Strong Museum, 1984), 2–4; Slater, *Children in the New England Mind*, ch. 2.

42. Phillip Greven, *Spare the Child: The Religious Roots of Punishment and the Psychological Impact of Physical Abuse* (New York: Knopf, 1991), 69.

43. Paul C. Rosenblatt, *Bitter, Bitter Tears: Nineteenth-Century Diarists and Twentieth-Century Grief Theories* (Minneapolis: University of Minnesota Press, 1983), 142. A possible explanation why Rosenblatt found evidence of corporal punishment lies in his pool of diary writers. He drew from writers of all classes, from sources covering the whole century, and included Canadian and Southern writers.

44. Mary Walker, manuscript journal, entries for 31 March and 2 April 1846, Walker Collection; Abigail Bailey, *Memoirs of Mrs. Abigail Bailey*, ed. Ethan Smith (1815; reprint, New York: Arno Press, 1980), 40–41; William Brown to "Dear Sister," 14 November 1851, William Brown Collection, Huntington Library. This phenomenon might be explained by this study's focus on correspondence rather than journals.

45. Stephen M. Frank, *Life with Father: Parenthood and Masculinity in the Nineteenth-Century American North* (Baltimore: Johns Hopkins University Press, 1998), 119.

46. Linda A. Pollock, *Forgotten Children: Parent-Child Relations from 1500–1900* (Cambridge, England: Cambridge University Press, 1983), ch. 5. Pollock's argument challenges an established contention that corporal punishment generally declined beginning in the eighteenth century. However, both Pollock's argument and the established version agree that corporal punishment was not the norm in the nineteenth century. See Degler, *At Odds*, 71–72.

47. Thomas Kilby Smith to Elizabeth Smith, 31 December 1851, Smith Collection.

48. Ann North to Ann Lewis, 1 January 1860, North Collection.

49. Greven, *Spare the Child*. See Chapter 6 for examples of this long-lasting tension.

50. William Edmond to Polly Edmond, 15 May 1796, in *Letters and Journals*, 18.

51. Thomas Lyon Hamer to Thomas Madison Hamer, 21 January 1837, Thomas Lyon Hamer Collection, Huntington Library.

52. Daniel S. Dickson to Manco Dickson, 5 January 1837, in *Speeches, Correspondence, etc., of the Late Daniel S. Dickson, of New York*, vol. 2, ed. John R. Dickinson (New York: G. P. Putnam & Son, 1867), 341–42.

53. William Edmond to Polly Edmond, 15 May 1796, in *Letters and Journals*, 18.

54. John Milton Putnam to Antoinette Putnam, 1 January 1840, Metcalf Family Papers.

55. Jane Elfreth to "Dear Father," 30 December 1836, in *The Elfreth Book of Letters*, ed. Susan Winslow Hodge (Philadelphia: University of Pennsylvania, 1985), 134.

56. Nicholas Longworth Anderson to his mother, 27 August 1856, in *The Letters and Journals of General Nicholas Longworth Anderson, 1854–1892*, ed. Isabell Anderson (New York: Flemin H. Revell Company, 1942), 92.

57. William Edmond to Polly Edmond, 4 June 1794, in *Letters and Journals*, 15–17.

58. Ibid., 15–17.

59. Jacob Elfreth to his children, 27 February 1837, in *Elfreth Book of Letters*, 149.

60. Altina Waller, *Reverend Beecher and Mrs. Tilton: Sex and Class in Victorian America* (Amherst: University of Massachusetts Press, 1982), 27. See Jay Fliegelman, *Prodigals and Pilgrims: The American Revolution against Patriarchal Authority, 1750–1800* (Cambridge, England: Cambridge University Press, 1982); Jan Lewis, *The Pursuit of Happiness: Family and Values in Jefferson's Virginia* (Cambridge, England: Cambridge University Press, 1983); Richard Sennett, *Families against the City: Middle Class Homes of Industrial Chicago, 1872–1890* (Cambridge, MA: Harvard University Press, 1970); Stephanie Coontz, *The Social Origins of Private Life* (London: Verso, 1988), 164; Laurel Ulrich, *A Midwife's Tale: The Life of Martha Ballard, Based on Her Diary, 1785–1812* (New York: Knopf, 1990), ch. 6.

61. Phillip Greven, *Four Generations: Population, Land, and Family in Andover, Massachusetts* (Ithaca, NY: Cornell University Press, 1970).

62. Michael Anderson, *Family Structure in Nineteenth-Century Lancashire* (London: Cambridge University Press, 1971), 79–97.

63. Thomas Lyon Hamer to Lydia Bruce Hamer, 1 January 1833, Hamer Collection.

64. Jane Elfreth to "Dear Father," 22 January 1835, in *Elfreth Book of Letters*, 38.

65. Thomas Butler Carter, "Some Facts and Incidents in the Early Life of Thomas Butler Carter, from Boyhood and on Until Now," typescript copy, 15 September 1888, Thomas Butler Carter Collection, Newberry Library.

66. William P. Eaton to "Dear Parents," 12 June 1838, William P. Eaton Collection, Huntington Library.

67. Ibid.

68. David Allmendinger, *Paupers and Scholars: The Transformation of Student Life in Nineteenth-Century New England* (New York: St. Martin's Press, 1975).

69. William P. Eaton to Joseph Eaton, 30 November 1842, Eaton Collection.

70. Sarah Cleveland to Jane and Wellington Cleveland Burnett, ca. 8 July 1860, Wellington Cleveland Burnett Collection, Huntington Library.

71. Maria Hodge to Lyman Hodge (on same letter as Benjamin Hodge to Lyman Hodge), 2 December 1853, Benjamin Hodge Collection, Huntington Library.

72. Maria Hodge to Lyman Hodge, 22 November 1854, Hodge Collection.

73. Arthur W. Calhoun, *A Social History of the American Family: From Independence through the Civil War*, vol. 2 (1918; reprint, New York: Barnes & Noble, Inc., 1960), 67.

74. Karen Lystra, *Searching the Heart: Women, Men, and Romantic Love in Nineteenth-Century America* (New York: Oxford University Press, 1989), 124.

75. William James Potter, manuscript diary, entry for 26 February 1847, Potter collection.

CHAPTER FIVE

1. Jacob Elfreth to Jane, Caleb and Sarah Elfreth, 13 November 1835, in *The Elfreth Book of Letters*, ed. Susan Winslow Hodge (Philadelphia: University of Pennsylvania Press, 1985), 83. Jacob Elfreth believed that letter-writing was a valuable educational activity for children and adults, so between 1835 and 1837, Elfreth and his young children wrote over 153 pages of letters in this book.

2. Mary P. Ryan, *Cradle of the Middle Class: The Family in Oneida County, New York, 1790–1865* (Cambridge, England: Cambridge University Press, 1981). Ryan also points to the voluntary associations that flourished during these years.

3. Jacob Elfreth to his children, 27 February 1837, in *Elfreth Book of Letters*, 149.

4. John Milton Putnam to Antoinette Putnam, 1 January 1840, Metcalf Family Papers, Newberry Library.

5. John Milton Putnam to Antoinette Putnam, 10 February 1846, Metcalf Family Papers.

6. Some might argue that the feminization of American Protestant religion during the nineteenth century reduced the accessibility of religious cultural forms to men. Thus, fathers' role in religious instruction declined, and a valuable conduit for the transmission of culture was closed off to men. However, such arguments rest on an assumption of separate spheres for men and women and an idea of gender determined personality traits. The so-called feminine characteristics associated with religion—compassion, deference to authority, altruistic love—also had a place in masculinity in the antebellum period largely because of religion. Regardless of the changes

affecting institutional religion, the middle-class culture of antebellum America remained dominated by Protestantism. See Anne Douglas, *The Feminization of American Culture* (New York: Knopf, 1977); Charles E. Rosenberg, "Sexuality, Class and Role in 19th-Century America," in *The American Man*, ed. Elizabeth and Joseph Pleck (Englewood Cliffs, NJ: Prentice-Hall, 1980), 219–54; E. Anthony Rotundo, "Learning about Manhood: Gender Ideals and the Middle-Class Family in Nineteenth-Century America," in *Manliness and Morality: Middle-Class Masculinity in Britain and America, 1800–1940*, ed. J. A. Mangan and James Walvin (New York: St. Martin's Press, 1987), 35–51.

7. Ryan, *Cradle of the Middle Class*, 65.
8. Ephesians 6:5.
9. Charles Rich to Albina Rich, 26 December 1853, Metcalf Family Papers.
10. John Joseph Craven to Catherine Trichnor Craven, 2 April 1849, California File, Huntington Library. See also Lucy Clark Allen to Harriet Ware, January 1827, in *Memorial of Joseph and Lucy Clark Allen*, edited by "Their Children" (Boston: George H. Ellis, Printer, 1891), 71–72.
11. Proverbs 22:6.
12. Joseph F. Kett, *Rites of Passage: Adolescence in America, 1790 to the Present* (New York: Basic Books, 1977), 107. See also Steven Mintz, *A Prison of Expectations: The Family in Victorian Culture* (New York: New York University Press, 1983).
13. Daniel S. Dickson to Manco Dickson, 5 January 1837, in *Speeches, Correspondence, etc., of the Late Daniel S. Dickson, of New York*, vol. 2, ed. John R. Dickinson (New York: G. P. Putnam & Son, 1867), 341–42.
14. Nathaniel Saltonstall to Leverett Saltonstall, 14 September 1798, in *The Saltonstall Papers, 1607–1815*, ed. Robert E. Moody (Boston: Massachusetts Historical Society, 1974), 56.
15. Nathaniel Saltonstall, Jr., to Nathaniel Saltonstall, 7 August 1801, in ibid., 71.
16. George Templeton Strong, *The Diary of George Templeton Strong: The Turbulent Fifties, 1850–1859*, vol. 2, ed. Allan Nevins and Milton Halsey Thomas (New York: The Macmillan Co., 1952), 178.
17. Keith Spence to Mary Spence, 22 June 1802, Spence-Lowell Collection, Huntington Library.
18. Mintz and Kellogg, *Domestic Revolutions*, 55; Carl N. Degler, *At Odds: Women and the Family in America from the Revolution to the Present* (Oxford: Oxford University Press, 1980), ch. 2; Nancy F. Cott, *The Bonds of Womanhood: 'Woman's Sphere' in New England, 1780–1835* (New Haven, CT: Yale University Press, 1977), 126–29; Sara M. Evans, *Born for Liberty: A History of Women in America* (New York: The Free Press, 1989), 70–71.
19. Keith Spence to Mary Spence, 7 July 1806, Spence-Lowell Collection.
20. Lincoln Clark to Catherine Clark, 15 April 1856, Lincoln Clark Collection, Huntington Library. See also Keith Spence to Mary Spence, 27 July 1807, Spence-Lowell Collection.
21. John Putnam to Antoinette Putnam, 12 May 1847, Metcalf Family Papers.
22. Maris A. Vinovskis, *An 'Epidemic' of Adolescent Pregnancy? Some Histor-*

ical and Policy Considerations (New York: Oxford University Press, 1988), 16.

23. Vinovskis, *An 'Epidemic'*, 9–16; Daniel S. Smith and Michael S. Hindus, "Premarital Pregnancy in America, 1640–1971: An Overview and Interpretation," *Journal of Interdisciplinary History* 5 (1975): 537–70.

24. Lincoln Clark to Julia Clark, 20 October 1851, Clark Collection.

25. Keith Spence to Mary Spence, 10 January 1801, Spence-Lowell Collection.

26. Thomas Lyon Hamer to Lydia Hamer, 3 June 1838, Thomas Lyon Hamer Collection, Huntington Library.

27. Simeon Baldwin to Rebecca Baldwin, ca. 1806, in *Life and Letters of Simeon Baldwin*, ed. Simeon E. Baldwin (New Haven, CT: The Tuttle, Morehouse & Taylor Co., 1919), 479.

28. See, for example, John Bodnar, *The Transplanted: A History of Immigrants in Urban America* (Bloomington: Indiana University Press, 1985); Rudolph Veccoli, "The Contadini in Chicago: A Critique of The Uprooted," *Journal of American History* 51 (December 1964): 404–17; Virginia Yans-McLaughlin, *Family and Community: Italian Immigrants in Buffalo, 1880–1930* (Urbana: University of Illinois Press, 1982); Michael Anderson, *Family Structure in Nineteenth Century Lancashire* (London: Cambridge University Press, 1971).

29. The number of families studied from rural, town, and urban situations were twenty-six, forty-one, and twenty-five, respectively, with eighteen unknown. Some families were counted twice because of moves. Families on farms were usually assigned rural status, but these families often had access to nearby towns. Urban status was given to those families that lived in New York, Philadelphia, Boston, and Western cities in the 1840s and 1850s, such as Chicago and Cincinnati. Town families generally lived in small, local population centers where basic services like schools and transportation systems existed.

30. Bernard Wishy, *The Child and the Republic: The Dawn of Modern American Child Nurture* (Philadelphia: University of Pennsylvania Press, 1968), 42.

31. William Edmond to Polly Edmond, 4 June 1794, in *Letters and Journals: Judge William Edmond, 1755–1838; Judge Holbrook Curtis, 1787–1858; Judge William Edmond Curtis, 1823–1880; William Edmond Curtis, 1855–1923; Dr. Holbrook Curtis, 1856–1920*, ed. Elizabeth Curtis (Hartford, CT: The Case, Lockwood & Brainard Co., 1926), 15–17.

32. Jacob Elfreth to Joseph Elfreth, 19 March 1835, in *Elfreth Book of Letters*, 68.

33. Benjamin Hodge to Lyman Hodge, 6 November 1850, Benjamin Hodge Collection, Huntington Library.

34. Ibid.

35. Benjamin Hodge to Lyman Hodge, 16 November 1850, Hodge Collection.

36. John Taylor Gilman to John Taylor Gilman, Jr., 9 March 1797, George Jacob Abbot Collection, Huntington Library.

37. Thomas Lyon Hamer to "My Dear Child," 21 March 1838, Hamer Collection.

38. William Eaton to Sarah Danielson, 11 [month unreadable, probably March] 1804, William Eaton Collection, Huntington Library.

39. Lincoln Clark to Julia Clark, 5 June 1852, Clark Collection.

40. For collections that provide a good range of instruction in these values, see the Hamer Collection; *The Life of the Late Gen. William Eaton*, ed. Charles Prentiss (Brookfield, MA: E. Merriam & Co., 1813); *Elfreth Book of Letters*; *Almon Danforth Hodges and His Neighbors* (Boston: n.p., 1909); *The Saltonstall Papers*; Wellington Cleveland Burnett Collection, Huntington Library.

41. Jacob Elfreth to "My dear children," 31 December 1837, in *Elfreth Book of Letters*, 174.

42. Ibid., 175.

43. Rotundo, "Learning about Manhood," 35–36; Rosenberg, "Sexuality, Class and Role," 219–54.

44. John Aikin, *Letters from a Father to His Son on Various Topics Relative to Literature and the Conduct of Life* (Philadelphia: James Carey, 1796), 255.

45. Rotundo, "Learning about Manhood," 35–36.

46. Joseph Eaton to William P. Eaton, 23 October 1854, William P. Eaton Collection, Huntington Library.

47. Keith Spence to Mary Spence, 23 December 1801, Spence-Lowell Collection; Lester Burnett to Wellington and Jane Burnett, 15 December 1859, Burnett Collection.

48. Austin C. Dunham, *Reminiscences of Austin C. Dunham* (Hartford, CT: The Case, Lockwood & Brainard Co., n.d.), 37–38, 40.

49. Jacob Elfreth to Jane Elfreth, 5 January 1835, in *Elfreth Book of Letters*, 25.

50. William Edmond to Polly Edmond, 23 February 1799, in *Letters and Journals*, 24–26.

51. Eliza Dwight, introduction, in *Caleb and Mary Wilder Foote: Reminiscences and Letters*, ed. Mary Wilder Tileston (Boston: Houghton Mifflin Co., 1918), 10.

52. Albina Rich to Isaac Metcalf, 9 September 1851, Metcalf Family Papers, Newberry Library.

53. See, for example, Thomas Butler Carter, "Some facts and incidents in the early life of THOMAS BUTLER CARTER, from boyhood and on until now" manuscript autobiography, typescript copy, 15 September 1888, Thomas Butler Carter Collection, Newberry Library; Charles Rich to Charlie and Josie Rich, 13 August 1854, Metcalf Family Collection; *Diary of William Sewall, 1797–1846, Formerly of Augusta Maine, Maryland, Virginia and Pioneer in Illinois*, ed. John Goodell (Beardstown, IL: Hartman Printing Co., 1930); Joseph Elfreth to Jacob Elfreth, 1 April 1835, in *Elfreth Book of Letters*, 73–74.

54. Keith Spence to Mary Spence, 8–9 June 1803, Spence-Lowell Collection.

55. Charles Penniman Daniell to Sarah Daniell, 5 July 1848, Charles Penniman Daniell Collection, Huntington Library; see also *Reminiscences of Austin C. Dunham*, 37–38.

56. For hints of the relationships between fathers and rebellious sons, see the Charles Henry Ray Collection, the Wellington Cleveland Burnett Collection, and the William James Potter Collections in the Huntington Library.

57. John Putnam to Antoinette Putnam Metcalf, 24 August 1846, Metcalf Family Papers. See Daniel T. Rodgers, "Socializing Middle-Class Children," in *Growing Up in America: Children in Historical Perspective*, ed. N. Ray Hiner and Joseph M. Hawes (Urbana, IL: University of Illinois, 1985), 121–25.

58. Thomas Lyon Hamer to Washington Hamer, 21 January 1837, Hamer Collection.

59. Thomas Kilby Smith to Bettie and Belle Smith, 24 February 1863, Thomas Kilby Smith Collection, Huntington Library.

60. Keith Spence to Mary Spence, 21 November 1797, Spence-Lowell Collection.

61. Thomas Kilby Smith to Bettie and Belle Smith, 24 February 1863, Smith Collection.

62. Rotundo, "Learning about Manhood," 41–42.

63. John North, "Random Sketches of a Crude Life," typescript autobiography written from 1888 to 1890, p. 9, John Wesley North Collection, Huntington Library.

64. Charles Henry Ray to "My Dear Children," 10 July 1861, Charles Henry Ray Collection, Huntington Library.

65. Thomas Lyon Hamer to Thomas Hamer, 31 August 1846, Hamer Collection.

66. William Eaton to Fritz Babbit, 4 August 1808, in *Life of the Late Gen. William Eaton*, 410–11; William Eaton, journal fragment, 17 March 1793, William Eaton Collection, Huntington Library. This fragment is a demand for satisfaction of personal honor, and there is no record in the collection that William Eaton actually fought the duel. Eaton, however, was clearly concerned with personal honor throughout his military career, and the concern seems to stem from pressures within the Army itself rather than self-imposed pressures. For other collections that reveal the exaggerated standards of honor in the military for this time, see the Spence-Lowell Collection and William Henry Allen Collection in the Huntington Library.

67. Thomas Lyon Hamer to Thomas Madison Hamer, 21 January 1837, Hamer Collection.

68. Ibid.

69. Lincoln Clark to Catherine Clark, 4 December 1850, Clark Collection.

70. William Edmond to Polly Edmond, 17 February 1799, in *Letters and Journals*, 22–24.

71. Ibid., 22–24.

72. Lincoln Clark to Julia Clark, 21 May 1847, Clark Collection.

73. Simeon Baldwin to Rebecca Baldwin, ca. 1806, in *Life and Letters*, 479.

74. John Pintard to Eliza Pintard Davidson, 23 September 1819, in *Letters from John Pintard to His Daughter Eliza Pintard Noel Davidson, 1816–1833*, vol. 1, *Collections of The New York Historical Society for the Year of 1937* (New York: J. J. Little & Ives Co., 1944), 226.

75. Lincoln Clark to Catherine Clark, 8 February 1856, Clark Collection.

76. Cott, *Bonds of Womanhood*, 104; Linda K. Kerber, *Women of the Republic: Intellect and Ideology in Revolutionary America* (New York: W. W. Norton & Company, 1986), ch. 7.

77. Lincoln Clark to Catherine Clark, 26 February 1856, Clark Collection.

78. Lincoln Clark to Catherine Clark, 5 February 1851, Clark Collection. Catherine eventually found an outlet for her talents; during the war she joined the United States Christian Commission working in hospitals and after the war in hospital reform. At one point she wrote home, "I wish I could help you, more than I do or have. Sometimes I think perhaps I ought not to have left home, but I reviewed the subject carefully on every side and thought it was my duty to come" (Catherine Clark to Lincoln Clark, 12 January 1864, Clark Collection). As long as Catherine remained unmarried, her duty could be broadly defined.

79. See, for example, David G. Pugh, *Sons of Liberty: The Masculine Mind in Nineteenth-Century America* (Westport, CT: Greenwood Press, 1983).

80. Cott, *Bonds of Womanhood*, 117–25; Mary Beth Norton, *Liberty's Daughters: The Revolutionary Experience of American Women, 1750–1800* (Boston: Little, Brown, 1980), 155–299; Kerber, *Women of the Republic*.

81. John Milton Putnam to Antoinette Putnam, 12 March 1846, Metcalf Family Papers.

82. William Edmond to Polly Edmond, 4 June 1794, in *Letters and Journals*, 15–17.

83. Cott, *Bonds of Womanhood*, 111. No father in the sources expressed this sentiment.

84. Lavina Watson to John Fanning Watson, 17 March 1835, John Fanning Watson Collection, Huntington Library.

85. John M. Putnam to Antoinette Putnam Metcalf, 1 December 1857, Metcalf Family Papers.

86. William Eaton to Sarah Danielson (step-daughter), 17 January 1804, William Eaton Collection.

87. Lincoln Clark to Catherine Clark, 5 April 1852, Clark Collection.

88. John Milton Putnam to Antoinette Putnam, 12 December 1844, J. M. Putnam to A. Putnam, 4 March 1849, J. M. Putnam to A. Putnam, 27 January 1846, Metcalf Family Papers; Thomas Lyon Hamer to Melvina Hamer, 7 October 1837, Hamer Collection; Jacob Elfreth to "Dear Children," 29 January 1837, in *Elfreth Book of Letters*, 139–41.

89. Cott, *Bonds of Womanhood*, 108–109; Ryan, *Cradle of the Middle Class*, 168–71.

90. Sheldon Colton to Carlos Colton, 24 May 1857, Sheldon Colton Collection, Huntington Library.

91. Keith Spence to Mary Spence, 21 November 1797, Spence-Lowell Collection.

92. Stephen M. Frank argues for a much stronger resistance of fathers to their sons' education, but he makes this contention based on only a few fathers, some of them probably working class. Limited resources in working-class families probably did produce more tension when it came to education than in middle-class families. Frank, *Life with Father: Parenthood and Masculinity in the Nineteenth-Century American North* (Baltimore: Johns Hopkins University Press, 1998), 149–60.

93. George Washington Strong, from unnamed source quoted in the introduc-

tion to *The Diary of George Templeton Strong: Young Man in New York, 1835–1849*, vol. 1, ed. Allan Nevins and Milton Halsey Thomas (New York: The Macmillan Co., 1952), xvii.

94. Ibid., xviii.
95. Hyman Clendenen to Clemens and James Clendenen, ca. 1857, Clemens L. Clendenen Collection, Huntington Library.
96. Clemens Clendenen to Louisa Shinn Clendenen, 9 April 1864, Clendenen Collection.
97. *Diary of William Sewall*, 244, 246.
98. Eliza Dwight, in introduction to *Caleb and Mary Wilder Foote*, 16.
99. Lucy Clark Allen to Harriet Ware, January 1827, in *Memorial of Joseph and Lucy Clark Allen*, 76.
100. Jacob Elfreth to "Dear Children," 29 January 1837, in *Elfreth Book of Letters*, 139–41; See also James Savage to his wife, 8 September 1842, in *Letters of James Savage to His Family* (Boston: n.p., 1906), 102; Ann North to George and Mary Ann Loomis, 23 October 1859, North Collection; Julia Clark to Catherine Clark, 12 November 1850, Clark Collection.
101. Benjamin Hodge to Lyman Hodge, 18 March 1850, Hodge Collection.
102. Elijah Grant to Eleanor Bissell, 4 September 1848, Mary Eleanor Bissell Collection, Huntington Library.
103. Nicholas Longworth Anderson to his mother, 8 March 1855, in *The Letters and Journals of General Nicholas Longworth Anderson, 1854–1892*, ed. Isabell Anderson (New York: Flemin H. Revell Company, 1942), 23.
104. Susan Winslow Hodge, introduction to *Elfreth Book of Letters*, 15.
105. See James Savage to his wife, 8 September 1842, *Letters of James Savage*, 101; Lucy Clark Allen to Catherine Thaxter, 8 November 1836, and Hiram Withington to a friend, April 1839, in *Memorial of Joseph and Lucy Clark Allen*, 97, 104; Sarah Cleveland to Jane Burnett, 1 December 1856, Wellington Cleveland Burnett Collection, Huntington Library.
106. Ann North to George and Mary Ann Loomis, 8–11 January 1854, North Collection.
107. Matthias Zahm, "Matthias Zahm's Diary," in *Papers Read before the Lancaster County Historical Society*, 47 (no. 4, 1947): 81.
108. Strong, *Diary*, vol. 2, 266–67.
109. Luther Trussell to Delia Page, 5 December 1859, in *Farm to Factory: Women's Letters, 1830–1860*, ed. Thomas Dublin (New York: Columbia University Press, 1981).
110. Erik H. Erikson, *Childhood and Society*, rev. ed. (New York: W. W. Norton & Company Inc., 1963), ch. 6.
111. Edward Everett to Anne Everett, 11 January 1830, in *Memoir of Anne Gorham Everett: With Extracts from Her Correspondence and Journal*, ed. Phillipa Call Bush (Boston: n.p., 1857), 28.
112. See, for example, William G. McLoughlin, "Evangelical Childrearing in the Age of Jackson: Francis Wayland's View on When and How to Subdue the Willfulness of Children," *Journal of Social History* 9 (fall 1975); Ann North to George and Mary Ann Loomis, 24 July 1853, 19 November 1854, 24 June 1860, and 12 August 1860, North Collection.
113. Orville Hickman Browning, *The Diary of Orville Hickman Browning:*

Volume I, 1850–1864, ed. Theodore Calvin Pease and James G. Randall (Springfield, IL: Illinois State Historical Library, 1925), 158.

114. Strong, *Diary*, vol. 1, 8.

115. Lucy Clark Allen to "Mrs. Lincoln," March 1837, in *Memorial of Joseph and Lucy Clark Allen*, 98.

116. Browning, *Diary*, vol. 1, 112.

117. See Steven Mintz and Susan Kellogg, *Domestic Revolutions: A Social History of American Family Life* (New York: The Free Press, 1988), 45.

118. Lincoln Clark to Catherine Clark, 22 November 1856, Clark Collection; See also Benjamin Hodge to Lyman Hodge, 1 December 1849, Hodge Collection.

119. Strong, *Diary*, vol. 2, 247; For mention of Santa Claus, see *Diary of Orville Hickman Browning*, vol. 1, 165.

120. Jane Elfreth to Jacob Elfreth, 4 December 1837, in *Elfreth Book of Letters*, 167. For other examples of gift giving, see Sarah Connell Ayer, *The Diary of Sarah Connell Ayer, 1805–1835* (Portland, ME: Lefavor-Tower Co., 1910), 343; Daniel S. Dickson to "Mrs. Dickson," 24 August 1835, in *Speeches*, 331; Ann North to George and Mary Ann Loomis, 8–11 January 1854, North Collection; Maria Hodge to Lyman Hodge, 21 January 1854, Hodge Collection; Thomas Lyon Hamer to Lydia Hamer, 22 January 1834, Hamer Collection; Charles Rich to Albina Rich, 10 November 1854, Metcalf Family Collection.

CHAPTER SIX

1. Daniel Dickson to Louise A. Hughan, 14 February 1836, in *Speeches, Correspondence, Etc., of the Late Daniel S. Dickson, of New York*, ed. John R. Dickinson (New York: G. P. Putnam & Sons, 1867), 333.

2. William P. Eaton to Joseph Eaton, 30 November 1842, William P. Eaton Collection, Huntington Library.

3. Steven Mintz, *A Prison of Expectations: The Family in Victorian Culture* (New York: New York University Press, 1983).

4. Joseph F. Kett, *Rites of Passage: Adolescence in America, 1790 to the Present* (New York: Basic Books), 31.

5. Mary Paul to Bela Paul, 13 September 1845, in *Farm to Factory: Women's Letters, 1830–1860*, ed. Thomas Dublin (New York: Columbia University Press, 1981), 100.

6. Jenny Putnam to Antoinette Putnam Metcalf, 31 March 1855, Metcalf Family Papers, Newberry Library.

7. Thomas Dublin, *Women at Work: The Transformation of Work and Community in Lowell, Massachusetts, 1826–1860* (New York: Columbia University Press, 1979).

8. John Milton Putnam to Antoinette Putnam, 12 July 1849, Metcalf Family Papers. Some young women who worked for wages outside the home retained control over their own wages. See Thomas Dublin, *Women at Work*.

9. John Milton Putnam to Antoinette Putnam, 30 June 1848, Metcalf Family Papers.

10. Robert L. Griswold, *Fatherhood in America: A History* (New York: Basic Books, 1993), 16.

11. E. Anthony Rotundo, *American Manhood: Transformation in Masculinity from the Revolution to the Modern Era* (New York: Basic Books, 1993), 168.

12. Rotundo, *American Manhood*, 174.

13. John Bodnar, *The Transplanted: A History of Immigrants in Urban America* (Bloomington: Indiana University Press, 1985), ch. 2.

14. Charles Cleveland to Jane Cleveland Burnett, 3 May 1856, Wellington Cleveland Burnett Collection, Huntington Library.

15. Nathaniel Saltonstall to Levi Saltonstall, 1 May 1805, in *The Saltonstall Papers, 1607–1815*, vol. 2, ed. Robert E. Moody (Boston: Massachusetts Historical Society, 1974), 241.

16. Levi Saltonstall, diary entry for 4 March 1805, in ibid., vol. 2, 232.

17. Nathaniel Saltonstall to Levi Saltonstall, 1 May 1805, in ibid., vol. 2, 241.

18. Kett, *Rites of Passage*, 170.

19. E. Anthony Rotundo, "Fatherhood in America," unpublished manuscript, 210.

20. See John Wesley North Collection, Huntington Library.

21. William P. Eaton to "Dear Parents," 12 June 1838, William P. Eaton Collection, Huntington Library.

22. George Templeton Strong, *The Diary of George Templeton Strong: Young Man in New York, 1835–1849*, vol. 1, ed. Allan Nevins and Milton Halsey Thomas (New York: The Macmillan Co., 1952), xxi.

23. Benjamin Stanton to William Stanton, 17 November 1851, William Stanton Collection, Huntington Library.

24. Thomas Butler Carter, "Some Facts and Incidents in the Early Life of Thomas Butler Carter, from Boyhood and on Until Now," 9, typescript copy, Thomas Butler Carter Collection, Newberry Library.

25. Ibid., 11.

26. Benjamin Stanton to William Stanton, 11 January 1858, Stanton Collection.

27. Benjamin Stanton to William Stanton, 16 June 1860, Stanton Collection.

28. Benjamin Stanton to William Stanton, 3 April 1856, Stanton Collection.

29. Stephen M. Frank, *Life with Father: Parenthood and Masculinity in the Nineteenth-Century American North* (Baltimore: Johns Hopkins Press, 1998), 140–60.

30. William James Potter, diary entry for 23 March 1847, William James Potter Collection, Huntington Library.

31. Ibid., 25 November 1847.

32. Ibid., 23 November 1847.

33. William James Potter to William Potter, 6 April 1856, Potter Collection.

34. William James Potter to William Potter, 6 July 1856, Potter Collection.

35. Mintz, *A Prison of Expectations*, 60.

36. Rotundo, "Fatherhood in America," 252.

37. Sarah Connell Ayer, *Diary of Sarah Connell Ayer, 1805–1835* (Portland, ME: Lefavor-Tower Co., 1910), 150.

38. Mary P. Ryan, *Cradle of the Middle Class: The Family in Oneida County, New York, 1790–1865* (Cambridge, England: Cambridge University Press, 1981), 192.

39. Carol Smith-Rosenberg, "The Female World of Love and Ritual: Relations between Women in Nineteenth-Century America," in *Women's America: Refocusing the Past*, ed. Linda Kerber and Jane De Hart Mathews (New York: Oxford University Press, 1982).

40. Elizabeth Babcock to Spooner Babcock, 13 August 1856, Potter Collection.

41. Elizabeth Babcock to Spooner Babcock, 19 November 1856, Potter Collection.

42. Almira Bidamon Swigart to Lewis Bidamon, 3 March 1855, Lewis Bidamon Collection, Huntington Library.

43. Almira Bidamon Swigart to Lewis Bidamon, 24 March 1854, Bidamon Collection.

44. B. H. Piper to Luther Trussell, 4 September 1860, in Dublin, ed., *Farm to Factory*, 168–69.

45. Luther Trussell to Delia Page, 7 September 1860, in ibid., 169–70.

46. Luther Trussell to Delia Page, 11 September 1860, quoted in ibid., 172–73.

47. Frank, *Life with Father*, 140–60. Frank probably exaggerates the amount of tension between middle-class fathers and sons. Much of his evidence comes from struggling fathers who needed their sons' labor on farms. Education was essential to the middle-class mindset, and most of the fathers studied here, even farming fathers, supported their sons' schooling.

48. E. Anthony Rotundo, "Romantic Friendship: Male Intimacy and Middle-Class Youth in the Northern United States, 1800–1900," *Journal of Social History* 23 (fall 1989): 18.

49. Sheldon Colton to Carlos Colton, 12 November 1854, Sheldon Colton Collection, Huntington Library. See also Samuel J. Watson, "Flexible Gender Roles during the Market Revolution: Family Friendship, Marriage, and Masculinity among U.S. Army Officers, 1815–1846," *Journal of Social History* 29 (fall 1995): 86–87.

50. Olive Cleveland Burnett to Jane Cleveland Burnett, March 1860; Lester Burnett to Wellington Cleveland Burnett, 17 September 1859, Burnett Collection.

51. Lester Burnett to Edward Burnett, 4 February 1859, 11 September 1859, 29 November 1860, and Lester Burnett to Wellington Cleveland Burnett, 17 September 1859, Burnett Collection.

52. Olive Cleveland Burnett to Jane Cleveland Burnett, March 1860, Burnett Collection.

53. The incidence of fathers and sons who separated and did not reconcile was probably higher in the population as a whole. Estranged fathers and sons would produce few letters for study. To partially compensate for this shortcoming of the sources, the correspondence of all family members was read. Such relationships, or lack thereof, can occasionally still be observed through the letters of other family members.

54. Charles Cleveland to Jane Cleveland Burnett, 19 May 1856, Burnett Collection. See also Charles Cleveland to Jane Cleveland Burnett, 3 May 1856.

55. Levi Ray to Charles Henry Ray, 8 June 1841, Charles Henry Ray Collection, Huntington Library.

56. Levi Ray to Charles Henry Ray, 26 October 1844, Ray Collection.

57. Harvey Hubbard to Charles Henry Ray, 9 June 1841, Ray Collection.

58. Levi Ray to Charles Henry Ray, 5 March 1845, Ray Collection.

59. Paul E. Johnson, *A Shopkeeper's Millennium: Society and Revival in Rochester, New York, 1815–1837* (New York: Hill and Wang, 1978).

60. Mintz, *A Prison of Expectations*; Robert Abzug, *Passionate Liberator: Theodore Dwight Weld & the Dilemma of Reform* (New York: Oxford University Press, 1980); Kathryn Kish Sklar, *Catherine Beecher: A Study in American Domesticity* (New Haven, CT: Yale University Press, 1973); Johnson, *A Shopkeeper's Millennium*.

61. Benjamin Hodge, manuscript journal, entry for 24 October 1824, Benjamin Hodge Collection, Huntington Library.

62. William Brown to Cornelia Brown, 29 February 1852, William Brown Collection, Huntington Library.

63. William Brown to Joseph Brown, 14 February 1852, and William Brown to "Dear Sister," 14 November 1851, Brown Collection.

64. Phillip Greven, *Spare the Child: The Religious Roots of Punishment and the Psychological Impact of Physical Abuse* (New York: Knopf, 1991), 123–24.

65. Linda Gordon, *Heroes of Their Own Lives: The Politics and History of Family Violence, Boston 1880–1960* (New York: Viking, 1988), 3.

66. Patty Johnson Garrett to Henry Johnson, 6 August 1849, Newcomb-Johnson Collection, Huntington Library.

67. Patty Johnson Garrett to Henry Johnson, 20 August 1849, Newcomb-Johnson Collection.

68. Greven, *Spare the Child*, 122–68.

69. William Brown to "Dear Sister," 14 November 1851, Brown Collection.

70. Steven Mintz and Susan Kellogg, *Domestic Revolutions: A Social History of American Family Life* (New York: The Free Press, 1988), 18–20, 46.

71. Henry Sewall to William Sewall, 2 April 1821, in *Diary of William Sewall, 1791–1846: Formerly of Augusta, Maine, Maryland, Virginia, and Pioneer in Illinois*, ed. John Goodell (Beardstown, IL: Hartman Printing Co., 1930), appendix II, 8.

72. William Sewall, journal entry for 17 January 1818, in ibid., 33–34.

73. Henry Sewall to William Sewall, 2 April 1821, in ibid., appendix II, 8.

74. Hamilton Colton to Carlos Colton, 12 June 1858, Colton Collection.

75. Dr. Gregory, *A Father's Legacy to His Daughters* (Philadelphia: Jacob Johnson, Pub., 1806), 93.

76. Keith Spence to Mary Traill Spence, 23 December 1801, Spence-Lowell Collection, Huntington Library.

77. John Milton Putnam to Antoinette Putnam Metcalf, 16 December 1852, Metcalf Family Papers.

78. John Milton Putnam to Isaac Metcalf, ca. 1857, Metcalf Family Papers.

79. Luther Trussell to Delia Page, 24 August 1860, in Dublin, ed., *Farm to Factory*, 166.

80. John Aikin, *Letters from a Father to His Son, On Various Topics Relative to Literature and the Conduct of Life* (Philadelphia: James Carey, 1796), 248.

81. Nancy Wolloch, *Women and the American Experience: A Concise History*, (New York: McGraw-Hill, 1996), 59.

82. John Taylor Gilman to Dorthea Gilman, 17 December 1809, George Jacob Abbot Collection, Huntington Library.

83. Luther Trussell to Delia Page, 24 August 1860, in Dublin, ed., *Farm to Factory*, 166.

84. Ann North to George and Mary Ann Loomis, 7–9 February 1851, North Collection.

85. John Wesley North to George Loomis, 30–31 May 1850, North Collection.

86. John Wesley North to George Loomis, 15 March 1850, and Ann North to George Loomis, 17 March 1850, North Collection.

87. John Wesley North to George Loomis, 9–10 February 1851, North Collection.

88. John Taylor Gilman to his son, John Taylor Gilman, 16 October 1814, Abbot Collection.

89. Levi Saltonstall to Anna Saltonstall, 5 November 1804, *The Saltonstall Papers, 1607–1815*, ed. Robert E. Moody (Boston: Massachusetts Historical Society, 1974), 219.

90. Jean H. Baker, *Affairs of Party: The Political Culture of Northern Democrats in the Mid-Nineteenth Century* (Ithaca, NY: Cornell University Press, 1983), 31.

91. Charles Penniman Daniell to Josiah Newell Daniell, 14 July 1852, Charles Penniman Daniell Collection, Huntington Library.

92. John Milton Putnam to Antoinette Putnam Metcalf, 16 December 1852, Metcalf Family Papers.

93. See, for example, the correspondence between John Taylor Gilman and Dorthea Gilman Nichols, Abbot Collection; also *Letters from John Pintard to His Daughter Eliza Pintard Noel Davidson, 1816–1833*, vol. 1, *Collections of The New York Historical Society for the Year of 1937* (New York: J. J. Little & Ives Co., 1940).

94. Thomas Kilby Smith to Eliza Bicker Smith, 5 February 1850, Thomas Kilby Smith Collection, Huntington Library.

95. Steven Ruggles, "The Transformation of American Family Structure," *The American Historical Review* 99 (February 1994): 103–28.

96. James Bell to Augusta Halleck, 11 September 1859, James Bell Collection, Huntington Library.

97. Lincoln Clark to Elisha Clark, 14 March 1838, Lincoln Clark Collection, Huntington Library.

98. Lincoln Clark to Julia Clark, 4 April 1847, Clark Collection.

99. John Milton Putnam to Isaac and Antoinette Metcalf, 26 February 1855, Metcalf Family Papers. See also Rotundo, "Fatherhood in America," 259–60.

100. John Milton Putnam to Isaac and Antoinette Metcalf, 23 February 1860, Metcalf Family Papers.

101. George Putnam to Antoinette Putnam Metcalf, 2 November 1861, Metcalf Family Papers.
102. Ibid.
103. Ayer, *Diary of Sarah Connell Ayer*, 253.

CONCLUSION

1. Abigail Bailey, *Memoirs of Mrs. Abigail Bailey*, ed. Ethan Smith (1815; reprint, New York: Arno Press, 1980), 32–34. While I question the veracity of some of this account, it graphically captures the patriarchal family culture of the early national period. Whether true in detail or not, it is an accurate account of the culture of the time.
2. Ibid., 40.
3. Although Abigail's emotional responses to the incest have a timeless quality to them—denial, followed by self-blame and then anger at her daughter, are all still part of a pattern seen in twentieth-century incest cases—her eventual turn to family and the community was very much an eighteenth-century solution to her problem. The account itself probably would have offended the Victorian sensibilities too much to have been produced sixty years later.
4. Ibid., 189. The editor of the account, a New Hampshire minister, recorded that after the settlement, Asa Bailey sunk into poverty and "married a vile widow,—a turbulent being, who in some degree repaid his cruelties to a better companion" (Ethan Smith, ibid., appendix, 197).
5. Harry Brod, "Introduction, Themes and Theses of Men's Studies," in *The Making of Masculinities: The New Men's Studies*, ed. Harry Brod (Boston: Allen & Unwin, 1987), 13–14; Eli Zaretsky, "Capitalism, the Family, and Personal Life," in *History of Women in the United States: Historical Articles on Women's Lives and Activities*, vol. 1, *Theory and Method in Women's History, Part I*, ed. Nancy F. Cott (Munich, Germany: K.G. Saur, 1992), 72–180.
6. Michael Grossberg, *Governing the Hearth: Law and Family in Nineteenth-Century America* (Chapel Hill: University of North Carolina Press, 1985), 235–49, chs. 3, 4.
7. Stephen M. Frank, *Life with Father: Parenthood and Masculinity in the Nineteenth-Century American North* (Baltimore: Johns Hopkins University Press, 1998), 60. Frank later retreats from this view somewhat, agreeing that economics "drew men out of their families" (p. 81).
8. Steven Mintz and Susan Kellogg, *Domestic Revolutions: A Social History of American Family Life* (New York: The Free Press, 1988), 120, 128.
9. John R. Gillis, *A World of Their Own Making: Myth, Ritual, and the Quest for Family Values* (New York: Basic Books, 1996). Unfortunately, Gillis' potentially helpful approach is undermined in his chapter on fatherhood by his acceptance of some fatherhood myths as fathering realities. Drawing from the limited secondary sources on fatherhood, he is heavily influenced by the separate spheres and domesticity constructions.
10. Keeping these categories clear as we study the family is a challenging task. Convention and behavior are closely intertwined, and it is often difficult to draw these distinctions with any precision. This study of fatherhood has

tried to explore behavior but has occasionally glanced over at the model family found in the minds of some fathers. Some of the advice from fathers to children, for example, probably should be seen as addressing an ideal family rather than illustrating actual behavior. In some cases children followed paternal admonitions, but in many of the sources it was not evident whether or not children wanted to conform to their fathers' view of how their family should be.

11. Stephanie Coontz, *The Way We Never Were: American Families and the Nostalgia Trap* (New York: Basic Books, 1992); Gillis, *A World of Their Own Making.*
12. Gillis, *A World of Their Own Making*, 4–5.
13. Ibid.; Coontz, *The Way We Never Were.*

Select Bibliography

Abelin, Ernst L. "Some Further Observations and Comments on the
  Earliest Role of the Father." *International Journal of Psycho-Analysis* 56
  (1975): 293–302.
Allmendinger, David. *Paupers and Scholars: The Transformation of
  Student Life in Nineteenth-Century New England*. New York: St.
  Martin's Press, 1975.
Barth, Gunther. *City People: The Rise of Modern City Culture in
  Nineteenth-Century America*. New York: Oxford University Press, 1980.
Benson, Leonard. *Fatherhood: A Sociological Perspective*. New York:
  Random House, 1968.
Bloch, Ruth. "American Feminine Ideals in Transition: The Rise of the
  Moral Mother, 1785–1815." *Feminist Studies* 4 (June 1978): 101–26.
Blumin, Stuart M. "The Hypothesis of Middle-Class Formation in
  Nineteenth-Century America: A Critique and Some Proposals."
  American Historical Review 90 (April 1983): 299–338.
———. *The Emergence of the Middle Class: Social Experience in the
  American City, 1760–1900*. Ithaca, NY: Cornell University Press, 1989.
Brady, Marilyn Dell. "The New Model Middle-Class Family, 1815–1930."
  In *American Families: A Research Guide and Historical Handbook*, ed.
  Joseph M. Hawes and Elizabeth I. Nybakken. New York: Greenwood
  Press, 1991.
Brod, Harry, ed. *The Making of Masculinities: The New Men's Studies*.
  Boston: Allen & Unwin, 1987.
Bushman, Richard L. "Family Security in the Transition from Farm to City,
  1750–1850." *Journal of Family History* 6 (fall 1981): 238–56.
Carnes, Mark C. *Secret Ritual and Manhood in Victorian America*. New
  Haven, CT: Yale University Press, 1989.
Carnes, Mark C., and Clyde Griffen, eds. *Meanings for Manhood:*

Constructions of Masculinity in Victorian America. Chicago: University of Chicago Press, 1990.

Cavallo, Dominick. "Growing Up Female in a Middle Class Household: The Childhood and Youth of Jane Addams." In *Family Life in America, 1620–2000*, ed. Mel Albin and Dominick Cavallo. St. James, NY: Revisionary Press, 1981.

Coontz, Stephanie. *The Social Origins of Private Life: A History of American Families, 1600–1900*. London: Verso, 1988.

———. *The Way We Never Were: American Families and the Nostalgia Trap*. New York: Basic Books, 1992.

Cott, Nancy F. *The Bonds of Womanhood: 'Woman's Sphere' in New England, 1780–1835*. New Haven, CT: Yale University Press, 1977.

Davidoff, Leonore, and Catherine Hall. *Family Fortunes: Men and Women of the English Middle Class, 1780–1850*. London: Hutchinson, 1987.

Degler, Carl N. *At Odds: Women and the Family in America from the Revolution to the Present*. New York: Oxford University Press, 1980.

D'Emilio, John, and Estelle B. Freedman. *Intimate Matters: A History of Sexuality in America*. Chicago: University of Chicago Press, 1988, 1997.

Demos, John, and Sarane Spence Boocock, eds. *Turning Points: Historical and Sociological Essays on the Family*. Chicago: University of Chicago Press, 1978.

Demos, John. *A Little Commonwealth: Family Life in Plymouth Colony*. London: Oxford University Press, 1970.

———. "The Changing Faces of Fatherhood." In *Father and Child: Developmental and Clinical Perspectives*, ed. Stanley H. Cath, Alan R. Gurwitt, and John Munder Ross. Boston: Little, Brown, 1982.

———. *Past, Present and Personal: The Family and Life Course in American History*. New York: Oxford University Press, 1986.

Doherty, William J. "The Best of Times and the Worst of Times: Fathering as a Contested Arena of Academic Discourse." In *Generative Fathering: Beyond Deficit Perspectives*, ed. Alan J. Hawkins and David C. Dollahite. Thousand Oaks, CA: Sage Publications, 1997.

Dublin, Thomas. *Farm to Factory: Women's Letters, 1830–1860*. New York: Columbia University Press, 1981.

Easterlin, Richard A. "Population Change and Farm Settlement in the Northern United States." *Journal of Economic History* 36 (1976): 45–75.

Faragher, John Mack. *Women and Men on the Overland Trail*. New Haven, CT: Yale University Press, 1979.

———. *Sugar Creek: Life on the Illinois Prairie*. New Haven, CT: Yale University Press, 1986.

Faragher, Johnny, and Christine Stansell. "Women and Their Families on the Overland Trail to California and Oregon, 1842–1867." *Feminist Studies* 2 (no. 2/3, 1975): 150–66.

Filene, Peter G. *Him/Her/Self: Sex Roles in Modern America*. Baltimore: Johns Hopkins University Press, 1986.

Fliegelman, Jay. *Prodigals and Pilgrims: The American Revolution against Patriarchal Authority, 1750–1800*. Cambridge, England: Cambridge University Press, 1982.

Frank, Stephen M. "'Rendering Aid and Comfort': Images of Fatherhood in the Letters of Civil War Soldiers from Massachusetts and Michigan." *Journal of Social History* 26 (fall 1992): 7–31.

———. *Life with Father: Parenthood and Masculinity in the Nineteenth-Century American North*. Baltimore: Johns Hopkins University Press, 1998.

Gillis, John R. *A World of Their Own Making: Myth, Ritual, and the Quest for Family Values*. New York: Basic Books, 1996.

Gordon, Linda. *Woman's Body, Woman's Right: A Social History of Birth Control in America*. New York: Grossman Publishers, 1976.

———. *Heroes of Their Own Lives: The Politics and History of Family Violence, Boston 1880–1960*. New York: Viking Press, 1988.

Gordon, Michael. "The Ideal Husband as Depicted in the Nineteenth Century Marriage Manual." *The Family Coordinator* 18 (October 1969): 226–31.

Greven, Phillip. *Four Generations: Population, Land, and Family in Andover, Massachusetts*. Ithaca, NY: Cornell University Press, 1970.

———. *The Protestant Temperament: Patterns of Child-Rearing, Religious Experience, and the Self in Early America*. New York: Knopf, 1977.

———. *Spare the Child: The Religious Roots of Punishment and the Psychological Impact of Physical Abuse*. New York: Knopf, 1991.

Griswold, Robert L. *Family and Divorce in California, 1850–1890: Victorian Illusions and Everyday Realities*. Albany: State University of New York Press, 1982.

———. *Fatherhood in America: A History*. New York: Basic Books, 1993.

Grossberg, Michael. *Governing the Hearth: Law and Family in Nineteenth-Century America*. Chapel Hill: University of North Carolina Press, 1985.

Hardyment, Christina. *Dream Babies: Three Centuries of Good Advice on Child Care*. New York: Harper & Row, 1983.

Hareven, Tamara K. "Cycles, Courses, and Cohorts: Reflections on the Theoretical and Methodological Approaches to the Historical Study of Family Development." *Journal of Social History* 12 (1978): 97–109.

———. "The History of the Family and the Complexity of Social Change." *The American Historical Review* 96 (February 1991): 95–124.

Heininger, Mary Lynn Stevens et al. *A Century of Childhood, 1820–1920*. Rochester, NY: Margaret Woodbury Strong Museum, 1984.

Hoffert, Sylvia D. *Private Matters: American Attitudes toward Childbearing and Infant Nurture in the Urban North, 1800–1860*. Urbana: University of Illinois Press, 1989.

Jackson, Kenneth T. *Crabgrass Frontier: The Suburbanization of the United States*. New York: Oxford University Press, 1985.

Jensen, Joan M. *Loosening the Bonds: Mid-Atlantic Farm Women, 1750–1850*. New Haven, CT: Yale University Press, 1986.

Johansen, Shawn. "Before the Waiting Room: Northern Middle-class Men, Pregnancy and Birth in Antebellum America." *Gender and History* 7 (August 1995): 1983–200.

Johnson, Paul E. *A Shopkeeper's Millennium: Society and Revival in Rochester, New York, 1815–1837*. New York: Hill and Wang, 1978.

Kerber, Linda K. "The Republican Mother: Women and the Enlightenment—An American Perspective." *American Quarterly* 28 (summer 1976): 187–205.

———. *Women of the Republic: Intellect and Ideology in Revolutionary America*. Chapel Hill: University of North Carolina, 1980.

———. "Separate Spheres, Female Worlds, Woman's Place: The Rhetoric of Women's History." *Journal of American History* 75 (June 1988): 9–39.

Kett, Joseph F. *Rites of Passage: Adolescence in America, 1790 to the Present*. New York: Basic Books, 1977.

Kimmel, Michael. *Manhood in America: A Cultural History*. New York: The Free Press, 1996.

Kimmel, Michael, and Michael A. Messner, eds. *Men's Lives*. New York: Macmillan, 1989.

Kuhn, Anne L. *The Mother's Role in Childhood Education: New England Concepts 1830–1860*. New Haven, CT: Yale University Press, 1947.

LaRossa, R. et al. "The Fluctuating Image of the 20th Century American Father." *Journal of Marriage and the Family* 53 (1991): 987–97.

LaRossa, Ralph. *The Modernization of Fatherhood: A Social and Political History*. Chicago: University of Chicago Press, 1997.

Laslett, Barbara. "The Family as a Public and Private Institution: An Historical Perspective." *Journal of Marriage and Family* 35 (August 1973): 480–92.

Leavitt, Judith Walzer. *Brought to Bed: Childbearing in America, 1750–1950*. New York: Oxford University Press, 1986.

Leverenz, David. *Manhood and the American Renaissance*. Ithaca, NY: Cornell University Press, 1989.

Lewis, Jan, and Kenneth A. Lockridge. "'Sally Has Been Sick': Pregnancy and Family Limitation among Virginia Gentry Women, 1780–1830." *Journal of Social History* 22 (fall 1988): 5–20.

Lewis, Jan. *The Pursuit of Happiness: Family and Values in Jefferson's Virginia*. Cambridge, England: Cambridge University Press, 1983.

Lewis, Robert A., and Robert E. Salt, eds. *Men in Families*. Beverly Hills, CA: Sage Publications, 1986.

Lystra, Karen. *Searching the Heart: Women, Men, and Romantic Love in Nineteenth-Century America*. New York: Oxford University Press, 1989.

MacFarlane, Alan. *The Family Life of Ralph Josselin: A Seventeenth-Century Clergyman.* London: Cambridge University Press, 1970.

Magnum, Garth L. "Technological Change and the Erosion of the Patriarchal Family." *Dialogue* 2 (Autumn 1967): 45–52.

Mangan, J. A., and James Walvin, eds. *Manliness and Morality: Middle-Class Masculinity in Britain and America, 1800–1940.* New York: St. Martin's Press, 1987.

Marsh, Margaret. "Suburban Men and Masculine Domesticity, 1870–1915." *American Quarterly* 40 (June 1988): 165–88.

———. "From Separation to Togetherness: The Social Construction of Domestic Space in American Suburbs, 1840–1915." *Journal of American History* 76 (September 1989): 506–27.

McKee, Lorna, and Margaret O'Brien. *The Father Figure.* London: Tavistock Publications, 1982.

McLoughlin, William G. "Evangelical Childrearing in the Age of Jackson: Francis Wayland's View on When and How to Subdue the Willfulness of Children." *Journal of Social History* 9 (fall 1975): 21–34.

Mechling, Jay. "Advice to Historians on Advice to Mothers." *Journal of Social History* 9 (fall 1975): 44–63.

Miller, Jacquelyn C. "An 'Uncommon Tranquility of Mind': Emotional Self-Control and the Construction of a Middle-Class Identity in Eighteenth-Century America." *Journal of Social History* 30 (fall 1996): 129–48.

Mintz, Steven. *A Prison of Expectations: The Family in Victorian Culture.* New York: New York University Press, 1983.

Mintz, Steven, and Susan Kellogg. *Domestic Revolutions: A Social History of American Family Life.* New York: The Free Press, 1988.

Morgan, D. H. J. *Social Theory and Family.* London: Routledge & Kegan Paul, 1975.

Morgan, Edmund. *The Puritan Family: Religion & Domestic Relations in Seventeenth-Century New England.* 1944. Rev. ed., New York: Harper & Row, 1966.

Norton, Mary Beth. *Liberty's Daughters: The Revolutionary Experience of American Women, 1750–1800.* Boston: Little, Brown, 1980.

———. *Founding Mothers and Fathers: Gendered Power and the Forming of American Society.* New York: Knopf, 1996.

O'Barr, Jean F., Deborah Pope, and Mary Wyer, eds. *Ties That Bind: Essays on Mothering and Patriarchy.* Chicago: University of Chicago Press, 1979, 1990.

Osherson, Samuel. *Finding Our Fathers: The Unfinished Business of Manhood.* New York: The Free Press, 1986.

Osterud, Nancy, and John Fulton. "Family Limitation and Age at Marriage: Fertility Decline in Sturbridge, Massachusetts, 1730–1850." *Population Studies* 30 (1976): 481–94.

Osterud, Nancy Grey. *Bonds of Community: The Lives of Farm Women in*

Nineteenth-Century New York. Ithaca, NY: Cornell University Press, 1991.

Parke, Ross D. *Fatherhood*. Cambridge, MA: Harvard University Press, 1996.

Parsons, Talcott et al. *Family, Socialization and Interaction Process*. Glencoe, IL: The Free Press, 1955.

Pleck, Elizabeth. "Two Worlds in One: Work and Family." *Journal of Social History* 10 (1979): 178–95.

Pollock, Linda A. *Forgotten Children: Parent-Child Relations from 1500–1900*. Cambridge, England: Cambridge University Press, 1983.

Popenoe, David. *Life without Father: Compelling New Evidence That Fatherhood and Marriage Are Indispensable for the Good of Children and Society*. New York: The Free Press, 1996.

Pugh, David G. *Sons of Liberty: The Masculine Mind in Nineteenth-Century America*. Westport, CT: Greenwood Press, 1983.

Reed, James. *From Private Vice to Public Virtue: The Birth Control Movement and American Society since 1830*. New York: Basic Books, 1978.

Rodgers, Daniel T. *The Work Ethic in Industrial America, 1850–1920*. Chicago: University of Chicago Press, 1978.

Rosenberg, Charles E. "Sexuality, Class and Role in Nineteenth-Century America." In *The American Man*, ed. Elizabeth and Joseph Pleck. Englewood Cliffs, NJ: Prentice-Hall, 1980.

Rosenblatt, Paul C. *Bitter, Bitter Tears: Nineteenth-Century Diarists and Twentieth-Century Grief Theories*. Minneapolis: University of Minnesota Press, 1983.

Rotundo, E. Anthony. "American Fatherhood: A Historical Perspective." *American Behavioral Scientist* 29 (September/October 1985): 7–25.

———. "Learning about Manhood: Gender Ideals and the Middle-Class Family in Nineteenth-Century America." In *Manliness and Morality: Middle-Class Masculinity in Britain and America, 1800–1940*, ed. J. A. Mangan and James Walvin. New York: St. Martin's Press, 1987.

———. "Romantic Friendship: Male Intimacy and Middle-Class Youth in the Northern United States, 1800–1900." *Journal of Social History* 23 (fall 1989): 1–26.

———. *American Manhood: Transformations in Masculinity from the Revolution to the Modern Era*. New York: Basic Books, 1993.

Ruggles, Steven. "The Transformation of American Family Structure." *American Historical Review* 99 (February 1994): 103–28.

Ryan, Mary P. *The Empire of the Mother: American Writing about Domesticity 1830–1860*. New York: Haworth Press, 1982.

———. *Cradle of the Middle Class: The Family in Oneida County, New York, 1790–1865*. Cambridge, England: Cambridge University Press, 1981.

Sather, Katheryn. "Sixteenth and Seventeenth Century Child-Rearing: A

Matter of Discipline." *Journal of Social History* 22 (summer 1989): 735–43.

Saum, Lewis O. "Death in the Popular Mind of Pre-Civil War America." *American Quarterly* 26 (December 1974): 477–95.

Scholten, Catherine M. *Childbearing in American Society: 1650–1850*, ed. with preface and introduction by Lynne Withey. New York: New York University, 1985.

Sennett, Richard. *Families against the City: Middle Class Homes of Industrial Chicago, 1872–1890*. Cambridge, MA: Harvard University Press, 1970.

Slater, Peter G. *Children in the New England Mind in Death and in Life*. Hamden, CT: Archon Books, 1977.

———. "'From the Cradle to the Coffin': Parental Bereavement and the Shadow of Infant Damnation in Puritan Society." In *Growing Up in America: Children in Historical Perspective*, ed. N. Ray Hiner and Joseph M. Hawes. Urbana, IL: University of Illinois Press, 1985.

Smith, Daniel S., and Michael S. Hindus. "Premarital Pregnancy in America, 1640–1971: An Overview and Interpretation." *Journal of Interdisciplinary History* 5 (1975): 537–70.

Smith, Daniel Scott. "Family Limitation, Sexual Control, and Domestic Feminism in Victorian America." In *Clio's Consciousness Raised: New Perspectives on the History of Women*, ed. Mary Harman and Lois W. Banner. New York: Harper & Row, 1974.

———. "Child-Naming Practices, Kinship Ties, and Change in Family Attitudes in Hingham, Massachusetts, 1640–1880." *Journal of Social History* 18 (summer 1985): 541–66.

Smith-Rosenberg, Carol. "The Female World of Love and Ritual: Relations between Women in Nineteenth-Century America." *Signs: A Journal of Women in Culture and Society* 1 (1975): 1–30.

Stannard, David E. *The Puritan Way of Death: A Study in Religion, Culture, and Social Change*. New York: Oxford University Press, 1977.

Stearns, Peter N. *Be a Man! Males in Modern Society*. New York: Holmes & Meier Publishers, Inc., 1979.

Stowe, Steven M. *Intimacy and Power in the Old South: Ritual in the Lives of the Planters*. Baltimore: Johns Hopkins University Press, 1987.

Strickland, Charles. "A Transcendentalist Father: The Child-Rearing Practices of Bronson Alcott." *Perspectives in American History* 3 (1960): 5–76.

———. *Victorian Domesticity: Families in the Life and Art of Louisa May Alcott*. Tuscaloosa, AL: University of Alabama Press, 1985.

Suitor, J. Jill. "Husbands' Participation in Childbirth: A Nineteenth-Century Phenomenon." *Journal of Family History* 6 (fall 1981): 278–93.

Sunley, Robert. "Early Nineteenth-Century American Literature on Child Rearing." In *Childhood in Contemporary Cultures*, ed. Margaret Mead and Martha Wolfenstein. Chicago: University of Chicago Press, 1955.

Thorne, Barrie, and Marilyn Yalom, eds. *Rethinking the Family: Some Feminist Questions*. London: Longman, 1982.

Ulrich, Laurel. *A Midwife's Tale: The Life of Martha Ballard, Based on Her Diary, 1785–1812*. New York: Knopf, 1990.

———. *Good Wives: Images and Reality in the Lives of Women in Northern New England, 1650–1750*. New York: Knopf, 1980.

Vinovskis, Maris A. *An 'Epidemic' of Adolescent Pregnancy? Some Historical and Policy Considerations*. New York: Oxford University Press, 1988.

Warner, Sam B., Jr. *Streetcar Suburbs: The Progress of Growth in Boston, 1870–1900*. Cambridge, MA: Harvard University Press, 1962.

Watson, Samuel J. "Flexible Gender Roles during the Market Revolution: Family, Friendship, Marriage, and Masculinity among U.S. Army Officers, 1815–1846." *Journal of Social History* 29 (fall 1995): 81–106.

Wells, Robert V. "Family Size and Fertility Control in Eighteenth-Century America: A Study of Quaker Families." *Population Studies* 25 (1971): 73–82.

———. *Revolutions in Americans' Lives: A Demographic Perspective on the History of Americans, Their Families, and Their Society*. Westport, CT: Greenwood Press, 1982.

Welter, Barbara. "The Cult of True Womanhood: 1820–1860." *American Quarterly* 18 (summer 1966): 151–74.

Wertz, Richard, and Dorothy C. Wertz. *Lying-In: A History of Childbirth in America*. New York: The Free Press, 1977.

Wishy, Bernard. *The Child and the Republic: The Dawn of Modern American Child Nurture*. Philadelphia: University of Pennsylvania Press, 1968.

Index

Manners, inculcation of, 102,
118–120, 129, 138
Market economy, 5
as corrupting influence, 18, 39–40
and decline of family ties, 166,
174
and fathers' time with children,
18–19, 31–44, 115–116,
174–75
and new patterns of work, 20–24,
36, 124–125, 144, 147, 175
and patterns of consumption, 6,
23–24, 124, 173, 177
and paternal authority, 18,
39–40, 85–86, 103, 144,
147–149, 166
and success, 20–23
Marriage
in colonial era, 4, 159
and conflict between fathers and
children, 152, 159
control over decision of, 9, 11,
85, 141, 152, 159–162, 174,
176
to maintain class status, 117
as source of emotional fulfillment,
48–49, 92, 159
as transition in father-child relationships, 139–141, 159,
162–165
within middle-class, 152, 150
See also Courtship
Masculinity
and childbirth, 46, 51–57, 61–62
and domestic sphere, 18
and dueling, 127, 217n.66
fathers' inculcation of in sons,
109–110, 122, 125–128
and fear of femininity, 130
historians' portrayal of, 3, 12, 25,
51, 122, 126–127, 144, 153,
and identity, 153
and 'Masculine Primitive',
126–127
types of, 122, 126–127, 213n.6

and war, 127
and work, 20, 74, 124–125
See also Father; Father-son relationships; Gender roles
Mather, Cotton, 5, 47
Mechling, Jay, 6
Merchants as fathers, 20–21, 74,
76,
Men. *See* Fathers; Masculinity
Metcalf, Antoinette Putnam, 30,
54–55, 101
and father, 168
and childrearing, 89
and illness, 78
and marriage, 160
and work, 143
Metcalf, Isaac
and career, 27
and childbirth, 54–55
and childcare, 35, 74
and domestic work, 29–30
and hiring of servants, 72
and infants, 73, 78
and views on family, 49
and work-related absences, 29
Metcalf, Mayo, 34–35
Metcalf, Wilder, 78
Mexican-American War, 127
Middle class. *See* Middle-class
family; Social classes
Middle-class family
and changing role of women and
children, 6–8, 32–34, 67, 104,
124
and communal ties, 118
and consumption, 23, 173, 177
and emotion, 48
and family wage, 87
and private sphere, 18
and schooling, 100, 103–105,
109–111, 133
size of, 49–50, 52
values of, 6–8, 111, 141, 154,
156, 159

Victorian Patriarch, 1
Vinovskis, Maris A., 117
Violence. *See* Child abuse

Walker, Mary Richardson, 96
Waller, Altina, 102
Warner, Sam Bass, Jr., 36
Wayland, Francis, 95–98, 100
Welfare, 167
Welter, Barbara, 3
West, the, 26, 27, 38, 59
Will breaking. *See* Childrearing
Wetnurses, 63, 72
Widowhood, 24
Wishy, Bernard, 118
Women
  and childbearing, 47–49, 54–62
  and patriarchy, 11–12
  perceived traits of, 7, 19, 51, 85,
    88, 115, 117, 121–125,
    128–132, 151, 161
  as primary childrearers, 5, 12, 63,
    84–85, 88, 91, 123–124, 142
  as providers, 177
  as repositories of virtue, 19, 85,
    88, 115, 117
  roles as producers and consumers,
    6
  subordination of, 12, 84, 92, 117,
    128, 140
  workload, 11–12, 49–50,
    142–144

  See also Mothers; Childbearing;
    Father–daughter relationships
Work
  children's, 32–34, 47, 67, 104,
    107, 115, 122–125, 133,
    142–149
  as contributor to declining father-
    hood, 4, 18–19, 31–44
  culture of, 20–23, 122–123
  division of labor in families,
    18–19, 28–32, 96–97, 104,
    107, 122–125, 142
  and gender specialization, 7,
    84–88, 122–125, 142–149
  and men's identity, 20–25, 54–57,
    153, 165–168
  and moral values, 19, 122–123
  play as learning about, 136
  and Protestant ethic, 21, 122
  and separate spheres, 18, 84–88,
    122–125, 142–149
  and time with children, 18–19,
    31–44, 115–116, 174–175
  See also Domestic chores
Working class, 111, 115, 131, 144,
  156

Yale, Gregory, 57, 67
Youth culture, 150–151, 173–174,
  176–177

Zahm, Matthias, 136